Homosexuality:
The Test Case for
Christian Sexual Ethics

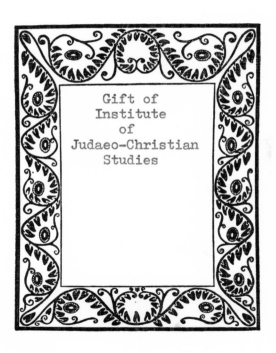

Theological Inquiries

Studies in Contemporary
Biblical and Theological Problems

General Editor
Lawrence Boadt, C. S. P.

PAULIST PRESS
New York • Mahwah

Homosexuality

The Test Case for Christian Sexual Ethics

James P. Hanigan

PAULIST PRESS
New York • Mahwah

Copyright © 1988 by James P. Hanigan

Library of Congress Cataloging-in-Publication Data

Hanigan, James P.
    Homosexuality : the test case for Christian sexual
ethics
    (Theological inquiries)
    1. Homosexuality—United States. 2. Homosexuality—
Religious aspects–Christianity. 3. Sexual ethics—
United States. I. Title. II. Title: Christian
sexual ethics. III. Series.
HQ76.3.U5H36   1987   261.8′35766   87-25907
ISBN 0-8091-2944-2 (pbk.)

Published by Paulist Press
997 Macarthur Boulevard
Mahwah, NJ 07430

Printed and bound in the
United States of America

CONTENTS

INTRODUCTION

Over the course of the almost twenty centuries of Christian history there have arisen many specific moral issues which Christian theologians have struggled to resolve. The issues themselves were generally not new to the human experience of life, but they were often raised anew for Christian believers because of the experience of the new life given and received through faith in Jesus the Christ. This conviction of the newness of life, of having been born again to live in the light rather than in the darkness, led to a process of ongoing moral questioning in light of the gospel message. This process of moral reflection is already vividly clear in many of the Pauline letters. Issues such as what to do about work, sex, legal appeals, eating and drinking, government and taxes, all had to be thought out afresh to determine the proper Christian attitudes and behaviors in regard to these fundamental human practices.[1]

But it was not only the newness of the life in Christ that provoked and even necessitated moral questioning. The developments and conflicts of human history, along with a deepening insight into the mystery of Christ crucified and risen, brought certain issues to the fore at different periods of history, and, at times, even raised entirely new issues, issues in both cases which were decisive for the future development of the Christian life. Contact with pagan philosophies, for example, raised the issue of the appropriateness of secular learning for Christian believers.[2] The recognition of the Church by the political authority of the Roman Empire led to the question of the Christians' responsibility for the well-being of society, and most acutely to the question of Christians' participation in war.[3] The growing sophistication of economic arrangements in the high Middle Ages necessitated reflection on the meaning of a just price, in time forced a relaxation of the ban on lending

1

money at interest, and eventually led to a reconsideration of the Christians' relationship to the entire economic order.[4] More recently, with the growing sense of human global interdependence, practices such as slavery, racism and imperialism have been seen as crucial moral issues for Christian faith and practice.

In regard to some of these issues the efforts of the theologians must be judged to have been largely successful, at least to the twofold extent that these issues no longer occupy a significant part of theologians' time and energy, and that there does exist today a substantial consensus in the Christian community in regard to them. Issues such as whether Christians should pay taxes and participate in the political life of their nation, or whether Christians should involve themselves in secular business activities, or whether Christians ought to pursue secular learning, while they may raise occasional questions of a particular nature, have generally been settled to affirm the propriety of such activities for Christian people as fundamental aspects of their service to their fellow human beings.

But there are other moral issues which have not achieved the same kind of consensus or for which a long-established consensus has broken down. Such issues continue to bedevil theologians to this day. In the present social and cultural setting of the United States, two such issues stand out as being particularly resistant to any kind of confident and common resolution.[5] One of these issues is the use of, or the threat to use, violence in pursuit of morally good ends.[6] This issue is highlighted and rendered critical for North American Christians today by the possession and possible use of nuclear weapons.[7] What makes the issue so problematic for the present age is the qualitatively new character of it, such that the traditional ways of analyzing and evaluating the use of violence as a means to an end do not seem at all pertinent in the face of the overwhelmingly destructive power of the new weaponry.[8]

Christian theologians have slowly but generally come to recognize that there is a clear biblical imperative for Christian believers to engage in the tasks of peace-making.[9] Many of them have also reached agreement that there is a present evangelical and moral urgency about working to establish and to preserve a social order in which freedom, justice and human dignity are both honored and protected.[10] There would appear to be a growing consensus about the general direction in which human beings should exert their moral energies or, in more technical language, about the formal ends[11] which it is morally incumbent upon Christian believers to seek in regard to their participation in and responsibility for the social ordering of human life.

When, however, it comes to a discussion about the morality of the means to these ends, the consensus fails.[12] How congruent or compatible with the gospel of God's love as revealed in Christ are certain practical and specific ways to realize the formal goals of peace and justice? Most pressing, are acts of violence ever morally justified in the pursuit of peace and justice? And if they are, are there moral limits on the kinds and the extent of violence the Christian may use to restore peace, defend freedom, and promote justice? Those remain the unsettled and much disputed questions. Since the achievement of peace and human survival seems at times to indicate one course of action, while the advancement of justice and the preservation of freedom often seem to require a contrary course, the lack of consensus can hardly be surprising. In addition, since the ends we seek are linked to the means we employ by no bond of necessity that can be clearly demonstrated, and the means themselves appear to be only doubtfully under our human ability to control, our judgments about the means to the ends are severely limited in both their practical certainty and their moral authority.[13]

The other issue, which will be the general concern of this study, has to do with the appropriate ends which the various possible uses of human sexuality should serve. This issue is highlighted for North American Christians today by a number of significant social developments.[14] Among these developments must be counted the spiraling growth of the world population, the widespread breakdown of marriages, the growing incidence of out of wedlock births and of abortions, especially among teenagers, and an increasingly explicit emphasis in the mass media upon all forms of sexual activity as morally innocent and humanly natural. But we must also take account of a number of positive developments which have accompanied the so-called sexual revolution.[15] One notices such things as the removal of a burden of false guilt from many people as a result of the new freedom to discuss sexuality; the very real, albeit quite incomplete, strides made in according full human recognition to women; and the slowly dying cult of male machismo. Also notable is the growing insistence by homosexual individuals upon their rights and dignity which have so often been denied at great human cost to members of the homosexual community and to the shame of homosexual and heterosexual individuals alike.[16]

This whole issue of sexual morality is problematic today, not because our traditional ways of analyzing and evaluating sexual conduct do not seem relevant to the issue, but because increasing numbers of thoughtful people have become convinced that those ways were seriously flawed,[17] or simply wrong.[18] It is now not a matter of debating what means will best and most honorably serve clearly acknowledged moral ends, but of trying to determine what ends human sexuality can and should serve. Debates about the morality of premarital sex, or divorce and remarriage, or any other sexual issue, are no longer debates about whether and to what degree such actions realize the purposes of human sexuality. They have become debates about the very meaning and purpose of human sexual behavior itself.

To draw the comparison between violence and sexuality as moral issues more tightly, it is clear that, in our reflections on the use of violence, both peace and justice are ends about which we must be concerned. No position on the use of violence can claim Christian backing if it does not appeal to these morally obligatory ends. While there is some dispute about what these ends really are and the degree to which human activity can achieve them,[19] our major struggle is to find morally acceptable ways to serve both ends when they often seem to require contrary means. If the possession and threat to use nuclear weapons serve to protect freedom and justice, the possession and threat also gravely imperil peace and reconciliation among the peoples of the world. If unilateral disarmament would serve the cause of peace, it might also serve the cause of tyranny and slavery. And it is also quite possible that these means, about which we argue so vehemently, might well have little or nothing to do with the ends they are supposed to achieve.[20]

In our contemporary reflections on sexuality, however, it is the traditional ends of procreation and unity, or inter-personal love, as well as the traditional relationship between them, that are subject to serious question. If the end of human sexual behavior is understood to be procreation, it is clear enough that any number of sexual practices do not serve this end. But is procreation the end? If the end of human sexuality is inter-personal love, it is also clear that any number of sexual practices ruled out by the end of procreation are now acceptable means to the end. But is inter-personal love the goal of human sexuality, and if it is, how is it related to the good of procreation? If the end of human sexual practice is simply mutual pleasuring or the sharing and enhancement of personal experience, even more sexual practices are acceptable as moral means to that end. But, among these possible ends, or others that could be mentioned, what is the proper end, and if there is more than one proper end, how are the plurality of ends related to one another? In short, in matters sexual, the consensus among Christians as to the ends sex is intended by God to serve has collapsed.

The basic thesis of the present study is that homosexuality has emerged today as the sexual issue or the test-case, as it were, on which any viable Christian sexual ethic will stand or fall. Consequently, while homosexual practice and relationships are the central focus of the book, its subject matter is really Christian sexual ethics in general and, more widely still, the place of sexuality and sexual behavior in the Christian life. The first chapter of the study will be devoted to explaining what it means to call homosexuality "the test-case" and to unfolding the reasons for thinking it is an issue of such general ethical importance. It is by no means self-evident that what Christian theology says about homosexual practices has decisive significance for its total view of human sexuality. But that is the claim I will be trying to support throughout this book. By the same token, although I will not argue it at any length here, our own attitudes and behaviors toward homosexual people may well be the decisive indicator of the integrity and truthfulness of our own sexual morality.

Both the biblical witness and the Christian theological tradition have been noted for their opposition to homosexuality.[21] This opposition has generally not taken the form of a mild distaste or a gentle rebuke, but has been vigorous and at times even vituperous. Accordingly, the second chapter will be concerned with an analysis and assessment of the biblical sources and theological reasoning on which this opposition has been based. In following the path of reasoning which the theological tradition has taken, I will be most concerned with the developments in that tradition which have led to the need to reconsider and reevaluate the historic opposition to homosexuality.

In the third chapter we will turn to a critical assessment, from a theological perspective, of the various contemporary proposals about the morality of homosexual behavior and relationships. This assessment will be made in light of both the challenge posed in the first chapter and the developments in the theological tradition itself which the second chapter will underscore. In making this evaluation, I will do so with an eye toward the fourth chapter of the study in which I will propose a position of my own on the moral status of homosexual acts and relationships.

Because the topic of sexuality is so multi-faceted and tied so closely to our deepest beliefs and doubts, hopes and fears, joys and disappointments, I have found it necessary to add three concluding chapters. In them I discuss, in a cautious and admittedly tentative way, some aspects of the Christian virtue of chastity, of sex and its relationship to sin and human freedom, and our limited knowledge of God's will, as well as the practical conclusions that can be drawn from the more theoretical analysis in the preceding chapters. I have also made extensive use of the end notes to each chapter in order to discuss certain aspects of both sexuality and morality when I judged that introducing these considerations into the text itself would interrupt the flow of the argument. Consequently, the book needs to be read and evaluated as a whole, and I ask the reader's patience in this matter.

As will be evident to those readers familiar with the literature on the moral status of homosexuality, I am plowing very little new ground in the present work. Although the position on the morality of homosexual acts and relationships which I will try to defend in the book accords in many ways with the traditional Catholic teaching, I do believe I am making a new suggestion, albeit one informed by the Christian theological tradition, on how we may best understand our sexual relationships in relation to Christian faith. But even there, I am deeply indebted to many theologians who have wrestled with these issues at greater length and depth than I have been able to do here. That debt I have tried to acknowledge in the notes accompanying each chapter. I am especially indebted to my colleague in the theology department at Duquesne University, Professor David F. Kelly, for the long hours he spent in conversation with me, helping to clarify many of the issues and arguments developed in the text. I am both grateful for and edified by his help, particularly since he does not at all share my conclusions. He has been for me a model of what a scholarly colleague and friend can be. I also am indebted to the editors and reviewers of Paulist Press, particularly Fr. Philip Keane, S.S., who provided me with some extremely helpful, critical suggestions for improving the first version of the manuscript.

I first became interested in the question of the morality of homosexual behavior a number of years ago. The interest was sparked by a conversation with a Jesuit friend about the pastoral work he had been doing in Atlanta with some members of the underground homosexual community there. Two aspects of his experience were particularly intriguing and noteworthy. Though he had not deliberately sought out or even thought about the kind of ministry to homosexuals in which he had become involved, he was often accused of taking up that ministry because he himself was a homosexual. As a matter of fact, he was not, but he had grown indifferent to defending himself against such a charge, as if that charge somehow tarnished or negated the worth of his ministry and impugned the need and the dignity of those whom he tried to serve. The second striking aspect of his experience was that he was ethically blind, in the sense that he had no clear idea or convictions about the ethical status of homosexual acts and relationships, nor of the ethical soundness of the advice and counsel he gave to the people with whom he worked. He knew, of course, what the formal teaching of the Church was on the matter and he had no practical desire or theological grounds to dispute it. It simply was of no practical relevance to his pastoral work.

The interest was further stimulated by a student I had in a theology seminar on the theological aspects of women's liberation. As the course unfolded, it turned out to be a rare educational experience. The students not only became involved with the issues of the course intellectually, but also in very existential ways which led them to become personally involved with one another. About halfway through the course the student in question bravely and openly acknowledged her own homosexual orientation and related some of the very difficult problems and questions it posed for her in trying to live out a Christian life. Her sharing of her experiences was a revelation for many of us in the class, for we had never confronted or even thought about some of the issues and dilemmas she faced. It became immediately evident to all of us that she held on to her faith at a great price, one that few of us were sure we would be willing to pay and most of us were convinced she should not have to pay.

In both of these situations, and in many others I have encountered since then, people, when confronted by the concrete reality of homosexual human beings as opposed to some abstraction called homosexuality, are often torn between what seems the most practical, humanly loving thing to do or say and what they think the demands of Christian morality are or should be. In time such a conflict becomes existentially unbearable and some kind of resolution must be sought. The resolution of the conflict can take a variety of forms. Often it involves an outright rejection of the homosexual person as somehow contagiously infected by sin. At times it leads to a choice in favor of concrete human beings over against what appears to be an abstract and heartless ethical code. For others the conflict is resolved by a selective reinterpretation of the Christian ethic in a way that seems more human and more compassionate.

I do not pretend to have any easy answers to resolve that apparent conflict, but I have tried to write with a compassionate attention to it. While I am extremely dubious about selective reinterpretations of any tradition, I am quite sure that personal rejection of homosexual people is no answer to any kind of conflict and can find no grounds in Christian faith. I am equally sure that the Christian ethic is neither abstract nor heartless. With that doubt and those two convictions I approach the present work. I can only ask the reader to bring a similar sympathetic and self-critical attention to the reading of the book.

This work deals, among other things, with love and friendship and their relationship to Christian faith. What any one person knows of these realities is inevitably limited, and is dependent far more on experience with friends and loved ones than on knowledge derived from books and academic study. I am greatly indebted to my family and various friends and colleagues over the years for what little I do know of these important realities. I wish to express a special word of thanks, however, to Professor Marilyn Schaub for her help in directing me to useful biblical commentaries, and to my other colleagues in the theology department at Duquesne, to the departmental secretary, Mrs. Mary Ellen Lewis, for her help in preparing the manuscript, and to my wife, Elizabeth Coulbourn Hanigan, to whom I am beyond indebtedness. Finally, I dedicate the book to two very dear friends of long and lasting value, from whom I have learned much about faith and love and friendship, John and Sally Sherrill.

NOTES

1. Examples of this ongoing moral questioning can be found throughout the New Testament. As illustrative of the point in the Pauline letters see, for work, 2 Thessalonians 3:6–15; for sex, 1 Corinthians 6:12—7:40; for legal appeals, 1 Corinthians 6:1–11; for eating and drinking, Romans 14:1–21; for government and taxes, Romans 13:1–8. The same process of moral questioning is also at work in the gospels and in other epistles, and not always with the same result. Perhaps the most notable example is the difference on the question of divorce and remarriage to be found in Matthew 5:31–32 and 19:9, Mark 10:10–12, and 1 Corinthians 7:12–16. This is one reason why the use of Scripture in Christian ethics or moral theology is not a simple business. Some helpful works in this regard are Bruce C. Birch and Larry L. Rasmussen, *The Bible and Ethics in Christian Life* (Minneapolis: Augsburg Publishing House, 1976); Raymond E. Brown, S.S., *The Churches the Apostles Left Behind* (New York/Ramsey: Paulist Press, 1984); Lisa Sowle Cahill, *Between the Sexes: Foundations for a Christian Ethics of Sexuality* (Philadelphia: Fortress Press; New York/Ramsey: Paulist Press, 1985), pp. 15–82; Robert J. Daly, S.J. *et. al., Christian Biblical Ethics: From Biblical Revelation to Contemporary Christian Praxis: Method and Content* (New York/Ramsey: Paulist Press, 1984); Thomas Ogletree, *The Use of the Bible in Christian Ethics* (Philadelphia: Fortress Press, 1983); William C. Spohn, S.J., *What Are They Saying About*

Scripture and Ethics (New York/Ramsey: Paulist Press, 1984). Reviews and evaluations of these works can be found in Kenneth R. Himes, O.F.M., "Scripture and Ethics: A Review Essay," *Biblical Theology Bulletin* 15, 2 (1985), pp. 65–73, and William C. Spohn, S.J., "Notes on Moral Theology: 1985: The Use of Scripture in Moral Theology," *Theological Studies* 47, 1 (March 1986), pp. 88–102. The need for ongoing reflection on the contemporary historical situation in light of the gospel message was one of the major affirmations of the Second Vatican Council. *Gaudium et spes* (The Church in the Modern World) 3–4, *Vatican Council II: The Conciliar and Post Conciliar Documents*, ed. Austin Flannery, O.P. (Collegeville: The Liturgical Press, 1975), pp. 904–905.

2. Francis X. Murphy, C.SS.R., *Moral Teaching in the Primitive Church* (Glen Rock: Paulist Press, 1968), p. 115. This question is still alive in a different form in the modern era. Today it takes the theoretical form of the relationship of revelation and reason. Its practical importance can be seen in the ongoing discussion on the nature of a Catholic or Christian university or college and how religious and secular truths are to be related to one another. Two clear, contemporary illustrations of this discussion are to be seen in the arguments over the proper canonical relationship of the Catholic university to the Church and the theologian's place and purpose in academic institutions. See, for instance, *Origins* 15, 43 (April 10, 1986), pp. 697–711 and *Origins* 15, 41 (March 27, 1986). But the question that concerned the early Church has been generally settled for most Christians; secular learning does have a place in the Christian life.

3. Roland H. Bainton, *Christian Attitudes Toward War and Peace* (Nashville/New York: Abingdon Press, 1960), pp. 85–100. While Bainton's views are rather one-sidedly pacifist, he does locate the issue historically very well. That the early Christians were not quite as passive in regard to violence as Bainton argues is confirmed in John Helgeland, Robert J. Daly and J. Patout Burns, *Christians and the Military: The Early Experience* (Philadelphia: Fortress Press, 1985). This issue is still alive today in terms of the proper role of religion and religious figures in public life. The agreement is that there is a place for Christian concern; what that place is remains a matter of hot dispute. Robert N. Bellah, *The Broken Covenant: American Civil Religion in Time of Trial* (New York: Seabury Press, 1975); David Hollenbach, S.J. *et al.*, "Theology and Philosophy in Public: A Symposium on John Courtney Murray's Unfinished Agenda," *Theological Studies* 40, 4 (December 1979), pp. 700–715; Richard John Neuhaus, *The Naked Public Square: Religion and Democracy in America* (Grand Rapids: William B. Eerdmans, 1984); Rembert G. Weakland,

"The Church in Worldly Affairs: Tensions Between Laity and Clergy," *America* 156, 10 (October 18, 1986), pp. 201–205, 215–216.

4. Alexander Grey, *The Socialist Tradition: Moses to Lenin* (New York: Harper and Row, Publishers, 1946), pp. 54–60; Ernst Troeltsch, *The Social Teaching of the Christian Churches*, II, trans. Olive Wyon (New York: Harper Torchbooks, 1960), pp. 554–560, 641–650; Jacob Viner, *Religious Thought and Economic Society*, eds. Jacques Melitz and Donald Winch (Durham: Duke University Press, 1978), pp. 8–72. The lending of money at interest is an interesting case of the development in ethical teaching. Usury today is still considered to be morally wrong, but it no longer simply refers, as it formerly did, to the practice of lending money at interest. Today usury means lending money at excessive interest. The end (of making money) and the means (by lending money at interest) become accepted; the manner of executing the end (the conditions under which one employs the means and so the concrete or specific means) is the debated point.

5. There are two other areas of major concern in contemporary moral theology. One is the question of economic justice, a question of particular urgency today because of our consciousness of the unacceptable inequality in the extremes of wealth and poverty. Recent Popes have frequently addressed this issue and, as I write, the American Catholic bishops have just completed the process of addressing themselves to the issue from the American perspective. See Donal Dorr, *Option for the Poor: A Hundred Years of Vatican Social Teaching* (Maryknoll: Orbis Books, 1983); National Conference of Catholic Bishops, "Economic Justice for All: Catholic Social Teaching and the U.S. Economy," *Origins* 16, 24 (November 27, 1986). The World Council of Churches has also addressed the issue on numerous occasions. See Ronald H. Preston, *Religion and the Persistence of Capitalism* (London: SCM Press, 1979). The other issue of great contemporary urgency is rooted in the area of medical and bio-ethics. It is provoked by the remarkable advances in medical science and technology. The best scholarly look at this particular story is David F. Kelly, *The Emergence of Roman Catholic Medical Ethics in North America: An Historical-Methodological-Bibliographical Study* (New York/Toronto: The Edwin Mellen Press, 1979).

6. Ralph B. Potter, *War and Moral Discourse* (Richmond: John Knox Press, 1969); John Howard Yoder, *The Politics of Jesus* (Grand Rapids: William B. Eerdmans, 1972), p. 158, puts the issue most clearly as one of means to a good end: "This refusal [to use violence] is not a withdrawal from society. It is rather a major negative intervention within

the process of social change, a refusal to use unworthy means even for what seems to be a worthy end." The just war theory is equally clear on the issue in that a just cause or just end is the first and most fundamental condition for any legitimate use of violence, but it is not a sufficient condition. See William V. O'Brien, "The Challenge of War: A Christian Realist Perspective," in Judith A. Dwyer, S.S.J. (ed.), *The Catholic Bishops and Nuclear War* (Washington, D.C.: Georgetown University Press, 1984), pp. 42–49.

7. National Conference of Catholic Bishops, *The Challenge of Peace: God's Promise and Our Response* (Washington, D.C.: United States Catholic Conference, 1983), 1–3, pp. 1–2. The same issue of the use of violence is highlighted for many non-Western Christians today by the demands for radical political and social change. The question for them becomes whether violence is ever a moral means in trying to effect the changes demanded by social justice. Hence, the question of violence becomes a central one for all forms of liberation theology. See, for instance, Juan Luis Segundo, *The Liberation of Theology* (Maryknoll: Orbis Books, 1976), pp. 154–182; Congregation for the Doctrine of the Faith, "Instruction on Christian Freedom and Liberation," *Origins* 15, 44 (April 17, 1986), pp. 723–726.

8. David Hollenbach, S.J., *Nuclear Ethics: A Christian Moral Argument* (New York/Ramsey: Paulist Press, 1983), pp. 47–62; and "Notes on Moral Theology: 1985—Whither Nuclear Deterrence? The Moral Debate Continues," *Theological Studies* 47, 1 (March 1986), pp. 117–133.

9. *The Challenge of Peace,* pp. 9–18: "Because we have been gifted with God's peace in the risen Christ, we are called to our own peace and to the making of peace in our world" (55), p. 17. Similar affirmations can be found in statements issued by many Christian denominations.

10. Stephen Charles Mott, *Biblical Ethics and Social Change* (New York/Oxford: Oxford University Press, 1982), pp. 59–81; Daniel C. Maguire, "The Primacy of Justice in Moral Theology," *Horizons* 10, 1 (Spring 1983), pp. 72–85; a now almost classic statement of this obligation is Synod of Bishops Second General Assembly, *Justice in the World* 6, in Joseph Gremillion, *The Gospel of Peace and Justice* (Maryknoll: Orbis Books, 1975), p. 514.

11. Formal ends, or formal norms, prescribe the attitudes and intentions human beings should bring to their actions, and so, in fact, norm human being rather than human action. In the present case, human beings should seek peace, intend justice and so on. See Richard M. Gula, S.S., *What Are They Saying About Moral Norms?* (New York/Ramsey: Paulist Press, 1982), pp. 55–58; more general discussions of norms can be found

in Charles E. Curran and Richard A. McCormick, S.J. (eds.), *Readings in Moral Theology No. 1: Moral Norms and Catholic Tradition* (New York: Paulist Press, 1979).

12. In addition to the works already cited, see Judith A. Dwyer, S.S.J., "Catholic Thought on Nuclear Weapons: A Review of the Literature," and David A. Hoekema, "Protestant Statements on Nuclear Disarmament," *Religious Studies Review* 10, 2 (April 1984), pp. 97–107. For a general overview of the different rationales behind the lack of consensus, see James P. Hanigan, "War and Peace: Christian Choices," *Today's Parish* (Nov/Dec 1983), pp. 21–24.

13. *The Challenge of Peace,* 282, p. 87: "At the same time, we recognize that the Church's teaching authority does not carry the same force when it deals with technical solutions involving particular means as it does when it speaks of principles or ends." This lack of certitude and authority in regard to means is not due simply to the religious nature of the Church's mission. It is due more basically to the nature of moral reality itself. It is also why people of good faith and good will may differ from one another in their concrete moral judgments.

14. The issue of the ends sexuality should serve is also a matter of concern to Christians in non-Western countries today, but different social circumstances bring different questions to the fore. In many African countries, for example, one of the key issues is polygamy. Eugene Hillmann, *Polygamy Reconsidered: African Plural Marriage and the Christian Churches* (Maryknoll: Orbis Books, 1975). A clear sense of the cultural, as well as moral, conflict that traditional western sexual morality can cause in other cultures can be had from reading Walter Trobisch, *I Loved a Girl* (New York: Harper & Row, Publishers, 1963).

15. Morton Hunt, *Sexual Behavior in the 1970s* (New York: Dell Publishing Company, 1974); Sol Gordon and Roger W. Libby, *Sexuality Today and Tomorrow* (North Scituate: Duxbury Press, 1976); David R. Mace, *The Christian Response to the Sexual Revolution* (Nashville: Abingdon Press, 1970), pp. 67–100; Reay Tannahill, *Sex in History* (New York: Stein and Day, Publishers, 1980), pp. 388–426.

16. Brian McNaught, *A Disturbed Peace: Selected Writings of an Irish Catholic Homosexual* (Washington, D.C.: A Dignity Publication, 1981), pp. 42–43, 68–69.

17. Charles E. Curran, "Sexuality and Sin: A Current Appraisal," *Contemporary Problems in Moral Theology* (Notre Dame: Fides Publishers, 1970); "Sexual Ethics: A Critique," *Issues in Sexual and Medical Ethics* (Notre Dame/London: University of Notre Dame Press, 1978); Philip S. Keane, *Sexual Morality: A Catholic Perspective* (New York:

Paulist Press, 1977); Andre Guindon, *The Sexual Language* (Ottawa: University of Ottawa Press, 1977); James P. Hanigan, *What Are They Saying About Sexual Morality?* (New York/Ramsey: Paulist Press, 1982).

18. Anthony Kosnik, *et al, Human Sexuality: New Directions in American Catholic Thought* (New York: Paulist Press, 1977); James B. Nelson, *Embodiment: An Approach to Sexuality and Christian Theology* (Minneapolis: Augsburg Publishing House, 1978); Michael Valente, *Sex, The Radical View of a Christian Theologian* (New York: Bruce Publishing Company, 1970).

19. There has been some needed discussion about what is actually meant by the justice and peace Christians should seek. See, for example, John Macquarrie, *The Concept of Peace* (New York: Harper & Row, Publishers, 1973); David Hollenbach, S.J., "Modern Catholic Teachings Concerning Justice," in John C. Haughey (ed.), *The Faith That Does Justice: Examining the Christian Sources for Social Change* (New York/Ramsey: Paulist Press, 1977), pp. 207–231. The degree to which the ends of our activity are under human control, or even should be, is a matter of considerable debate. The debate has its sharpest theological form in the debate over the relationship of human action to the coming of the kingdom of God. The practical importance of this debate for ethics has to do with the weight one gives to consequences in assessing moral responsibility and determining the rightness or wrongness of certain actions. If the ends of our activity are entirely in the hands of God, then even unhappy or disastrous consequences are of no account in determining moral responsibility. Most theologians give some weight to consequences and to the likely outcomes of human action. The critical question is how much weight and how to determine what else, if anything, should be taken into account. On the kingdom of God see Bruce Chilton (ed.), *Kingdom of God in the Teaching of Jesus* (Philadelphia: Fortress Press, 1984); John Gray, *The Biblical Doctrine of the Reign of God* (Philadelphia: Fortress Press, 1985).

20. Bruce M. Russett, "The Doctrine of Deterrence," in Philip J. Murnion (ed.), *Catholics and Nuclear War* (New York: Crossroad, 1983), pp. 149–151. There is a certain irony in the fact that we argue so bitterly over means to ends when we often cannot even be sure that the particular means we defend will, in fact, achieve the end. It is always important, therefore, to remember that not all ends have a necessary or even directly causal relationship to the means we advocate. This lack of clear causal connection has important consequences for claims made about sexual behavior, as well as for claims made for defense policies. The inescapable ambiguity of the nuclear issue is clearly reflected in the conclusions of *The*

Challenge of Peace, 147–199, pp. 46–62, in which a practical pacifism in regard to the use of nuclear weapons is joined with an acceptance of the possession and deployment of such weapons for the purposes of deterrence as morally tolerable on a short term basis while serious efforts are made to find an alternative way of keeping the peace and safeguarding freedom.

21. Derrick Sherwin Bailey, *Homosexuality and the Western Christian Tradition* (London: Longmans, Green, 1975); John Boswell, *Christianity, Social Tolerance and Homosexuality* (Chicago: University of Chicago Press, 1980).

One

THE HOMOSEXUAL SITUATION

To begin this study, let us pose a question. What does it mean to call homosexuality the moral issue on which Christian sexual ethics in general will stand or fall? For, after all, even on a very liberal estimate, it is an issue of direct and immediate concern to only one out of every four or five members of the human family.[1] While it is certainly not an issue theologians should ignore because of the minority status of homosexual individuals, why should it become the central focus of our ethical attention to sexual matters? Why make it the test-case for all Christian sexual ethics?

THE PROBLEM

By referring to homosexuality as the test-case I mean to affirm that, whatever understanding of human sexuality Christian theologians propose, whatever norms they generate to guide sexual behavior, whatever goods or values they associate with our being sexual creatures, whatever rituals, institutions and ways of life they develop to realize and protect these values, all of them must be tested for their truthfulness and Christian authenticity against both the fact of homosexuality and the experiential capacities of homosexual people themselves. Christian sexual ethics cannot legitimately ignore or bypass or exclude a minority of people. Its ethic must be one that is at least possible for all Christians—indeed, in principle, for all human beings—to embrace and live in good faith with a reasonable hope of success.[2] If it is not possible for a minority group of people to live, it cannot be obligatory for anyone, even acknowledging that the possibility may be only and always a graced possibility.[3]

17

At the same time that the ethic must be a universal possibility, it must also be a proclamation of the good news of Jesus the Christ. Both theologically and pastorally, Christians are summoned to proclaim a message of joyful hope and to express in their words and deeds a loving concern for others that bears witness to the truth and the reality of the hope that is in them (1 Pet 3:13–17). What Christians say about sexuality and sex must express this joyful hope and loving concern to homosexually oriented individuals as well as to those of heterosexual inclination. Something better than "You are a sinner; repent," or "Tough luck; that's the way things are," or "Resign yourself to a life of sexual abstinence," or "The rules do not apply to you" has to be said. Paul wrote to the Corinthians that it was better to marry than to burn (1 Cor 7:9). While it is not fashionable today to speak about sex and marriage in such negative terms,[4] there is, nonetheless, a measure of truthfulness about the human experience of sexuality in Paul's words. The human sexual drive can be and often is surprisingly imperious and unruly; it can manifest itself in many bizarre, aberrant, and humanly harmful ways. Is the only choice Christian sexual ethics can offer to homosexuals the choice to burn? And if there are other choices open to homosexuals, why should not these options be available to heterosexuals as well? Thus, homosexuality may well serve as the test-case of Christian sexual ethics since, among all the issues of sexual morality, it poses today the clearest challenge to the universal and evangelical character of that ethic.

Numerous stories emerging from pastoral practice can illuminate the point being made here. One such story, reported to me by a priest-student of mine and suitably camouflaged, will serve as one illustration. A man came to him in confession—I do not say to celebrate the sacrament of reconciliation for reasons that will appear. The man was in his mid-thirties, married and the father of three children. He had first become consciously aware of his homosexual inclinations in his late teens. He had tried to fight them off and to repress them without much success. He had been advised by a priest, ignorantly and tragically, to find a good woman, get married, and all that foolishness would disappear. He took that advice, but, of course, "the foolishness" did not disappear. His homosexual bent continued to exert itself, over-riding any lingering heterosexual inclinations and desires, and leading him into periodic homosexual episodes. These shamed him personally, and he also regarded them as acts of marital infidelity. Finally, in tears and at the edge of despair, the man cried out to the priest hearing his confession, "Father, help me; I don't want to be this way."

The priest, though deeply moved by the man's sincerity and full of compassion for him and his family, was baffled. What should he do or say, not along the lines of pastoral or psychological counseling, but from the perspective of religious faith, sexual ethics and moral responsibility?[5] Even acknowledging the terribly mistaken advice from the past, what, from an ethical perspective, does one say to this man about his future responsibilities and his own sexual conduct?

HOMOPHOBIA

There are certain aspects to the whole phenomenon of homosexuality that make it especially difficult to deal with and which, I suggest, support the contention that it is, indeed, the test-case for Christian sexual ethics. Several of these aspects are worth mentioning here. There is, first, the extensive cultural mythology about and resulting social antipathy toward homosexual individuals that create for them an inevitably distorted social situation. Homosexual persons have been forced to live in a situation of hiding, of relating to others under false pretenses, except in situations where their sexual orientation is known or can be openly proclaimed. And then, too often, they become either the butt of jokes or something of an odd curiosity.

Combined with this distorted social situation, and closely related to it, is the incomprehension of the majority heterosexual community. It is almost impossible without a studied effort—some would say it is altogether impossible—for the heterosexual person to comprehend the outlook and the problems of the homosexual individual who is like him or her in all things except sexual orientation. The "unnaturalness" of homosexual attraction and desire and the consequent immorality of homosexual acts seems almost self-evident to the heterosexual individual. The prospect of an intimate physical relationship with a member of one's own sex is not only not appealing to the heterosexual person, it is often repulsive. While that repulsion may well be culturally induced and sustained to a large degree, it is nonetheless real, causing in many people an almost pathological fear of homosexuality and homosexual people which we have come to call homophobia.[6] Parents have been known to disown children, friend to reject friend, when homosexual attraction reared its head. It is, then, little wonder that most homosexual persons are not initially eager to admit to others or even to acknowledge to themselves the true state of their sexual feelings and inclinations.

We sometimes gloss over this difference in experience for heterosexual and homosexual people too readily which is surely a mistake. It is worth some time to reflect upon the difference, for it reveals some important things about human sexuality and the process of its moral ordering. Heterosexual individuals enter into personal relationships or engage in daily social interaction without any need either to hide or to proclaim their sexual orientation. They simply take it for granted, just as they take for granted the sexual orientation of those with whom they interact, unless or until someone does or says something to cause them to wonder and question. Such personal relating or social interaction that takes place flows naturally, as it were, from this taken for grant ed, unreflexive preconsciousness.[7]

Though we rarely pay attention to the fact, heterosexual women relate differently to men and heterosexual men relate differently to women than they do to members of their own sex. I do not refer here to the subjects they talk about, or to the language they use, or to the social and cultural roles they play, or even to the social chauvinistic or sexist attitudes and biases they bring to their relationships. I refer rather to the emotional tone and unspoken feeling quality of the relationship, the physical and emotional comfortableness or dis-ease one feels in the presence of the other. When one stops to think about it, one attends differently to members of the opposite sex than one attends to members of the same sex. I find, for one instance, that in classes or lectures before a sexually diverse audience, I usually become aware that there are physically attractive women in the audience, and some not so attractive. But I do not have a clue as to whether there are physically

attractive men present. From the depths of preconscious awareness springs the unreflexive knowledge[8] of and consequent relatedness to members of the opposite sex as potentially desirable or
undesirable sexual partners or sexual aggressors which generates a
range of feeling and emotional tone toward them which is simply
different than what is felt toward members of the same sex.

Furthermore, in learning to order and discipline our sexual
curiosity, desiring and energy, to direct our sexual drives into chan-
nels that will be socially acceptable, respectful of the human autonomy and dignity of others, and personally enriching, it is the opposite sex, or, more precisely, particular persons of the opposite sex,
who become the focus of this difficult and never finished learning
process. Being a Christian, in the present author's case a Roman
Catholic Christian, I have that faith community and its religious
tradition to support and guide me and provide me with models in
the learning process. A normative direction which expresses the
meaning and worth of my sexual desiring and energy is made clear.
Sexuality, I am taught, has been ordered by the Creator, either
toward a life of consecrated celibacy witnessing to God's universal
love in the service of his people and to their eschatological hope, or
to marriage as the sacramental sign of Christ's union with and
fidelity to his Church and God's passionate love for each individual
member of the human family. Numerous historical examples of
holy men and women are offered to me for inspiration and imita-
tion, and unless my local community is morally bankrupt beyond
imagining, I have living examples of happy and fulfilled individuals
witnessing to the truth and reality of these meanings.[9]

As is common knowledge, the struggle to achieve some measure of psycho-sexual integration is not an easy one. The learning
process is fraught with difficulties, both personal and social, and
few people, if any, ever achieve perfect integration. But the struggle is certainly made easier and a measure of success is at least
possible for the heterosexual individual for a number of reasons
implicit in the experience just described. But the person with a
genuine homosexual orientation finds himself or herself in an
upside-down world. It is not members of the opposite sex but of
the same sex who become the dominant focus of one's sexual
curiosity, desiring and energy. And few of them welcome this atten-

tion or respond to the homosexual person in kind. One's sexual curiosity is met with hostility and contempt, labeled perverse, and given no acceptable social form in which to develop. One so oriented quickly comes to feel different[10] and alone,[11] and simply cannot take his or her sexual orientation and identity for granted, or anyone else's for that matter.

Unlike the heterosexual individual, therefore, the person of homosexual orientation is most commonly involved in a constant struggle to fight and deny his or her own sexual orientation and feelings, or to acknowledge them but keep them carefully hidden, revealing them only with the greatest care and discretion, or to proclaim one's sexual orientation openly as the central truth of one's personal identity, since it is so obviously of primary psychological and social importance.[12] Furthermore, even if and when one's sexual orientation is acknowledged to be dominantly homosexual, what is the normative direction in which to channel one's sexual desires and energies? The community of sexual love and procreative life called marriage is not a real possibility, or so the Church and society at large declare. The life of consecrated celibacy in community appears to be more of a fated condemnation or an occasion of sin than a personal calling to witness and service. What meaning and worth are to be found in homosexual desiring and energy? Who are the models, past or present, from whom the homosexual individual can take inspiration and guidance? And to whom can one speak about these troublesome feelings and questions in order to find some guidance and direction in life?

Given this difference in the heterosexual and homosexual experience, and the problems resulting from the difference for the homosexual person, it should not be surprisiing that an alternate life-style[13] develops around the homosexual orientation, just as a life-style different than married life develops around the life of consecrated celibacy and around the still uncommitted life of the single heterosexual person in the world. But it is only in the case of the homosexual person that one's sexual orientation is the explicit, conscious focus of that life-style and so of one's personal identity, as well as being the focus of social hostility and personal attack. Heterosexual people, as a rule, neither do, nor feel the need to, go about proclaiming themselves as such. Their sexuality and sexual orientation are, of course, a fundamental part of their personal identity, but hardly the central focus and core of that identity as mother or father, wife or husband, priest or nun, man or woman. Part of, indeed a fundamental part of, my own self-identity, for instance, if I may be excused the personal reference for the moment, is as a professor of theology. But I find I have no need, either personal or social, to say that I am a heterosexual professor of theology. The homosexual individual very frequently does have the need to include his or her sexual orientation in every affirmation of self-identity, and understandably so. But in that case, sexuality and sexual relationships tend to become excessively important in one's understanding of what it is to be human.[14]

This difference in experience, therefore, leads to a basic question. Should the moral norms that govern the sexual life of heterosexual people be the same as those which order the sexual existence of homosexual people? More basic still, not only should they be the same, but can they be the same? The traditional answer, generally still affirmed today from both sides of the sexual spectrum,[15] is that they can and should be the same because, whatever people's sexual orientation may be, they are all still human, they are all actual or potential members of the body of Christ. Christian sexual ethics guides everyone toward the full, responsible, human and Christian living of his or her life as a sexual being. To exclude, in principle, a minority from the possibility of living such a life, however small that minority may be, is simply unacceptable for a faith that is catholic or universal in principle and outreach. It is, then, the special situation of homosexual individuals, as sketched above, that is one more reason for suggesting that homosexuality is the test-case today for Christian sexual ethics.

SCIENTIFIC UNCERTAINTY

There are two other aspects to the issue of homosexuality which bear on its status as test-case that need to be mentioned before turning our attention to the question of moral evaluation. Both aspects have to do with our knowledge, or lack thereof, about human sexuality from the perspective of modern scientific investigation. Up to this point I have written as if the homosexual and heterosexual orientations were in polar contrast to one another, as conceptually and analytically they are. But from the evidence accumulated from the social sciences, existentially this does not appear to be the case. The scale developed by Alfred Kinsey and his associates for their reports on male and female sexual behavior[16] reflects the actual experience of human sexual attraction and desire more accurately than does a radical opposition between homosexual and heterosexual experience.

On a scale of zero through six, with exclusive homosexual and heterosexual orientations at either extreme, most human beings fall somewhere between the two extremes. In terms of their fantasies, dreams, feelings, curiosity, experiences of sexual attraction and interest, as well as their overt behavior, some degree of homosexual and heterosexual attraction and desire is known to most people. One does not have to understand or accept the Freudian theory that everyone at birth is polymorphously perverse,[17] that any object will serve to satisfy sexual desire, to recognize the truth manifested in Kinsey's scale. The evidence, for example, of fairly widespread homosexual behavior in places like prisons, seminaries, single-sex boarding schools and the military, that is, in places where there are no members of the opposite sex to whom one may relate in one's social setting, which behavior then ceases when individuals return to a two sex environment, is a confirmation of homosexual inclination and desire in many people whose sexual orientation is fundamentally heterosexual. Conversely, the desire and ability of many homosexually inclined people to enter into and sustain for a period of time a heterosexual relationship confirms Kinsey's findings as well.

This range in the spectrum of human sexual orientation brings us to the second aspect of the issue reflected in the scientific data.[18] Despite the growing interest in and research about the phenomenon of homosexuality, we still do not know what cause or combination of causes accounts for a person's sexual orientation, be it homosexual or heterosexual. We do know that individuals do not consciously and deliberately choose their sexual orientation nor can they simply decide to change the orientation they find themselves to have. That is the reason, incidentally, why we must conclude that there can be no moral stigma attached to being a person homosexually oriented any more than there is any moral merit to being a person of heterosexual bent. It is also the reason why one's own sexual orientation, whatever it may be, seems, from a purely subjective view, to be so entirely natural or, for people of a religious mind-set, God-given, and why the desires and actions arising from that orientation appear altogether appropriate and rightly immune from moral restraint, until the social prohibitions of one's culture are internalized by the super-ego.[19] We do know that a person's sexual orientation is basically established at a very early age, even though it may take years for the person to recognize and acknowledge it. But we do not know why these things are so with the result that we do not know, beyond serious question, how to evaluate homosexuality or how to classify it theologically, psychologically or sociologically.[20]

While there are a number of different theories about the causes of homosexuality, none have sufficient supporting evidence to be fully persuasive or to have won wide acceptance. While the American psychological community no longer classifies homosexuality as a psychological abnormality, a form of emotional immaturity or neurotic disorder, considering it now to be an alternate, albeit incomprehensible, sexual preference, that change was by no means unanimous among the professionals nor was it made with complete scientific detachment.[21] The inability of psychiatry and psychoanalysis, as well as other forms of psychological and behavioral therapy, to effect any change in the sexual orientation of individuals, their inability to cure the sickness, as it were, along with their inability to find specific symptoms of psychological abnormality associated with homosexuality,[22] were certainly factors in the decision to reclassify homosexuality psychologically. But political and social factors also played a part. To summarize, then, we do not know the causes of people's sexual orientation; we do not know how to change people's sexual orientation; we do not even know whether such a change is possible in theory; and even if it were possible, we do not know whether such a change would be desirable in practice. Consequently, as the authors of the study *Human Sexuality* expressed it, it is "difficult to say anything about homosexuality that is not of a provisional nature."[23] Another reason, then, for taking homosexuality as the test-case of sexual ethics today is our uncertainty about its psychological and social import, and so about the ethical directions human sexual expression should take.

PASTORAL DIFFICULTIES

There is a final factor about the situation of the homosexual individual which needs some attention. This factor can best be appreciated by contrasting the situation of the homosexual person to the dilemmas faced by other people who are caught up in one or another morally problematic sexual situation. I have in mind here such situations as the following: the person who is divorced and happily remarried outside the Church but whose longing is for a renewed communion with the ecclesial community; the person living with a beloved partner who for one reason or another refuses to have the relationship formally witnessed and blessed by the Church, and prefers to continue the relationship without the so-called benefit of clergy; the person who is physically separated from a spouse by human or natural necessity such as imprisonment or natural disaster; the person living a vowed celibate life which he or she is finding impossible to honor with any degree of spiritual tranquillity; the person married to a spouse who is physically or mentally so ill that no hope of recovery and no normal marital relationship are possible; and so on.

In all of the above situations and others similar to them, while courage and sacrifice may be required for faithful Christian living, there is always the possibility, at least, of a resolution of the situation for the people involved. The circumstances which make their situation morally problematic and personally difficult, and which may call into question their full communion with the Church, can be altered in various ways. Following the above examples in consecutive order, there is the possibility that an annulment of the previous marriage will be granted and a subsequent marriage in the Church will be possible; there is the possibility of a change of heart on the part of the reluctant partner and a willingness to marry publicly; there is the chance that time will bring an end to the separation; there is the opportunity to request a release from one's vows to enter upon a new way of life; there is the possibility that death will put an end to the suffering of the ill spouse; and in some cases, where public scandal can be avoided, there is the possibility for a solution in the internal forum when no solution in the external forum is available or possible.[24]

But none of these possible solutions are available to the homosexual person. In the present state of affairs in the Church, the homosexual person in a relationship is asked to separate and live without hope. No change in social circumstance will make any difference; no decision to submit oneself to the judicial or sacramental authority of the Church will win approbation for the continuance of an old sexual relationship or the inauguration of a new one. Nor is a solution to be found in the internal forum, since it is not the limits on juridical competence that render the public blessing of the relationship impossible. It is not a matter of surprise, then, that many active homosexual people are alienated from the Christian community and see the Church as an enemy, since nothing can be done to bless, approve, and strengthen their relationships, and nothing can be said or done which will change the homosexual person's condition. "I am sorry; I cannot help you," may well be the kindest words a homosexual individual will hear who seeks counsel and guidance from a priest or minister on how to live a richer and more faithful Christian life.[25] The question, then, of how the Christian sexual ethic can be good news for the homosexual individual is still another reason for considering homosexuality to be the test-case for Christian sexual ethics.

BIBLICAL ANALOGIES

Given all that has been said to this point, it is clear, I trust, why homosexuality is the test-case for Christian sexual ethics. Knowing as little as we do about its causes and consequences, knowing how central sexuality is to the healthy development of the human person and to the human capacity to love God and neighbor, knowing that we are called to minister the good news of Jesus Christ with both truthfulness and compassion so that ethical burdens are not to be laid upon people without clear warrant, and keeping in mind God's special concern for the outcast and oppressed, what should Christian ethics say about human sexuality and sexual behavior that does not ignore or gainsay the condition and experience of homosexual people themselves?

To express the same question in a different way, who is the analogue or model for the homosexual individual to follow? Is it the married couple, the consecrated celibate, or the single heterosexual in the world? While all three are called to practice the formal virtue of chastity in their particular ways of life, the concrete meaning and material norms of the virtue differ for each of them relative to their different life situations.[26] Marital chastity, for example, includes a number of sexual activities that would violate chastity for both celibate and single people. The chastity proper to the single heterosexual allows for forms of sexual expression and relating that would be neither morally appropriate nor humanly wise for the celibate. Or is the homosexual person in a fourth situation so that the material content of the virtue of chastity means something different for him or her?

To conclude this discussion of the homosexual situation and why it is the test-case for Christian sexual ethics, I refer the reader to the Gospel according to Matthew and the hard words there about the inadequacy of loving only one's friends (Mt 5:43–48). The clear intent of the admonition in the Gospel text is not that we should stop loving our friends or cease to greet those who greet us. The point of the text is rather to make love for one's enemies the test-case of what authentic Christian love is all about.[27] In a very practical and concrete sense, it is the love one has for one's enemies that reveals whether or not all one's loving is modeled on the form of God's love for us, who loved us while we were yet sinners (Rom 5:9). What Christian love ought to be and what it really is, in fact, are revealed most sharply in the relationship with one's enemies. It is not that loving one's enemies is the most frequent or most essential or the most joyful aspect of one's Christian life. Surely it is not. But it does serve to test the integrity and truthfulness of one's more common, ordinary experiences of loving the neighbor.

In a similar way, the truthfulness and integrity of Christian sexual morality, or so I am suggesting, is best tested, not by the more ordinary and common forms of human sexual relationships, but by the hard cases which somehow do not seem to fit into what we have accepted so comfortably and uncritically as normal and proper. If the destitute poor challenge our economic ethics and are the test of our Christian use of material wealth, and they are;[28] if the powerless and the voiceless are the test of our political ethics and the uses we make of our talents and power, and they are;[29] if the newly conceived and helpless aged are the test-cases for our ethics of life and the respect and protection we accord innocent life, and they are;[30] then I would argue that the homosexual person is the test-case for our Christian sexual ethic.

Lest the reader assume that the previous paragraph unduly prejudges the morality of homosexual acts and relationships in their favor, let me add that it does not and was not intended to do so. The good news that is the Gospel of Jesus Christ does not find its power and goodness in simply blessing whatever human beings find desirable or in bowing to what appears to be necessary. Nor does the Gospel become good news for the poor by making them rich in the things of this world, or for the powerless by giving them worldly prestige and status, or for the weak and the enfeebled by making them physically strong. It is quite possible for the Gospel of Jesus Christ to be good news for homosexual people without blessing homosexual acts or transforming a homosexual orientation into a heterosexual one.

What the challenge of the homosexual situation should do is to make us search our sexual ethic more critically and profoundly to be sure that we are not emphasizing trivial matters, while ignoring the weightier matters of justice, truth and love. Human hypocrisy runs rampant in sexual matters,[31] and there is no reason to think it might not also affect our sexual ethic, our sexual attitudes and our sexual purposes. Living in the individualistic, affluent and success-oriented society that we do,[32] it is understandable why many people might feel a certain revulsion upon looking into the face of the destitute poor, the incompetent voiceless, the deformed infant or enfeebled aged, or even the homosexually oriented individual. But such revulsion is not natural; it is a manifestation of the power of sin to limit and warp our willingness and ability to love one another as Jesus loved us.[33] We may not be guilty of or even responsible for these feelings of revulsion, but we are at fault if we allow them to dictate our behavior and shape our ethics.

It is in the light of what I have referred to here as the homosexual situation, though, truth to tell, it is the situation of us all, that I suggest we must face the biblical witness, the theological tradition and contemporary evaluations about the morality of homosexual behavior. The immediate task before us as we undertake this analysis is not to praise or blame, defend or criticize, but to understand both the whats and the whys of the Christian tradition. Whether or not one eventually esteems and adheres to this tradition, it is only fair first to allow that tradition to speak for itself before challenging or upholding it.

NOTES

1. Estimates of the number of people in the population whose sexual orientation is exclusively or predominantly toward members of the same sex vary rather widely, often in accord with the sexual orientation of those making the estimates. Complicating the question of numbers still more is the problem of what one means by a homosexual orientation. Even if we use the most restrictive definition and take the most conservative statistics, about four to five percent of the population has to be counted as predominantly homosexual in orientation. See Robert T. Francoeur, *Becoming a Sexual Person* (New York: John Wiley & Sons, 1982), pp. 513–516; Gordon and Libby, pp. 261–268; Michael R. Peterson, M.D., "Psychological Aspects of Human Sexual Behaviors," *Human Sexuality and Personhood* (St. Louis: Pope John XXIII Medical-Moral Research and Education Center, 1981), pp. 86–110. If we allow for parents, brothers and sisters, relatives, friends, and teachers in relationship to the homosexual individual, it is clear that the issue of homosexuality touches directly at least twenty percent of the population.

2. The notion of reasonable hope of success as a moral condition is borrowed from Just War Theory. The intent of the condition is to point out that one cannot be obliged to do what it is not possible to do, and that one ought not to risk serious harm in trying to do something that it is highly unlikely one will be able to achieve. Admittedly the notion of "reasonable hope of success" is less than precise, but it is not entirely amorphous. For an interpretation of this condition in regard to war see James F. Childress, "Just-War Criteria," in Thomas A. Shannon (ed.), *War or Peace? The Search for New Answers* (Maryknoll: Orbis Books, 1980), pp. 47–48.

3. Theologically, all good intentions and actions are inspired by

grace. See Karl Rahner, "Grace," in *Encyclopedia of Theology: The Concise Sacramentum Mundi,* ed. by Karl Rahner (New York: The Seabury Press, 1975), pp. 593–594. For the importance of recognizing the graced quality of human actions from a psychological viewpoint, see Rollo May, *Power and Innocence: A Search for the Sources of Violence* (New York: W.W. Norton & Company, Inc., 1972), pp. 256–257.

4. Philip S. Keane, S.S., *Sexual Morality: A Catholic Perspective* (New York/Ramsey: Paulist Press, 1977), pp. 5–11. The negativity of the Christian tradition toward sexual matters is often attributed to Augustine and with good reason. See David F. Kelly, "Sexuality and Concupiscence in Augustine," *The Annual of the Society of Christian Ethics* (1983), pp. 81–116. For a defense of Augustine against the charge see John J. Hugo, *St. Augustine on Nature, Sex and Marriage* (London: Scepter, 1969). The unpopularity of speaking negatively of sex and marriage today was reflected in the outcry in the popular press over the statement of Pope John Paul II that a husband could, and should not, lust after his wife. The present Pontiff's lectures on the Book of Genesis recognize both the positive giftedness of sexuality as well as its infection by the power of sin. See Richard M. Hogan and John M. LeVoir, *Covenant of Love: John Paul II on Sexuality, Marriage and Family in the Modern World* (New York: Crossroad, 1985) and Mary G. Durkin, *Feast of Love: Pope John Paul II on Human Intimacy* (Chicago: Loyola University Press, 1983).

5. Stanley Hauerwas, *Vision and Virtue* (Notre Dame: Fides/Claretian, 1974), pp. 103–105, has an excellent discussion and an example of the difference between a response based upon pastoral compassion and one based upon ethical criteria. He also alerts the reader to the dangers of confusing the two responses and the uselessness of Christian pastoral ministry if it has no grasp on the ethical issues involved in a person's situation. To stress the importance of this difference seems to be the major purpose of the recent letter to bishops from the Vatican's Congregation for the Doctrine of the Faith, "The Pastoral Care of Homosexual Persons," *Origins* 16, 22 (November 11, 1986), pp. 377, 379–382.

6. Jeannine Gramick, "Prejudice, Religion, and Homosexual People," in Robert Nugent (ed.), *A Challenge to Love: Gay and Lesbian Catholics in the Church* (New York: Crossroad, 1983), pp. 3–19.

7. For a brief discussion of the notion of unreflexive, preconscious knowledge and additional bibliographical references see George M. Regan, C.M., *New Trends in Moral Theology* (New York/Paramus: Newman Press, 1971), pp. 163–171.

8. *Ibid.,* especially p. 166.

9. The importance of symbolic or representative figures in shaping

our moral convictions and aspirations is difficult to overemphasize. This factor is all the more crucial to Christian faith which summons its adherents to follow a person and imitate a life. Without actual examples of what such a life is it is next to impossible for a person to embrace such a life. Here is to be found the theological and practical significance of the saints in the Catholic tradition. Little work has been done on the dynamics of this process and its relevance to Christian ethics. A start has been made by Philip S. Keane, S.S., *Christian Ethics and Imagination* (New York/ Ramsey: Paulist Press, 1984).

10. Richard Woods, *Another Kind of Love: Homosexuality and Spirituality* (Garden City: Image Books, 1978), p. 23.

11. McNaught, p. 9.

12. There is an interesting parallel between the importance sexuality takes on for homosexuals and the importance race takes on for black people in racially discriminatory societies. The social world, if it discriminates against people on the basis of sex or race, makes these factors of a person's existence of primary importance to individuals. One's color, or race, or sexual orientation is something one must come to grips with as a central feature of one's own identity and place in the world. See James P. Hanigan, *Martin Luther King, Jr. and the Foundations of Nonviolence* (Lanham: University Press of America, 1984), pp. 162–163. Obviously the same problem lies at the root of male machismo. If one's manhood is so closely tied to one's sexual prowess or ability to father children, then sex takes on an excessive psychological and social significance for the individual.

13. Edward A. Malloy, *Homosexuality and the Christian Way of Life* (Washington, D.C.: University Press of America, 1981), pp. 106–136, indicates the variety of social patterns in the homosexual way of life. This is a very valuable book to which I am indebted in a number of ways.

14. Woods, p. 37.

15. Woods, pp. 96–97; "Declaration on Certain Questions Concerning Sexual Ethics (*Persona Humana*)" in Kosnik, pp. 299–313.

16. Alfred Kinsey, Wardell Pomeroy and Clyde Martin, *Sexual Behavior in the Human Male* (Philadelphia: Saunders, 1948); *Sexual Behavior in the Human Female* (Philadelphia: Saunders, 1953).

17. Sharon MacIsaac, *Freud and Original Sin* (New York: Paulist Press, 1974), pp. 80–81, gives a clear explanation of what Freud meant by this claim and the rationale for it.

18. How theologians deal with the data of the social sciences is as difficult a question as how they deal with Scripture. For a careful analysis

of the problem and some sound suggestions see Cahill, *Between the Sexes,* pp. 83–104.

19. Gregory Zilboorg, M.D., "Superego and Conscience," in C. Ellis Nelson (ed.), *Conscience: Theological and Psychological Perspectives* (New York: Newman Press, 1973), pp. 210–223; John J. Glaser, "Conscience and the Super-Ego," *Theological Studies* 32, 1 (March 1971), pp. 30–47.

20. To classify homosexuality theologically would involve a determination as to whether or not a homosexual orientation is a consequence of original sin; to classify it psychologically would be to determine whether it is a psychological abnormality or within the range of psychic normality; to classify it sociologically would be to determine whether it serves a constructive social purpose or is socially dysfunctional. None of this do we know how to do with any degree of certitude.

21. Edward Batchelor, Jr., *Homosexuality and Ethics* (New York: Pilgrim Press, 1980), Introduction, pp. 2–3; Charles N. Socarides, M.D., "Homosexuality Is Not Just an Alternative Life Style," in Ruth Tiffany Barnhouse and Urban T. Holmes III (eds.), *Male and Female: Christian Approaches to Sexuality* (New York: Seabury Press, 1976).

22. Arlo Karlen, *Sexuality and Homosexuality: A New View* (New York: W.W. Norton & Company, Inc., 1971); see also Kosnik, *Human Sexuality,* p. 211.

23. Kosnik, p. 187.

24. The distinction between the internal forum and the external forum is made in canon law. Canon 130 of the new code reads as follows: "The power of governance is normally exercised in the external forum, but sometimes it is exercised in the internal forum only, but in such a way that the effects which its exercise normally has in the external forum are not acknowledged in this forum except as is established by law in certain instances." Briefly the external forum refers to the visible, public order of the Church or society. The internal forum refers to such things as the forum of conscience, sacramental confession, and so on. See James A. Coriden, Thomas J. Green, Donald E. Heintschel (eds.), *The Code of Canon Law: A Text and Commentary* (New York/Mahwah: Paulist Press, 1985), pp. 93–94: "A few examples of the exercise of this power only in the internal forum may be helpful: dispensation of certain occult impediments to marriage in special circumstances; secret marriages; remission of reserved censures in certain cases."

25. Pastoral sensitivity in this matter is slowly changing. Several dioceses have tried to develop pastoral guidelines for people working with homosexual individuals. See, for one specific example, "Guidelines for

Ministry to Homosexuals in the Diocese of San Jose," *Origins* 15, 40 (March 20, 1986), pp. 649–652. A collection of such documents can be found in John Gallagher (ed.), *Homosexuality and the Magisterium* (Mt. Rainier: New Ways Ministry, 1986). The most recent directive from the Congregation for the Doctrine of the Faith on "The Pastoral Care of Homosexual Persons," *Origins* 16, 22, leaves much to be desired in this regard. For a good critique of its pastoral shortcomings see Editorials, "Consulting Stephen's Experience: Pastoral Care of Homosexuals," *America* 155, 15 (November 22, 1986), pp. 313–314.

26. *Persona Humana,* 11, in Kosnik, p. 309.

27. Pheme Perkins, *Love Commands in the New Testament* (New York/Ramsey: Paulist Press, 1982), pp. 27–40.

28. National Conference of Catholic Bishops, "Economic Justice for All," *Origins* 16, 24, 48–52, pp. 417–418; Mott, *Biblical Ethics and Social Change,* pp. 60–61.

29. In addition to the references above, which rightly tie economic and political power together, see James P. Hanigan, "Spiritual Life and the Uses of Power," *Studies in Formative Spirituality* V, 3 (November 1984), pp. 335–344.

30. Cardinal Joseph Bernardin, "Enlarging the Dialogue on a Consistent Ethic of Life," *Origins* 13, 43 (April 5, 1984), p. 707.

31. Hypocrisy in sexual matters and in sexual ethics runs more deeply and widely than personal self-deception or personal bad faith. It can also be profoundly social as many recent studies have begun to argue. For one example of this sort of argument see Beverly Wildung Harrison, *Our Right To Choose: Toward a New Ethic of Abortion* (Boston: Beacon Press, 1983), pp. 154–186.

32. Robert N. Bellah, *et al., Habits of the Heart: Individualism and Commitment in American Life* (Berkeley: University of California Press, 1985).

33. James P. Hanigan, *As I Have Loved You: The Challenge of Christian Ethics* (New York/Mahwah: Paulist Press, 1986), pp. 105–113.

Two

THE BIBLICAL AND
THEOLOGICAL TRADITION

SOME PRELIMINARY DISTINCTIONS

Before beginning an analysis of the teaching about homosexuality in both the biblical and the theological traditions, it is first necessary to recall two basic distinctions. The two distinctions can be simply stated. First, there is a difference between an irreversible homosexual orientation and the occasional experience of homosexual attraction, desire, or even overt behavior. While a particular individual at a particular point in life might well have trouble telling the difference in his or her own case, the difference is and can be made both theoretically and clinically clear. A homosexual orientation involves the being and the personality of an individual in a much more fundamental way than does the occasional feeling of homosexual attraction or the occasional homosexual act. A sexual orientation defines a person in a way that a feeling or an action cannot. A sexual orientation is a constitutive element of who and what one is; a passing feeling or an occasional action is not, or at least need not be, constitutive of the self.[1]

Furthermore, one's sexual orientation is not a matter of conscious and deliberate volition. It has, as we have seen, the character or the appearance of being a given of one's human nature. This is the case even if it turns out on further investigation that one's sexual orientation is learned in some unconscious fashion. Sexual feelings, on the other hand, and even more so sexual acts, are susceptible in significant ways to conscious control and free choice.² While sexual feelings and desires may at times be almost overwhelming in their intensity and lead us to act in ways that appear to have been inevitable, there are, in fact, purposeful disciplines that one can adopt to control sexual desire and channel it in directions of one's own choosing.

This distinction between a homosexual orientation and homosexual feelings and acts represents a morally significant difference since the ethical demands for personal honesty with others and subjective authenticity with oneself mean that one is called upon in conscience to know and acknowledge the truth about the self one is. Whatever one's dominant sexual orientation may be, there is an ethical requirement that one not deceive others, or one's self, about it in relationships where such truthfulness is due the other.³ In addition, the moral virtue of prudence requires that we not take up activities and relationships when we have strong reasons to believe we will not be able to exercise proper responsibility for them. Prudence, however, does not ask us to refrain from responsibility simply on the grounds that its exercise will be challenging or difficult for us.

Second, there is the distinction, applicable to both homosexual and heterosexual individuals alike, between orientation and behavior, between what one is and what one does. Since, as has already been mentioned, one does not freely choose one's own sexual orientation, one cannot properly be held morally responsible for it. To be a person whose sexual orientation is predominantly homosexual or heterosexual is neither morally praiseworthy nor blameworthy. Therefore, the focus of ethical concern in discussions of sexual morality is not on one's sexual orientation but on overt, voluntary behavior, on what one does rather than on what one is, on the way in which a person acts out sexual feelings and desires, no matter what one's sexual orientation may happen to be.

But being and doing are not unrelated. The ethical concern with acts is partly because the human person becomes morally good or morally evil in and through attitudes, intentions and actions, in and through what the person loves, the ways in which he or she loves, and the concrete ordering one gives to the various objects of one's loving.⁴ Hence, in making moral evaluation of any human behavior, it is necessary to keep a number of things in mind. It is not enough to attend exclusively to the attitudes and intentions of the moral agent, that is, to the complex of reasons which motivate an action and give it its moral form, despite the central importance which intentionality undoubtedly has in the moral life.[5] It is also essential to attend to the object of moral choice, what one loves, and to the ordering of what one loves in the total context of one's life. What we do must be morally congruent with what we intend and our intentions are not capable in and of themselves of effecting this harmony between intention and action in every situation. More simply put, it is possible to mean well and do badly.

The first distinction between homosexual orientation and occasional experiences of homosexual attraction and desire, and the second related distinction between being and action in general, often affect the range of acceptable moral choices or possibilities available to the moral agent. Concretely expressed, heterosexual marriage may be an acceptable object of moral choice for a heterosexual individual for a number of specifiable reasons in a number of different circumstances,[6] but it is highly unlikely that it would often, if ever, be such a choice for the person with an irreversible homosexual orientation.

OLD TESTAMENT TESTIMONY

With these distinctions in mind, we can address the biblical and theological tradition. At first reading there would appear to be a quite clear condemnation of homosexual behavior in both the Old and the New Testaments, the normative source but not the sole source of Christian ethics.[7] The classical texts from the Hebrew Scriptures referring explicitly to homosexual behavior are the Sodom and Gomorrah story (Gen 19:1–29), and two texts from the Holiness Code (Lev 18:22; 20:13). The New Testament texts are Romans 1:26–27, Corinthians 6:9–10, and 1 Timothy 1:9–10. It is not to the point here to rehearse the history of the exegesis of these texts nor to propose some new interpretation of them.[8] Some brief attention to the texts, however, is required.

The story of Sodom and Gomorrah needs to be read in the context of God's determination to destroy these cities for their

great but unnamed wickedness (Gen 18:21) and Abraham's inter-
cession with God to save the cities if but ten just men could be
found living there (Gen 18:23–32). The two angels, who are taken
to be men by the townsfolk in Sodom, are on a tour of inspection,
as it were, to see if the just men can be found. The events which
follow upon their welcome by Abraham's nephew Lot are a confirmation that ten just men cannot be found and so lead to the
destruction of the cities. The idea lying behind the story is a common biblical theme. As Nahum Sarna has pointed out,

> As with the Flood, the Sodom and Gomorrah narrative is
> predicated upon the existence of a moral law of universal
> application for the infraction of which God holds all men
> answerable. The idea that there is an intimate, in fact,
> inextricable, connection between the socio-moral condi-
> tion of a people and its ultimate fate is one of the main
> pillars upon which stands the entire biblical interpretation
> of history.[9]

On even the most conservative reading of the particular pas-
sage in question (Gen 19:4–11), what is condemned as sinful in the
story is not simply homosexuality in general or even homosexual
acts as such, but the intent to commit homosexual rape in the
context of an abuse of hospitality against a background of general
depravity and disrespect for God.[10] The story certainly finds the
homosexual aspect appalling as evidenced by the offer, especially
strange to our modern ears, to give up to the crowd Lot's virgin
daughters in place of the two men. It is also clear that the author
designates homosexual activity, as it was understood at the time, as
the specific sin of Sodom.[11] But it must be remembered, as the
story sees it, that the two men are, in fact, not men but angels, a
fact known to God and the author of the story, albeit not known to
the townspeople. The story, then, can hardly be read as a condemnation of all homosexual activity in general and without qualification. Rape is rape and sinful, and gang rapes all the more so even
to our modern moral sensibilities, whether it be homosexual or
heterosexual rape. Furthermore, to abuse hospitality and to treat

messengers of God in this way would be particularly horrifying to the biblical authors.[12]

The two texts from the Holiness Code in the Book of Leviticus, however, are another matter. The texts themselves are brief and can be usefully quoted here. "You must not lie with a man as with a woman. This is a hateful thing" (Lev 18:22). "The man who lies with a man in the same way as with a woman: they have done a hateful thing together; they must die, their blood shall be on their own heads" (Lev 20:13). What is expressly forbidden in these texts is for a man to lie with another man as with a woman. This is seen, for no given reason, as an abomination before God, the penalty for which is death. It is worth noting that this is hardly the only sexual offense condemned so strongly in the Holiness Codes. Adultery, a great number of incestuous relationships, and bestiality are treated in similar fashion, with even the poor animal in the last case suffering the death penalty (Lev 20:15). The reasons for the strong opposition to such practices remain unexpressed except for the vague reference to the holiness of God (Lev 20:8), the unexamined belief that such actions are contrary to nature,[13] and an implicit concern for the stability and well-being of the family.[14]

There is no mention at all in the Old Testament of female homosexuality, which fact is not without interest since, for the biblical authors, it was the male seed alone which was thought to be the carrier of the new potential child, in whom rested the future of Israel and its possible Messiah. Consequently, seed-wasting, as male homosexual relations inevitably entails, was a crime against the welfare of the nation,[15] in a way that female homosexual relations could not be. These texts clearly show the Old Testament judgment about homosexual relations between men. And it can be safely assumed that the same judgment was shared by most of the New Testament authors, which accounts in part for the silence of so much of the New Testament on sexual matters.[16] What the texts do not make clear by themselves, as Robin Scroggs has recently demonstrated,[17] is what model of homosexual relations the texts intend to condemn and the reasons for the condemnation. That the texts envisage and intend to condemn all homosexual relations within the purview of the author's knowledge and understanding seems clear enough. That they also condemn all possible homosexual acts and relationships without qualification is an assumption that has been frequently made, but one for which there is no clear biblical or rational warrant.[18]

NEW TESTAMENT TESTIMONY

Similar difficulties beset the interpretation of the New Testament texts. There is certainly a clear-cut condemnation of homosexual relations between both men and women in Paul's Letter to the Romans. What renders the condemnation problematic as a universal condemnation is the context of lust, free choice, and a possible relationship to idolatry in which the condemnation takes place. In reading the first chapter of Paul's Letter to the Romans, one is struck by Paul's main theme: "The upright man finds life through faith" (Rom 1:17). It is the human refusal to honor the God they know that leads human beings into idolatry and then into moral depravity. "That is why God has abandoned them to degrading passions: why their women have turned from natural intercourse to unnatural practices and why their menfolk have given up natural intercourse to be consumed with passion for each other, men doing shameless things with men and getting an appropriate reward for their perversion" (Rom 1:26–27). Paul pictures people who have turned away from the true God and as a consequence are consumed with lust, people who knew what he called natural intercourse, but in the height of their rebellion against God have chosen homosexual intercourse instead. In short, what Paul portrays is a life which rejects God and takes as its object of worship the satisfaction of disordered human desires.[19]

Since Paul manifests no knowledge of an irreversible homosexual orientation, and never even considers the possibility of a caring, committed homosexual relationship, it is simply impossible to know what he would have said about our contemporary questions in regard to homosexuality. We cannot be sure that he wishes to rule out all homosexual activity as incompatible with Christian faith, unless we make the assumption that a homosexual orientation is always and everywhere a consequence and a manifestation of an idolatrous choice.[20] The reasons for not making such an assumption are to be found in the distinctions made at the beginning of this chapter.

The same problems involved in finding a universal or absolute condemnation of homosexuality in the Letter to the Romans pertain to the other New Testament texts as well. The First Letter to the Corinthians and the First Letter to Timothy both list sodomy or immoral relations between men and boys as among the practices which exclude one from the kingdom of God. Both letters assume such practices are similar to other behaviors like adultery, thievery, usury, murder, perjury and sacrilege. Not only do the texts not tell us why all homosexual behavior is wrong or in what ways it is similar to these other practices; they do not make explicit just what sexual practices in what contexts they have in mind when they condemn certain homosexual behaviors. Again, it is an unwarranted assumption that the biblical authors, had they the knowledge about the nature and variety of forms of homosexuality we have today, would wish to condemn without qualification all homosexual acts and relationships. It would be an equally unwarranted assumption to think that they would not wish to condemn all such acts and relationships.

While the Scriptures, then, yield at most a strong presumptive bias[21] against homosexual acts, the texts alone, as we must read them today,[22] do not settle the issue of the morality of homosexual behavior and relationships beyond all question. One is forced to agree, at least in a qualified way, with Scroggs' conclusion that "biblical judgments against homosexuality are not relevant to today's debate. They should no longer be used in . . . discussions about homosexuality . . . not because the Bible is not authoritative, but simply because it does not address the issues involved."[23] What seems to be needed for the contemporary task is a positive understanding of the nature and purpose of human sexuality, a need the Scriptures can certainly help meet. But that leads us to the second consideration of this chapter, the inherited theological teaching on the nature and purpose of human sexuality.

THE TRADITIONAL VIEW

Based upon a reading and an interpretation of a whole range of biblical texts, an understanding of human sexuality emerged and was developed in the Christian world which saw monogamous, indissoluble marriage between a male and a female to be the normative ideal to which human sexuality had been ordered by God. "This is why a man leaves his father and mother and joins himself to his wife, and they become one body" (Gen 2:24). The purpose of this sexual union was perceived to be the procreation and rearing of children. "God blessed them, saying to them, 'Be fruitful, multiply, fill the earth and conquer it' " (Gen 1:28). This reading of the Scriptures, which took Adam and Eve to be the prototypical couple symbolizing the divine purpose for human sexuality, led to an exquisitely clear and logically coherent sexual ethic that can be stated as follows.[24]

The relationship of marriage between a male and a female is the normative context for human sexual activity, most especially for genital, coital activity. Marriage is by its very nature—and in time for Roman Catholicism by its sacramental character[25]—monogamous and indissoluble. Therefore, all deliberately willed and pursued venereal pleasure outside the context of marriage is contrary to nature, against God's will, and consequently sinful. Within marriage the primary purpose of sexual activity is the procreation of children. Therefore, all forms of contraceptive intercourse, all intercourse during pregnancy or after menopause,[26] and all sexual activity leading to orgasm outside the act of genital intercourse contradict this purpose, are against God's will as revealed in nature, and so are seriously disordered. There are, of course, other secondary purposes to be realized in and through the sexual relationship, but these are never to be realized at the expense of the primary purpose. Among such secondary purposes are the releasing of sexual tension (the famous *remedium concupiscentiae*),[27] and the mutual comforting of one another. Given this basic sexual ethic, all homosexual acts are clearly morally wrong, for they occur outside the context of marriage and cannot be aimed at procreation. There could be no question about the immorality of such acts, though there could be differing views on the moral gravity of them.[28]

Over the centuries that inherited tradition on sexual morality was qualified in some ways, but those qualifications did not affect the judgment about the morality of homosexual acts. In the last sixty years, however, some important qualifications of the inherited tradition have been made which do affect the moral evaluation of homosexuality, though they were not made for that reason, but in the interests of a more biblically and empirically adequate understanding of human sexuality. I wish to mention three such qualifications here, and their unforeseen implications, using the official magisterial teaching of the Roman Catholic Church where these qualifications can be most readily detected and explored.

CASTI CONNUBII

The first important qualification can be found in the 1931 encyclical letter, *Casti Connubii,* of Pope Pius XI.[29] This letter was written, in part, as a response to an action of the Anglican bishops at the Lambeth Conference of 1929.[30] The bishops accepted the practice of contraceptive intercourse within marriage as a matter for conscientious Christian decision and left the means of contraception up to the tastes and needs of individual couples. Pius XI rejected that position of the Anglican Church but he did, in a highly qualified way, accept as morally permissible the so-called rhythm method of birth control.[31] The immediate consequence of that acceptance for moral theory on sexuality was that a Christian intentionality toward sexual activity is not morally required to include a procreative intent, only a loving intent in the context of committed marital fidelity. Insofar as the good or end of procreation is concerned, all that the nature of human sexuality requires of a Christian intentionality is an openness to the possibility of that good. One does not have to seek the good; one must only be willing to accept it. Hence, the Pope continued to oppose artificial, or humanly contrived, means of contraception as being radically opposed to such willingness.[32]

Though this was not explicitly emphasized in the encyclical, it seems clear on hindsight that sexual relations are now being understood to have a meaning and purpose other than procreation, a purpose which, while remaining hierarchically subordinate to the procreative purpose in the Pope's view,[33] can be legitimately sought in independence of either procreative intent or procreative possibility. In simple, if somewhat crude terms, there is more to sex than having babies, and this more can be morally pursued with at least intentional independence from the good of procreation, as well as natural, if temporary, biological independence. The sticking point for many people was why this temporary biological independence had to be natural and in no way artificial or humanly aided or contrived. The most obvious, if not altogether persuasive, response was that a natural independence showed respect for God as the author of nature and the giver of life, in a way that a humanly contrived independence did not.[34]

GAUDIUM ET SPES

This implication about a meaning to sexual relations independent of the good of procreation received explicit official confirmation in the second important qualification of the tradition which can be readily seen in a document of the Second Vatican Council.[35] In their discussion of marriage the council fathers reaffirmed the double purpose of sexual relations to be unitive and procreative, to involve both the making of new love and new life. But they refused to order the two purposes hierarchically, to say that one always took precedence over the other.[36] They were also explicit in recognizing the integral goodness of sexual acts in marriage even when procreation was neither possible nor desired,[37] and in acknowledging that at times the two goods could and did, in fact, come into conflict through no fault of the couple. Hence, they insisted upon the responsible control of births as a moral imperative of a couple's sexual life.[38] Due to the request of John XXIII and then Paul VI, both of whom had established commissions to study the question of artificial means of birth control, the council fathers did not pursue the question of the acceptable moral means to exercise this responsibility.[39]

Once again there is an implication in their position which was not spelled out, and was quite possibly not even foreseen. If there is an integral goodness to marital sexual relations apart from and independent of both procreative possibility and procreative intent—as, for example, in the relations between a husband and wife when the woman is past menopause or the man is known to be sterile—then the primary purpose, the continuous and pervasive meaning of sexual activity, is not procreation but must be found in the unitive purpose. Sex finds its deepest and lasting meaning as an expression, celebration and deepening of the two-in-one flesh unity of the couple. The moral worth of sexual acts is based upon their relationship to the couple's mutual love for and shared life with one another, and not upon either their procreative intent or their procreative openness. The order of the two goods of procreation and union must now be reversed and a new task is set for moral theologians. That task is to explain the relationship of the procreative good to the more basic, more pervasive unitive good.

HUMANAE VITAE

The third qualification of the inherited theological teaching on sexual morality can be seen in Pope Paul VI's encyclical letter, *Humanae Vitae*.[40] In this letter Paul attempted to carry out the new task, to explain the relationship of the procreative good to the unitive good. He accepted Vatican II's position. He repeated it explicitly[41] and insisted still more strongly on what he called the duty of responsible parenthood, even going so far as to explain the objective conditions of the responsibility.[42] He attempted to argue in the letter that there is an indissoluble link, established by God and revealed in nature, between the two goods of interpersonal unity and procreation.[43]

This is not the place to enter into an analysis and critique of *Humanae Vitae*.[44] I merely wish to point out that in emphasizing both the duty and the conditions of responsible parenthood, Pope Paul made it clear that there are circumstances and conditions which make it morally irresponsible for even a faith-filled married couple to bring children into the world, insofar as that activity is subject to their control. In not simply forbidding sexual relations between a husband and wife when such circumstances obtain[45]—abstinence, after all, is the only 100% sure-fire method of birth control short of surgical sterilization—he, too, gave an independent status to the unitive meaning and good of sexual relations. He, too, acknowledged the more basic and pervasive meaning of sexual acts to lie in love-making.

Married couples, of course, have long known that the meaning of their sexual life together is hardly centered upon or exhausted by procreative intent and consequence. But even the practice of the Church itself in regard to sacramental marriage should have revealed this basic truth. The Church does not refuse marriage to couples incapable of having children, be it for reasons of age or physical condition. Nor does the Church insist that married couples cease all sexual congress once the wife has passed her child-bearing years or some disease or accident has made procreation a physical impossibility. The impediment to marriage and to the sexual relations appropriate to marriage is not sterility. The impediment is impotence, the physical inability to engage in sexual intercourse at all.[46] Furthermore, while the traditional teaching has at times bordered on it,[47] it has not in general held it to be morally wrong for courting couples to hold hands, embrace, kiss, and engage in other forms of affective sexual expression, provided only that such expressions be mutually agreeable and not so excessively passionate as to carry the couple beyond rational, moral control, in which case such actions would be proximate occasions of sin, and themselves sinful when freely done.

What these qualifications of the inherited theological tradition on sexual morality all lead to is the conclusion that human sexuality finds its deepest and perduring meaning as an expression and deepening of interpersonal love in a context of committed fidelity. The good of procreation is not unrelated to the unitive good, but it is also not absolutely essential to it. The mere fact of an intentional and biological inability to procreate can no longer be considered a moral barrier to sexual intimacy where the integral goodness of the unitive end of sexuality is possible of realization—at which point in the developing theological tradition the morality of homosexual acts and unions is open for moral re-evaluation.

REASON FOR DEVELOPMENT OF THE TEACHING

It is not an accident of history that so much of the theological tradition on sexuality in this century has been concerned with the issue of birth control. The thoughtful reader will quickly realize that the good of procreation, regarded as the over-riding purpose to which human sexuality was divinely ordained, was indeed the lynch-pin which held the sexual ethic together. Once that pin is removed, there is no human sexual practice that does not require reevaluation, and many supporters of the traditional position are convinced that nothing else can take its place.[48] Once contraceptive intercourse is tolerated as an at times morally acceptable practice in the Christian life, there remains, it is suggested, no moral barrier to any other form of sexual expression. Whether that fear proves to be correct or not, what I have been concerned to show in the theological tradition is that the move away from procreation as the primary purpose of human sexual activity goes back a number of years. It is a move that was made much more rapidly, even precipitously, by most mainline Protestant denominations than by other Christian churches, but it has comparable, if more cautiously tentative steps, in the Roman Catholic tradition itself.

Our reflections on the theological tradition would not be complete if we did not inquire briefly into what accounts for this move. Certainly several non-theological factors must be acknowledged. The growing global population in an increasingly industrialized world made children into an economic liability rather than an economic asset. Large families became increasingly burdensome in terms of parents' economic, psychic and spiritual resources, to say nothing of the demands on their time and energy. This development made it increasingly difficult to care well for a large number of children, even for people of good will. Industrialization, and its inevitable partner, urbanization, meant dwellings were smaller, land for outdoor activity was less available, and the possibility for extended family living was more restricted. The burdens of child care became the exclusive responsibility of the parents, and in most cases fell squarely on the shoulders of the mother.

Second, the technological development of reasonably safe and effective birth control devices seemed to make procreation a real human choice rather than a matter of resignation to a seemingly arbitrary divine will.[49] This technical achievement promised to bring welcome relief from a series of unwelcome pregnancies and to reduce the problems of child care to more manageable proportions. Having a child now appeared to be a matter of human choice and responsibility, only tangentially and subjectively related to one's marital or sexual relationships. Sex, which is, or should be, a private, interpersonal act, began to lose its obvious social meaning when it was no longer understood to have as its primary rationale the procreation of children. We have seen the impact of these two developments on the theological tradition itself as it began to give increasing importance to the unitive good of marriage.

Third, a whole complex of cultural developments in the West conspired[50] to shift the meaning of life from social well-being to individual self-fulfillment.[51] This emphasis on the individual was accompanied by a product of medical science, a longer life-expectancy. These two developments had their most noticeable impact upon women, who now sought their fair share of the social and cultural goods of society, education, job satisfaction, economic independence and political participation. Motherhood, no matter how important to an individual woman, was no longer capable of exhausting a woman's identity. There had to be more to a woman's life than mothering, if for no other reason than that women were facing an additional thirty to forty years of life after the tasks of motherhood were completed. Nor, for the same reason, could children be the cement which held the marital relationship together "until death do us part." Consequently, the bearing and rearing of children became but one part of a woman's life project, and, with the advent of reasonably safe contraceptives, a voluntary part at that.[52]

But there are also theological reasons which account, in part, for the development in the traditional teaching. At least one of those reasons we have already seen: the critical-historical method[53] of reading and interpreting biblical texts. The attention paid to the social and cultural contexts in which the various biblical materials were written and transmitted makes it clear that some traditional teachings are not as well-founded biblically as we once thought.[54] This is the case especially with moral teachings, precisely because morality is so context-dependent. Human actions do not take place in a vacuum; they are dependent for their meaning on the context or situation in which they occur, just as the consequences of those actions often vary in relationship to changing contexts. That does not mean that moral principles and general moral teachings cannot be formulated; it does mean that the application of moral principles and general moral teachings varies with the situation to which they are applied.

A second, and to my mind even more critical, theological reason which accounts for the development in the tradition is a renewed appreciation for and a new insight into the centrality of human dignity and what it requires in theological thought. This is especially noticeable in the Roman Catholic tradition in both the official papal encyclicals on social justice issues[55] and in the writings of major theologians who have explored the intimate relationship between theology and anthropology.[56] It would be beyond the scope of the present work to explore this new emphasis in any detail, but one example may serve to illustrate and confirm this claim.

Christian theology has always placed a high value on the human person in its insistence on such doctrines as the creation of human beings in the image and likeness of God, their redemption in the blood of Christ, the inviolability and sacredness of the human conscience, and their eternal destiny of communion with the Trinitarian God. Doctrines such as these led to a strong, Roman Catholic[57] ecclesiastical and theological insistence upon the human obligation to respond to such overwhelming grace by worshiping God, keeping the commandments of God, practicing the theological and moral virtues, and in general showing oneself to be worthy and appreciative of the grace one had received. Rarely, if ever, were the doctrines thought out from the other side of the coin, in terms of the rights and respect due to the person so graced by God. People who failed to fulfill their obligations and show proper respect to God were regarded as ungrateful, unworthy, and fit subjects for divine and human justice. Such an attitude can be summarily captured in a traditional expression, "Error has no rights."[58]

This attitude and manner of understanding have changed. More and more, Christian theology is thinking through what is due to human persons in virtue of their dignity. Workers have a right to a just wage; children have a right to an education; women have a right to participate fully in the social order; all persons have a right to freedom and a fair share of the goods of society. These are rights one has in virtue of who and what one is; they are not privileges which have to be earned. While it may remain true that error has no rights, people do have rights even if they are in error.[59] Criminals may be the best illustration of this insistence on human dignity. Despite their crimes and the punishment properly due to them, criminals remain human beings and have a right to be treated as such. Difficult as it may be to achieve, the criminal justice system, if it is to meet the demands of justice, must be humane.

In regard to our present topic of homosexuality, whether or not homosexual behavior is to be judged as contrary to God's will, all homosexual people have rights as persons, rights which their sexual behavior, and even less their sexual orientation, do not negate. In more explicitly theological terms, sin does not invalidate or overcome God's creative and redemptive work, nor does sin excuse human beings from their moral obligations to one another. The sinner still has a just claim to be treated with dignity and respect, not because he or she is a sinner, but because he or she is and remains human. Whatever judgment one may make on the morality of homosexual acts and relationships, there is simply no theological or moral reason to deprive homosexual individuals of their human, civil and legal rights, or to deny their human dignity.

It is not easy to think out all the implications of human dignity in a complex social world and to give specific meaning and concrete form to the rights and obligations human dignity morally entails. It is even more difficult to determine which, if any, of these moral rights and obligations should also be legally protected and enforced. But recognizing that sexuality is an intrinsic component of human personhood means, among other things, that sex, to be morally appropriate, must be fully human; it must not be coerced; it must not be bought and sold as a product; it must not be used as a means to some end extrinsic to the dignity and worth of people. That is to say, sexuality and sex, while they certainly have both social meaning and social consequence, must be thought out first in terms of how they participate in and contribute to the dignity of the human person. Hence, the focus of moral thought in regard to sexuality has turned toward an examination of the personal and inter-personal goods of sex, rather than beginning with the social goods of procreation and marriage. It is that development which I have tried to uncover in the theological tradition and which I ask the reader to keep in mind as we turn to an examination of the various proposals currently being made about the morality of homosexual acts and relationships.

NOTES

1. I use constitutive here in the strong sense of being an essential element of a reality, without which it would not be what it is. As *Persona Humana* 1 expresses it, "According to contemporary scientific research, the human person is so profoundly affected by sexuality that it must be considered as one of the factors which give to each individual's life the principal traits which distinguish it." See the agreement and commentary in Kosnik, pp. 82–83. Sexuality, however, is not generic in reality, but specific. Biologically, one is not simply sexual, but male or female. And as a dynamic reality, one's sexuality includes an orientation toward the other, an orientation which is, at the very least, biologically and physically complementary to the opposite sex. Sexuality is not, of course, the only factor in human self-definition, but without a sexual orientation, human beings would not be human.

2. The degree of control human beings have over their sexual feelings is both limited and varied, but nonetheless real. Sexual feelings can be consciously stimulated, as the pornography business knows so well, and they can be repressed or supplanted. While we cannot deliberately make ourselves feel sexual attraction toward someone to whom we are not attracted, nor simply will away an attraction we do feel, we can control to a degree the intensity and frequency with which the attraction moves us. Actions are subject to even greater purposeful control.

3. The classic definition of the moral fault of lying includes the stipulation of telling a falsehood to one to whom the truth is due. That definition recognizes that not everyone has a right to know everything. Hence, one's sexual orientation is frequently nobody's business but one's own. But in entering into certain kinds of relationships, one might well have the obligation to make one's sexual condition clear. A courtship would be one obvious example of such a relationship.

4. Henry Fairlie, *The Seven Deadly Sins Today* (Notre Dame/London: University of Notre Dame Press, 1979), pp. 34–36, illustrates very well the traditional Augustinian notion that all sin starts in love and is love gone astray in one way or another. Germain Grisez, *The Way of the Lord Jesus: Vol. 1 Christian Moral Principles* (Chicago: Franciscan Herald Press, 1983), pp. 573–598, gives a more thorough account of human love

and its relationship to God that confirms the same view. On pp. 127–128, Grisez indicates the inadequacy of Augustine's view of the goods appropriate to love.

5. Timothy E. O'Connell, *Principles for a Catholic Morality* (New York: Seabury Press, 1976), pp. 78–82. O'Connell speaks of motive rather than intentionality but goes on to explain that by motive he means the meaning the action has to the individual.

6. No human choice can be judged to be a moral choice apart from the consideration of the concrete circumstances in which the choice is made; hence the language of "may be" in the text. In the case of a person homosexually oriented, the homosexual orientation is a circumstance which most likely precludes the choice of heterosexual marriage.

7. Cahill, *Between the Sexes,* pp. 4–6.

8. The best recent commentary on these texts is to be found in Robin Scroggs, *The New Testament and Homosexuality* (Philadelphia: Fortress Press, 1983); commentaries on the same texts by two moralists with quite different conclusions on the question of homosexual activity can be found in John McNeill, S.J., *The Church and the Homosexual* (Kansas City: Sheed, Andrews and McMeel, 1976), pp. 43–74 and Malloy, pp. 186–211.

9. Nahum M. Sarna, *Understanding Genesis: The Heritage of Biblical Israel* (New York: McGraw-Hill Book Company, 1966), pp. 146–147; author's italics omitted.

10. Bruce Vawter, *On Genesis: A New Reading* (Garden City: Doubleday and Company, Inc., 1977), pp. 233–234; Sarna, pp. 144–145.

11. Vawter, pp. 234–235.

12. *Ibid.,* p. 235.

13. For an explanation of what it meant in the Old Testament for something to be contrary to nature, see J. R. Porter, *Leviticus* (London/New York: Cambridge University Press, 1976), pp. 83–85. The author makes it clear that it is ritual purity which calls for harmony with or conformity to nature, but there are also overtones of moral purity involved.

14. Martin Noth, *Leviticus: A Commentary* (Philadelphia: The Westminster Press, 1965), pp. 146–151; W. Gunther Plant, Bernard J. Bamberger, and William W. Hallo, *The Torah: A Modern Commentary* (New York: Union of American Hebrew Congregations, 1981), pp. 877–880.

15. Edward Schillebeeckx, O.P., *Marriage: Human Reality and Saving Mystery* (London: Sheed and Ward, 1965), pp. 83–84.

16. Stephen Sapp, *Sexuality, the Bible and Science* (Philadelphia: Fortress Press, 1977), p. 37; R. K. Harrison, *Leviticus: An Introduction and Commentary* (Downers Grove: Inter-Varsity Press, 1980), p. 251.

17. Scroggs, pp. 123–129.

18. There may be theological reasons for drawing conclusions from the biblical texts that sustain an absolute prohibition on homosexual acts and relationships, but that is different than simply claiming a biblical warrant for the prohibition. One should be clear about the difference. The recently issued letter of the Congregation for the Doctrine of the Faith, "The Pastoral Care of Homosexual Persons," 6, *Origins* 16, 22, pp. 379–380, is less than clear about the dialectical relationship that should exist between the Scripture and present theological reflection. Grisez, *The Way of the Lord Jesus,* pp. 831–870, especially pp. 848–849, is very clear on the difference between the exegesis of biblical texts and the theological claims which appeal to, yet go beyond the texts. Whether one agrees with his theological views or not, he cannot be faulted in this regard.

19. C. K. Barrett, *A Commentary on the Epistle to the Romans* (New York/Evanston/London: Harper & Row, Publishers, 1957), pp. 38–40; John Murray, *The Epistle to the Romans* (Grand Rapids: William B. Eerdmans, 1968), pp. 43–47. Both commentators are clear that the depravity of homosexuality for Paul is based on its departure from the divine plan of creation. As a rebellion against what Paul sees as natural, homosexual behavior is also a rebellion against God. And because Paul sees it as a chosen rebellion, one can understand the hostility toward those who make such a choice. I have deliberately chosen commentaries here that were written before the contemporary problematic in regard to homosexuality was commonly recognized. What Paul says is clear. What he would say, were he faced with the contemporary problematic, is another question. The pastoral epistles in this matter merely borrow from Paul and the views of most of their contemporaries. See A. T. Hanson, *New Century Bible Commentary: The Pastoral Epistles* (Grand Rapids: William B. Eerdmans, 1982), pp. 44–45, 58–59.

20. The Council of Trent spoke of concupiscence, which affects both heterosexual and homosexual desire, as a consequence and a manifestation of original sin, not simply homosexual desire. "*Hanc concupiscentiam . . . ex peccato est et ad peccatum inclinat.*" Denzinger-Schonmetzer, *Enchiridion Symbolorum,* 1515.

21. The most complete explanation and use of presumption in moral analysis and argument can be found in J. Philip Wogaman, *A Christian Method of Moral Judgment* (Philadelphia: Westminster Press, 1976), pp. 38–215. In Catholic moral theology, presumptive bias is granted to the magisterial teaching of the Church, not simply on authoritarian grounds but because of the graced office the magisterium is. As Paul VI expressed it in *Humanae Vitae* (On the Regulation of Birth), 28, "Be the

first to give, in the exercise of your ministry, the example of loyal internal and external obedience to the teaching authority of the Church. That obedience, as you know well, obliges not only because of the reasons adduced, but rather because of the light of the Holy Spirit, which is given in a particular way to the Pastors of the Church in order that they may illustrate the truth." Cited from Gremillion, *The Gospel of Peace and Justice*, p. 441.

22. This book rests on the conviction that a-historical, fundamentalist readings of the scriptural text are both religiously and intellectually flawed. See Raymond E. Brown, *Biblical Exegesis and Church Doctrine* (New York/Mahwah: Paulist Press, 1985; Terence Keegan, *Interpreting the Bible: A Popular Introduction to Biblical Hermeneutics* (New York/Mahwah: Paulist Press, 1986).

23. Scroggs, p. 127; author's italics omitted. The text suggests agreement with Scroggs in a qualified way since it does not seem warranted that we dismiss or ignore the biblical texts altogether in any contemporary consideration of homosexuality.

24. The ethical view to be summarized in the text can be found at much greater length and detail in Bernard Häring, C.SS.R., *The Law of Christ*, III, trans. Edwin G. Kaiser, C.SS.R. (Westminster: The Newman Press, 1966), pp. 267–376.

25. Theodore Mackin, S.J., *Marriage in the Catholic Church: What Is Marriage?* (New York/Ramsey: Paulist Press, 1982), pp. 20–26.

26. Häring, *The Law of Christ*, III, pp. 346–347, in speaking of intercourse during pregnancy, points out that this is no longer the case in current theological teaching: "In antiquity and even up to modern times, moral theology was largely more severe in its judgment on this point. The attitude was an altogether logical conclusion from the premise that marital union must be motivated by the actual or virtual intention of generating children." The same logic and the same position follow in regard to intercourse after menopause.

27. The notion of marriage as a *remedium concupiscentiae* is often misunderstood to mean a license to satisfy sexual desire without limit or as the institutional legitimation of lust. In either case it understands the remedy to mean permission to satisfy an urge which cannot otherwise be safely controlled. This interpretation ignores the meaning of *remedium*. It is a healing of concupiscence or of lust, not a giving into it. See Häring, *The Law of Christ*, III, p. 335.

28. Boswell, pp. 207–266.

29. Pius XI, *Casti Connubii*, in Odile M. Liebard (ed.), *Love and Sexuality: Official Catholic Teachings* (Wilmington: McGrath Publishing

Company, 1978), pp. 23–70. The letter is actually dated December 31, 1930.

30. John T. Noonan, *Contraception* (Cambridge: Harvard University Press, 1965), p. 424.

31. *Casti Connubii,* 85, p. 42: "Nor are those considered as acting against nature who in the married state use their right in the proper manner although on account of natural reasons of time or of certain defects, new life cannot be brought forth. For in matrimony as well as in the use of matrimonial rights there are also secondary ends, such as mutual aid, the cultivating of mutual love, and the quieting of concupiscence which husband and wife are not forbidden to consider so long as they are subordinated to the primary end and so long as the intrinsic nature of the act is preserved."

32. *Ibid.,* 80–82, p. 41.

33. Philip Keane has pointed out to me that in *Casti Connubii,* 50, p. 31, Pius XI had referred to a sense in which the unitive meaning of marriage was primary. To cite the Pope's words, "This mutual inward moulding of husband and wife, this determined effort to perfect each other, can in a very real sense, as the Roman Catechism teaches, be said to be the chief reason and purpose of matrimony, provided matrimony be looked at not in the restricted sense as instituted for the proper conception and education of the child, but more widely as the blending of life as a whole and the mutual interchange and sharing thereof." If one is looking for an authoritative theological source to support the view of many contemporary theologians in regard to the purpose of sexuality, here it is.

34. Paul VI, *Humanae Vitae* 13, in Gremillion, *The Gospel of Peace and Justice,* pp. 433–434: "To make use of the gift of conjugal love while respecting the laws of the generative process means to acknowledge oneself not to be the arbiter of the sources of human life, but rather the minister of the design established by the Creator. In fact, just as man does not have unlimited dominion over his body in general, so also, with particular reason, he has no such dominion over his generative faculties as such, because of their intrinsic ordination towards raising up life, of which God is the principle."

35. *Gaudium et spes* (The Church in the Modern World), in *The Gospel of Peace and Justice,* 47–52, pp. 282–290.

36. *Ibid.,* 48, pp. 285–286.

37. *Ibid.,* 50, p. 287: "Therefore, marriage persists as a whole manner and communion of life, and maintains its value and indissolubility, even when offspring are lacking—despite, rather often, the very intense desire of the couple."

38. *Ibid.*, 51, p. 288.

39. *Ibid.*, 51, p. 288, and p. 332, note 118. For an interesting, if rather biased, account of the work of these birth-control commissions see Robert Blair Kaiser, *The Politics of Sex and Religion* (Kansas City: Leaven Press, 1985).

40. Paul VI, *Humanae Vitae* in *The Gospel of Peace and Justice*, pp. 427–444.

41. *Ibid.*, 7–9, pp. 430–431.

42. *Ibid.*, 10, p. 432.

43. *Ibid.*, 11, pp. 432–433.

44. For readers who would review or catch up on the debate, see Charles E. Curran *et al.*, *Dissent in and for the Church: Theologians and Humanae Vitae* (New York: Sheed and Ward, 1969); William H. Shannon (ed.), *The Lively Debate: Response to Humanae Vitae* (New York: Sheed and Ward, 1970).

45. *Humanae Vitae*, 16, p. 435.

46. *The Code of Canon Law*, Canon 1084, pp. 765–766.

47. David Knight, *The Good News About Sex* (Cincinnati: St. Anthony Messenger Press, 1979), pp. 233–247, gives practical moral advice that comes very close to ruling out the sexual expressions mentioned in the text. Knight's advice is carefully expressed and is not as extreme as first impressions might suggest.

48. The newly-elected vice-president of the National Conference of Catholic Bishops expressed this view before his recent election. See Daniel E. Pilarczyk, "On Preaching Heresy," *America* 154, 7 (February 22, 1986), p. 137: "The real force of the teaching of the Church's tradition . . . lies in seeing that the connection between intercourse and procreation is the very linchpin of societal sexual morality, and that once this connection is broken, there is no real basis for any kind of restraint. If contraceptive relations are morally acceptable in marriage, why not outside of marriage? If there is no essential connection between sexual activity and the generation of new life, what is wrong with recreational sex? What about homosexual activity?"

49. From the perspective of human understanding, we simply do not know why God permits conception in cases of rape and incest, or in situations where couples are manifestly irresponsible and indifferent to fetal welfare, and yet couples who are responsible and greatly desire children sometimes do not conceive. In this perspective the divine will appears to be arbitrary. In the light of such an appearance, it becomes a very real question of how much control and responsibility God invites us

to assume for the processes of life and death. To urge upon people the slogan that they should not play God is to beg a very real question.

50. I borrow the word conspire from John Courtney Murray, S.J., *We Hold These Truths: Catholic Reflections on the American Proposition* (Garden City: Image Books, 1964), pp. 33–35. As Murray points out, the original meaning of the term lacks the invidious connotations usually associated with it. It means a coming together, a breathing together which results in a concord of opinion and feeling. The word captures rather well what occurred in western civilization in regard to sexuality and procreation.

51. Individual self-fulfillment is a modern goal of liberal and pluralistic democracies. Henry Fairlie, *The Seven Deadly Sins Today,* pp. 29–33, blames psychiatry for its ascendance. Stanley Hauerwas, *A Community of Character: Toward a Constructive Christian Social Ethic* (Notre Dame/London: University of Notre Dame Press, 1981), pp. 72–86, blames political liberalism with its cult of individual freedom. Whatever the cause, the pursuit of individual self-fulfillment as a worthy and supreme life goal stands in fundamental contradiction to the biblical injunction "Anyone who finds his life will lose it; anyone who loses his life for my sake will find it" (Mt 10:39).

52. Sidney Callahan, "A Case for Pro-Life Feminism: Abortion and the Sexual Agenda, *Commonweal* CXIII, 8 (April 25, 1986), pp. 232–238, shows the extent to which the insistence on voluntary child-bearing has gone.

53. Raymond E. Brown, *The Critical Meaning of the Bible* (New York/Ramsey: Paulist Press, 1981), pp. 23–44; Robert J. Daly, S.J., *Christian Biblical Ethics,* pp. 17–34.

54. To say that a traditional Church teaching is not as well-founded biblically as we once thought is not automatically to declare it to be in error. It may be well-founded on other grounds. A good example is the frequent use of the story of Onan (Gen 36:6–14) to support the traditional teaching on the ban against artificial contraception. See *Casti Connubii,* 81, p. 41. This understanding of the biblical story has been rather decisively rejected today, even by many authors who would continue to defend the teaching. See Noonan, *Contraception,* pp. 527–528. For an interesting view of the continued relevance of the misinterpretation see Grisez, *The Way of the Lord Jesus,* p. 200, n.12.

55. David Hollenbach, S.J., *Claims in Conflict: Retrieving and Renewing the Catholic Human Rights Tradition* (New York/Ramsey: Paulist Press, 1979), pp. 41–106; Kenneth R. Overberg, *An Inconsistent Ethic?: Teachings of the American Catholic Bishops* (Lanham: University Press of

America, 1980), pp. 99–170, shows the central place of human dignity in the teaching of the bishops on social matters. He questions how consistently they have used the same norm in matters of sexual morality.

56. Karl Rahner, *Foundations of Christian Faith,* trans. William V. Dych (New York: Crossroad, 1984), is the leading exponent of this development.

57. The Roman Catholic emphasis on obligation and obedience was strongly tied to its regnant ecclesiology and its model of the Church as hierarchical institution. See Avery Dulles, S.J., *Models of the Church* (Garden City: Doubleday and Company, Inc., 1974), pp. 40–42. As the operative model of the Church changes, so does the ethical emphasis.

58. For the meaning of and the development away from this claim, as well as its practical importance, see John Courtney Murray, S.J., "The Problem of Religious Freedom," *Theological Studies* 25, 4 (December 1964), pp. 503–575.

59. Second Vatican Council, *Dignitatis Humanae* (Declaration on Religious Freedom) 2, in Gremillion, *The Gospel of Peace and Justice,* p. 339: "The right to religious freedom has its foundation, not in the subjective disposition of the person, but in his very nature. In consequence, the right to this immunity continues to exist even in those who do not live up to their obligation of seeking the truth and adhering to it."

Three

MORAL EVALUATIONS

INTRINSICALLY EVIL ACTS

When one reads the literature on the morality of homosexual behavior and relationships, four general positions seem to dominate, and indeed to exhaust, the discussion.[1] The first position to be discussed here may be called the traditional position. It is still embraced and insisted upon by official Roman Catholic teaching, by Eastern Orthodoxy, as well as by a number of other Christian denominations.[2] This position holds that all homosexual acts are always intrinsically disordered and objectively grave evil because by their very nature they contradict the design of creation, as well as being forbidden by the revealed will of God. The major and decisive indications of their disordered character are that, first, the physical structure of homosexual acts violates the complementary structure of male and female anatomy, and, second, such acts are closed by their very nature to the procreative good. In religious language they are contrary to God's will, however one arrives at a knowledge of that will.

Given this understanding of sexuality and the divine purpose for it, such acts can never be fit objects for deliberate moral choice and no intention of the moral agent can make them fit objects. To express the same idea in less technical and less precise language, an act of homosexual sex can never be an act of Christian love which proceeds from faith (Rom 14:22–23), no matter what the intentions of the actors may be. When such acts are deliberately chosen, therefore, they constitute mortal sin.

This last point may be difficult to understand. It may even be impossible to take seriously, especially if one is accustomed to thinking that actions mean whatever the conscious, psychological reasons of the agents performing the acts intend them to mean. So, for instance, if a sex act is mutually intended as an expression of shared love, it is thereby an act of love, and nobody else can gainsay that claim. Only the agents (and possibly God) know for sure what their actions mean.[3] Some additional words of explanation will be in order, then, so that it becomes clear just what this traditional position is trying to affirm.

There are two ways in which one can understand the claim that, despite the apparent intentions of the actors, an act of homosexual sex cannot be an act of love. Only one of those ways is essential to understanding the traditional position. The first way one can understand such a claim is to have recourse to hidden, possibly unconscious motivations to account for why people do what they do. In this way of understanding the matter, the reason why homosexual acts cannot be acts of love lies in a defect in the agent. Because of some sickness or abnormality (physical or psychological), or some social determinism, or even some previous moral flaw, the homosexual agent is moved to act by some force other than his or her free, conscious decision to love, to wit lust, even while thinking consciously that the choice is one's own free and loving decision.[4] Hence, the action is objectively wrong because the intention which informs it is inevitably wrong, even though the wrongness neither of the act nor of the intention is consciously apparent to the agent.

In this way of accounting for the immorality of homosexual acts, it is clear that homosexuals may not be subjectively guilty for what they do, even while they ought not to be doing it. A useful analogy to this way of understanding homosexuality would be the disease of alcoholism. It is the subjective condition of the alcoholic that blinds him or her to the abnormal and destructive nature of his or her drinking behavior. While the alcoholic may not be subjectively responsible and so morally guilty for such behavior, the behavior itself, for the alcoholic, is not innocent but destructive. It is not the satisfaction of thirst nor some other innocent desire, but some destructive and uncontrollable physical or psychological impulse which drives the alcoholic to drink as he or she does. Whether subjectively innocent or guilty, the alcoholic ought not to drink, even though drinking may be a perfectly acceptable moral behavior for an non-alcoholic. The analogy obviously breaks down, and so this way of understanding the objective disorder of homosexual acts breaks down, when one asks for the irrational signs and destructive consequences of homosexual behavior which parallel those of alcohol addiction and so mark the action as gravely disordered.

It is the case, in point of fact, that many defenders of the traditional position on homosexual morality would argue their position on the grounds I have just laid out. On the assumption that homosexual acts are known to be absolutely forbidden by God, there must be something amiss in the character and in the intentionality of the agent who wills them as acts of love. To choose to act contrary to the loving will of God cannot be a decision of love and to think that it is must be perverse, even if that perversity is hidden from the individual who so chooses. But that is only one way of understanding the claim that homosexual acts cannot be acts of love, and it is not the way essential to the first or traditional position.[5]

A second and more accurate way to understand the claim that homosexual acts can never be acts of love, despite the intentions of the agents, requires us to ask what it is that determines the moral form of our intentions. The answer to that question is evident: both our reasons for intending an action and the object of our intentionality give our intentions their moral form. To intend a moral evil, even for an ultimately good purpose, is to intend evil, no matter what other rationalizations may be offered in defense of that choice. Such an intention cannot be an act of love, not because of a defect in the agent, but because of the nature of the object intended. And no mere intention of the agent can change the nature of reality.

The act of rape can serve as a good example. It has become clear that the motivation behind an act of rape has little if anything to do with a desire for sexual intimacy and pleasure. What motivates rapists, what they intend, is not love and pleasure, but domination and control over women.[6] The very nature of the act of rape means that it can never be an act of love, no matter what the rapist may say or think he intends, no matter how misinformed he may be by his culture in regard to the nature of women and sexuality. Precisely because, in failing to respect something so central to the dignity of the other person, namely bodily integrity and personal freedom, the rapist must intend violation of the person, it becomes clear to us that there is no way any human intentionality can turn such violation into an act of love. Again, the reason why the rapist's intention is flawed is because of the object he intends; there is simply no way his intention can change the reality of what he intends. Circumstances beyond his control might mitigate or even abolish his subjective culpability, but they cannot make his intention to do this action morally right.

This way of understanding the claim of the traditional position that homosexual acts cannot be acts of love because of the very nature of the object of one's intending is the appropriate way to grasp what the claim means. There remains, of course, the more fundamental question as to whether the claim is true. How do we know, in fact, that homosexual acts are necessarily objectively disordered acts so that to choose them freely and deliberately is inevitably to intend moral evil and so to sin? How can it be established that homosexual acts are what an older theological tradition referred to as *intrinsece malum* or *peccatum mortale ex genere suo*?[7]

Reason, revelation and tradition, either separately or in conjunction, are all appealed to in support of this position, or more precisely they are held up as the sources of our knowledge of the intrinsic malice of such acts. In reviewing the biblical and theological tradition in Chapter II, we saw the reasons why homosexual acts were thought to be intrinsically evil. Either they were expressly forbidden by God as the divine will was revealed in Scripture, or they were shown by reason to contradict the inherent purpose of sexuality manifested in nature to be procreation. Supporting both these claims was the uninterrupted tradition of the Church, a tradition guided by the Holy Spirit, that such acts were always wrong.

CRITIQUE

While some considerably nuanced version of this position may one day prove to be defensible, and I will attempt to provide an argument in Chapter IV which supports some of the same conclusions as the traditional position, it has not yet been defended in a way that takes into account the scriptural problems and the qualifications of the tradition mentioned above. The refusal to address these problems and qualifications makes all appeals to revelation and tradition as secure sources of our knowledge about the intrinsic malice of all homosexual acts somewhat arbitrary and authoritarian.[8] We are, in effect, asked to accept that such acts are wrong because someone says so, even while the someone is unable or unwilling to say how or from where this knowledge is derived. In writing this, I do not intend to demean the very legitimate role of the teaching authority of the Church, nor the substantive theological significance of tradition. I only wish to point out that an authority which acts in arbitrary and authoritarian ways loses its legitimacy, its right to obedience and credibility. And a tradition incapable of development and critical scrutiny has ceased to be a living tradition inspired by the Holy Spirit, but has become a form of historical bondage.

The appeals to reason, even to reason informed by faith, have not generally been found to be very reasonable. This lack of reasonableness is largely because such appeals argue for a link between sex and procreation which is neither biologically well-founded nor rationally necessary, to say nothing about its absurdity in common human experience. Biologically, human nature is not so ordered that every act of sexual intercourse has the potential for procreation. Nor does reason require procreative possibility to make sense out of sexual intercourse. Indeed, it is this very point the recent theological tradition itself has so reasonably argued in accepting contraceptive intent in sexual relations as a moral responsibility at times without insisting on abstinence as the essential ethical consequence.

The traditional position, furthermore, is one which takes the single heterosexual as the model or analogue for the homosexual individual, but then proceeds to put much more severe restrictions on him or her.[9] Since dating and affective sexual expressions short of excess passion between homosexuals have no place to go, that is, they cannot have in view the committed, lasting sexual relationship called marriage, they can have no reasonable justification.

They can only be seen as occasions of sin which, if deliberately willed, are themselves sin. In effect, then, this first position we have discussed asks the homosexual person to model himself or herself on the committed celibate, without providing the social and religious meaning and support which undergird that way of life.

Logically, then, this traditional way of evaluating homosexual acts and relationships must either see in an irreversible homosexual orientation a profound physical, psychological, or spiritual abnormality, or else recognize in it a call from God to a life of celibacy. It is either a cross to be carried, like any other incurable disease, or a gift of grace to be honored and celebrated. Few exponents of this position regard homosexuality in the latter way,[10] and it is, it must be noted, a unique abnormality which does not deprive its victims of some basic human good essential to human well-being and wholeness, or compel them to do something destructive to themselves or others.

MORALLY NEUTRAL ACTS

There is a second position discernible in the literature which stands at the opposite extreme from the first position. It is only fair to inform the reader at the outset that I find it hard to take seriously as an ethical position. It is the position taken by a number of organized, secular homosexual groups as well as by a number of radical revisionists of the Christian ethical tradition.[11] Basically it regards homosexual attraction and desire to be as entirely natural and unambiguous as heterosexual attraction and desire. It argues that all acts following upon either form of sexual desire are natural and good and need no moral limitation beyond the sole norm of being non-coercive. In the words of the authors of *Honest Sex,* which proclaims itself to be a Christian sex manual, "every kind of sensual-sex experience can be legitimate, just as every kind of food may be eaten."[12] Homosexual acts are no more problematic than heterosexual ones morally, and neither form of sexual activity need concern itself with anything other than the free consent of the sexual partners and the avoidance of unwanted and undesirable consequences.

From my perspective this is simply an indefensible position on any grounds, but most especially on Christian ones. Its defense requires one to embrace a radical situation ethic which ignores or disclaims the revelatory character of both creation and Scripture, the disordering of human life by sin,[13] as well as the social nature of the human person. Each of these three charges merits some brief elaboration.

CRITIQUE

This second position in regard to the morality of homosexual acts and relationships views sexual activity as having no meaning or purpose in the divine plan other than being a play toy, a source of fun and pleasure to be used as human beings see fit. The natural complementarity of male and female anatomy, the real biological link between human sexuality and the continuation of the human species, the natural human selectivity and discrimination in choosing sexual partners, none of this carries any significance for the human meaning of sexuality. The divine will is in no way revealed to us in the things God has made nor are human beings in any way answerable to God for the use they make of the divine gifts.

The biblical witness that sees in sexual love a sign of the divine passion for union with human creatures and in procreation a natural sign of love's desire to create new life also counts for little in assessing the moral meaning of human sexuality. The co-responsibility for the continuation and well-being of creation which the Book of Genesis depicts God as handing over to Adam and Eve is also ignored. Hence sex is looked upon as being of no human consequence morally beyond whatever meaning and consequence the human agents choose to bestow upon it. The only meaning that can be said to be intrinsic to human sexual activity is that it is one of life's few renewable pleasures.[14]

Also ignored entirely in this second position is the disorderly nature of human sexual desires.[15] More accurately, perhaps, there is a simple equation of lust and sexual desire in this view, and it consequently finds lust to be humanly unambiguous and morally neutral. The only problems confronting the expression of sexual desire are to be found in the social world outside the self, for it is the situation in that social world which determines the existence and kind of unwanted consequences to be avoided in sexual expression. Sexual behavior is morally problematic only because the inhibitions and expectations of other people, social customs and rules, economic conditions, or physical and psychological well-being make it so. Love, fidelity, children, stability in a relationship, may all be welcome accompaniments to sexual pleasure, but they need not be.

Finally, this second position considers sex to be entirely personal or inter-personal and so treats its inescapable social dimension (marriage and family) as accidental and rarely fortuitous. Sex is a private matter and the satisfaction of sexual desire is a matter solely of personal taste and consequence, as in masturbation, or of inter-personal preference and mutual agreement. The decision as to how to conduct one's sexual affairs and life is of no concern to society as long as one extends the same courtesy to others. Social intrusions into the domain of sexuality are unwarranted, except where they are essential to preserve the personal or legal rights of individuals, as in the case of laws against rape, child abuse and pornography, or laws supporting divorce, alimony payments, the division of property after divorce, and abortion.[16]

The logical consequence of such a view is that there is no value in either a life of consecrated celibacy or a life of marital fidelity beyond their being the free, idiosyncratic choices of the people who choose, for private reasons of their own, to live in that way. Such choices, moreover, which ground the possibility of stable and lasting ways of life, do not have the potential value of being a sign or a witness, nor do they have the capacity for enabling and fostering essential human moral virtues. In sum, this second position takes the single heterosexual as the analogue for all homosexual individuals and proceeds to remove from both all moral limits on sexual behavior except those of personal sincerity and non-coercion. Sexual attraction and desire become altogether natural or biological phenomena and sex finds its properly human meaning only in the human ability to enhance physical pleasure and to multiply the occasions for satisfying physical desire. Human sexuality differs from animal sexuality in its liberation from cyclical and procreative necessity, and in the intensification of pleasure as a result of self-conscious experience. But, morally, sex need not and does not serve any higher purpose in humans than in animals.

LESS THAN IDEAL ACTS

A third position to be found in the current discussion about the morality of homosexual behavior is ethically both subtle and serious. It begins by insisting that we retain the heterosexual relationship in a committed marriage as the normative Christian ideal for sexual behavior. Taking the biblical and theological tradition with critical seriousness, it insists that human sexuality finds its fullest expression and meaning in a relationship of love between a male and a female in which there is both procreative and unitive intent and possibility. To this point it is in substantial agreement with the traditional position previously described.

A new consideration, however, now enters into the picture. This third position asks us to recognize that the normative ideal[17] cannot always be realized in human life. At times the inability to realize the ideal is due to circumstances external to the moral agent that can be changed. In such cases there is a moral obligation to work to effect the necessary change so that the ideal will become, in time, possible of realization.[18] At other times the realization of the normative ideal would require an interior conversion on the part of the moral agent, a reorientation of the self in terms of one's newly found convictions, values and goals.[19] But sometimes external change is not possible and interior conversion is not the issue, so that we are forced to accept, albeit with reluctance, something less than the ideal, not as a moral evil but as the best that can be had under the prevailing conditions.

When this analysis is applied to the matter of homosexuality, it is clear that neither a change in external circumstances nor an interior conversion of heart alters an irreversible homosexual orientation. Therefore, "it may be necessary at times to accept, albeit reluctantly, homosexual expressions and unions as the lesser of two evils, or as the only way in which some persons can find a satisfying degree of humanity in their lives."[20] This third position would, therefore, accept committed, stable homosexual unions as morally permissible under the specified conditions, though never as the ideal of what human sexuality should be. As a result of this less than ideal condition, it would certainly not accord such unions the status of sacramental marriage.[21]

In this view, then, some homosexual individuals, at least, are flawed in their humanity, through no fault of their own, since they are judged, by themselves or others,[22] to be incapable of living out the Christian sexual ideal of either consecrated celibacy or sacramental marriage. For that reason a different set of moral norms is appropriate for these homosexual individuals, although the model of heterosexual marriage is what they should strive to approximate. The dating and courtship rituals in which heterosexual couples engage would also be open to homosexual couples, who found celibate existence impossible, with a view toward forming a lasting, stable relationship on the analogue of marriage. The promiscuous sex often rashly assumed to be characteristic of the homosexual way of life would find no moral justification in this third position,[23] as it clearly does in the second position.

The position on homosexual acts and relationships just presented is sometimes referred to as an example of the theology of compromise. Its realism in the face of sin and human weakness is often considered by its advocates to be its strength, by its critics to be its weakness. Certainly it merits the same critical appraisal we have given to the first two positions. But because it is similar in many ways to the fourth position to be discussed, and its critique involves the introduction of some new considerations, I will defer the critical appraisal of the third position until the fourth position has also been expounded.

QUALITY OF RELATIONSHIP

There has appeared most recently in the literature on the morality of homosexual acts and relationships a fourth position which is gaining wide acceptance from theologians.[24] It is similar in many ways to the third position but has one major difference. This fourth position rejects the second-class status which the third position implicitly assigns to homosexual relationships. It argues that, if a committed heterosexual relationship open to the good of procreation is an ideal impossible of realization by homosexual individuals because of factors that cannot be altered either by changes in society or by interior conversion, factors so central to the personal identity of these individuals that a heterosexual relationship would be both dishonest and harmful to all parties involved, how can it be an ideal for homosexual persons, or even for those heterosexual individuals who are physically and/or psychically incapable of the ideal? Some other kind of relationship must be the normative ideal for Christian people.

On the basis of that kind of argument, which insists that a normative ideal be both concrete and possible, the fourth position concludes that homosexual relationships must be given equal normative status with heterosexual relationships. For what is important in determining a moral ideal for sexual relationships is not the sexual form of the relationship, which is only an abstraction, but the concrete impact the relationship has on human persons. Accordingly, both homosexual and heterosexual unions are judged to have meaning and value precisely inasmuch as, and to the degree that, they contribute to the personal well-being and human development of the partners. It is, then, the quality of the personal relationship between the partners, not its sexual character or form, that is seen to be morally significant in making an assessment of the moral quality of a sexual relationship.[25]

Hence, in the fourth position, the model of the faithfully committed married couple, as both the biblical and theological traditions have urged, can serve as the analogue for both homosexual and heterosexual couples. And the same moral criteria would then apply to both alike. Procreative possibility and intent cease to be significant moral considerations in the justification of any sexual acts, as does the biological sex of the partners. The moral criteria for inter-personal relationships are now seen to be the most important, even exclusive consideration. Such value-adjectives as personally enriching, other-regarding, faithful, socially responsible, life-serving and so on would be the applicable moral norms.[26]

The question of whether homosexual unions should be accorded the status of sacramental marriage, or, at the least, be blessed by the Church in a public ceremony, remains an open and debated one among the proponents of this view. Some moralists, still recognizing the traditional link between marriage and procreation, would reserve sacramental marriage for those relationships in which the traditional twofold end of union and procreation is possible.[27] The logic of the fourth position, however, which wants to accord full and equal rights in all areas of human life to all homosexual people, would seem to entail, as a minimum, a public recognition and celebration of homosexual unions.[28]

To this point I have tried to avoid any critical comment on either the third or fourth positions. I have described the first position as possibly defensible but not yet defended in any acceptable way, and I have excoriated the second position as morally bankrupt. To complete the analysis of the moral evaluations of homosexual acts and relationships. I wish to introduce here some additional considerations about human sexuality which will serve to critique the third and fourth positions as well as prepare the way for the formulation of a position of my own in the following chapter.

In addition to the thoughts and observations that have already been advanced in regard to the moral evaluation of human sexuality in general and homosexuality in particular, I find three additional considerations to be both germane and helpful to such an evaluation. The three considerations focus on the human right to marry, the kind of value which sex is in human life, and the notion of a way of life. The first consideration about the human right to marry is particularly helpful in critiquing the third position described above. The second consideration is germane to a criticism of the fourth position. The third consideration will be a central component in the position I wish to propose for the reader's consideration in the chapter which follows.

CRITIQUE OF COMPROMISE

The Christian religious tradition has consistently taught, despite some internal resistance to the teaching,[29] that human beings have a natural right to marry.[30] What is the meaning and basis of this teaching? It means that a human being, simply in virtue of being human, in virtue of his or her creation by God in the divine image and likeness, is authorized, has the authority or the right, without any need for approval from anyone else, to enter freely into a sexual relationship with another human being. To speak of marriage as a natural right is another way of saying that sexuality and sex are good gifts to human beings from a loving God, gifts which no human authority has the right to gainsay or try to negate.

Hence, the exercise of the right to marry, or, in the more expanded sense in which I have interpreted it, the exercise of the right to enter into a sexual relationship, ought not to be denied or made impossible to realize by the Church, the state, the family, or anyone else.[31]

Grasped in its concrete, practical reality, a person's right to marry is a claim made upon society to immunity from coercion, from either the coercion to enter a sexual relationship against one's will or from coercion not to enter a relationship of one's own choosing. The right is what is sometimes called a negative right[32] in that it entitles the subject of the right to no positive, substantive good in addition to the claimed immunity, and directly obliges the rest of us human beings to refrain from doing something rather than to do something. The right to enter into a sexual relationship, therefore, does not mean that one is entitled to or guaranteed a sexual partner, nor does it entitle a person to sexual satisfaction, or children, or the joys of interpersonal intimacy. One may well desire such goods, seek to enter into a relationship in the hope of achieving these goods, but strictly speaking he or she has no right to them. The substantive realization of such goods remains a gift, and in Christian understanding a gift of grace. The right to marry is simply a right not to be actively[33] impeded by others in the pursuit of the goods.

Because we have no positive right to these goods, we may not do just anything to achieve them. We may well have the right to enter into a sexual relationship, and certainly nobody has the right to prevent us from seeking to do so. But by the same token nobody has the corresponding obligation to enter into a sexual relationship with us in return, or to find us a willing sexual partner, or even to agree to the terms we lay down for entering into a sexual relationship. The right to marry, therefore, even construed as broadly as I have understood it here, has never been interpreted in a manner that denied the legitimate interest of society in regulating sexual relationships in a number of significant ways. More directly expressed, the right to enter into a sexual relationship, or to marry, carries with it important personal and social responsibilities in regard to the ways one achieves one's sexual ends. The right does deny society's authority to prevent such relationships altogether or to regulate them arbitrarily. It has been clear in the Church from very early days, for example, that the first moral condition limiting the exercise of the right in question, and so limiting human sexual behavior and the human desire for sexual satisfaction, is the condition of free mutual consent.[34]

I find this consideration especially relevant to a critique of the third position sketched above. Since, strictly speaking, there is no positive right to sexual satisfaction, sexual fulfillment and sexual happiness,[35] the human desire for such things and the pursuit of these goods, even the natural human orientation to these goods, cannot itself be a justification for doing just anything to achieve them. Certainly the desire for and the pursuit of these goods is both natural and right. Hence, no one has the right to stand in the way of or make impossible the pursuit of these goods by another human being. But the means one employs in the pursuit of these goods is not justified, not made morally right, simply because it is, or appears to be, the only means by which the goods can be realized. That, of course, is the truth and the import of the slogan that the end does not justify the means.

Therefore, just because a homosexual relationship may possibly be[36] the only way some people can find, or think they can find, a satisfying degree of humanity in their lives does not make such a relationship morally right by that very fact. The right to enter a sexual relationship is an immunity, not a positive entitlement. Unless it can be shown that free mutual consent is the only moral condition limiting human sexual behavior,[37] the mutual desire of two people for a satisfying human life by means of a sexual relationship cannot be judged to be a sufficient ground for justifying any sexual activity or relationship, be it a heterosexual or a homosexual relationship. The goodness of what they desire as a means (the sexual relationship) must be established as a worthy object of moral choice by something other than an end they may or may not realize in and through this choice.

Consequently, the reasoning of the third position which sees homosexual expressions and unions as the lesser of two evils and so morally permissible appears to me to be seriously incomplete and mistaken. The moral permissibility, the rightness, or at least the moral indifference of homosexual acts and unions must first be established, and not merely assumed or accepted by default, before they can be judged to be moral ways of pursuing what are unquestionably ontically good ends.[38] Still more, if homosexual acts and unions are to receive Christian blessing, even as something less than the normative ideal, their positive significance for the life of Christian individuals and the life of the Christian community will have to be demonstrated. I might point out in passing that, while a satisfying human life is by no means antithetical to Christian faith, it is not held out to the disciples of Jesus as the goal to which they should at all cost aspire.

If homosexual expressions and unions are to be morally justified, therefore, it must be on the same basic grounds that heterosexual unions are justified. Both forms of sexual union would have the same moral status for the same reasons. Both would be rooted in a Christian vision of life and sexuality ordered to eternal union with God and lived out as a response to the gift of God's grace. To this extent the fourth position outlined above can be said to be working along the proper theoretical lines when it insists upon the equal moral status of any sexual ideal for both homosexuals and heterosexuals.

In addition, we have reached a point in our historical understanding of human sexuality, or so this book has argued, where we simply have to give up all talk about sexual behavior being justified by procreation, or, more accurately, by procreative intent and some vague openness to the good of procreation, even while one is deliberately and properly intent on not procreating or is biologically incapable of doing so. While I would agree with Paul VI that there is an intrinsic connection between authentic sexual love and the generation of new life, or that sexual intimacy is ordered by God in the creation to both love-making and life-giving, the connection is not the kind he tried to defend in *Humanae Vitae*.[39]

CRITIQUE OF QUALITY OF RELATIONSHIP

In what, then, lies the moral and religious meaning of our sexual acts and sexual unions? This question leads to our second consideration: the kind of value sex is, a consideration which will be helpful in our critical analysis of the fourth position.[40] It is quite clear in the human story that human beings can and do value sex in all sorts of ways for all kinds of reasons. One general form such valuing takes is to value sex simply as a means to some other end and so to engage in sexual activity whenever, wherever and however sex can achieve the desired end. Sex, in this accounting, is accorded a purely instrumental worth deriving its entire value from the end to which it is a means, and the ends being sought in the activity of sex can be as various as the people who engage in the activity. So, for instance, sex may be a way to earn a living, a means by which to acquire extra income for life's luxuries, a tool by which to manipulate and control other persons for various reasons, a way to enhance one's self-esteem or gain attention or be popular or feel alive, or even the means by which to achieve the release of sexual tension in order to get to sleep, or, finally, the way to have a baby.[41]

In viewing the value of sex in this way, it seems obvious that there are only two significant considerations concerning the morality of one's sexual acts. The first consideration looks to the circumstances in which sex is performed, since the circumstances may well negate or seriously detract from the ability of the means here and now to achieve the desired end. If, for example, the end being sought in sex is one's livelihood, then pregnancy, personal fidelity, the free gift of self, strong emotional attachments, are all circumstances to be avoided inasmuch as they interfere with the end being pursued. The second consideration looks to the freedom of choice of the agents participating in the action, since coercion of any person against his or her will already violates the moral dignity of the person entirely apart from the sexual nature of the act itself.[42] Given this perspective on the meaning and value of human sexual activity, the end does justify the means[43] for the means has only instrumental worth. And whether the end does justify the means in any particular case all depends upon the situation or the circumstances in which the act is performed.

If sex were a commodity apart from persons, an object which one could use and then discard, or set aside until it was needed or wanted again, such a way of valuing it might have some validity. But one's body is not simply an object without relationship to one's personhood or subjectivity. The human person not only has a body, but he or she is that concrete body. Sex, as a bodily reality, is therefore inescapably associated with persons and inextricably tied up with human subjectivity. To value it *only* as a means is inevitably to treat persons as mere means to an end. It is to reify persons, to treat them and oneself as less than human. To value sex, therefore, only as an instrumental value is to misvalue it or to devalue it and so to engage in an intrinsically dehumanizing, and so unloving, practice.[44] It might be well to point out here in passing that this way of valuing sex is shared by the extreme forms of the first position which allow only the end of procreation as a justification of sexual activity and, to a lesser degree, by the third position which reluctantly accepts homosexual sex acts as a means to human fulfillment.

Another general form the valuing of sex can take is to value sex for its own sake or to accord it an intrinsic worth. Like all pleasures, sex can be regarded as simply good in and of itself. It is fun, it is pleasurable, it feels good, it is a gift, and that is its worth.[45] Like all gifts, sex is simply to be received and enjoyed with no strings attached. It has no meaning or purpose beyond the satisfaction of sexual desire and the pleasure that entails, so that its entire worth is intrinsic to the act itself. It has no symbolic meaning, no ritual meaning, no social meaning. It is seen as a substantive activity of human life, one that is worth doing for its own sake and to which only criteria of efficiency apply. Since it is an activity that is worth doing for its own sake, the only relevant moral criteria, in addition to free consent, are whether it is done badly or well, and whether the pleasure achieved is or is not outweighed by harmful, extrinsic consequences such as an unwanted pregnancy. The only important learning that takes place in sexual activity is the learning of technique which enhances the goodness of the end to be realized in and through the action.[46] On such an accounting of the value of sex, the most moral sex is the most physically pleasurable sex, and the most sexually virtuous person is the one most proficient in sexual techniques.

This way of valuing sex is certainly not altogether wrong. There can be no question but that a significant aspect of the unitive good of sexuality is realized in and through the pleasure-bonding of sexual activity.[47] An informed concern for sexual technique and a sensitivity toward what pleases one's partner greatly contributes to the shared pleasuring and can be a most significant, concrete way of expressing one's love for and to one's sexual partner. Indeed, total indifference toward this important dimension of human sexual experience is highly dehumanizing and bespeaks a pathetic moral blindness.

To value sex only in this way, however, seems to be both untrue to human experience and ultimately self-defeating. For if sexual activity had its entire meaning in the experience of satisfying sexual desire and mutual pleasuring, any partner who was willing and skilled would do as well as any other. Indeed, a machine would serve the purpose most adequately of all.[48] But this claim is not only not confirmed in human experience; it is radically contradicted by human experience. All things being equal, we much prefer persons as sexual partners to machines or animals, and we have very clear preferences among possible sexual partners which are not at all based on their sexual prowess or mastery of sexual technique. Since all things are rarely, if ever, equal, we may well settle for less than we would prefer simply in order to have a sexual partner, on the dubious principle that something is better than nothing. But in doing so, we are well aware that we are missing out on an important meaning of the activity we perform.

To value sex, therefore, only as an intrinsic value, as a substantive activity worth engaging in for its own sake, is to overvalue sex and, oddly enough, once again to depersonalize it and to engage in an intrinsically dehumanizing practice. As Rollo May has found in his clinical practice, sex simply for the sake of sex quickly becomes desiccated, uninteresting and incapable of bearing the weight placed upon it.[49] Divorced from its personal, human meaning, sex ceases to be the pleasure it was originally valued to be. It loses its free and fully human dimension and becomes something of a compulsion or obsession. Again we may note in passing that this way of valuing sex is common to the second position which regards sex as a mere biological instinct and to many popular sex therapy manuals which regard sexual technique as the only important human capacity involved in sexual activity.

It would appear, then, that sex is not the sort of value money is, a purely instrumental value, nor is it the sort of value that friendship and truth and love are, intrinsic values. It rather has aspects of both kinds of values. Sex is neither an activity that is merely a means to some other end nor a substantive activity engaged in simply for its own sake. Sex finds its fully human meaning, its religious and moral meaning as a symbolic or ritual activity.[50] It is an activity we can rightly value for its own sake to the degree that it means more and expresses more than itself. Sex, then, finds its proper value as an act which focuses, celebrates, expresses and enhances the meaning of our substantive activities and relationships. The fourth position on the morality of homosexual acts and unions is right on the mark when it stresses that the most significant aspect of all sexual relationships is the quality of the personal relationship between the sexual partners, for it is precisely this relationship which sexual activity focuses, celebrates and confirms.

In the Christian tradition, of course, genital sexual intercourse has come to be understood as the ritual appropriate to committed, interpersonal love. But sex cannot be the ritual simply of committed, interpersonal love, for we have many such loves—father, mother, brothers and sisters, other relatives, friends—which loves we also celebrate ritually in various ways without overt sexual expression, or at least without passionate sexual intimacy, being a factor. Sex, expecially in its fullest, most intimate expression in sexual intercourse, is not a ritual simply of committed, interpersonal love, and would, in fact, deeply wound, if not altogether destroy, some of these relationships. Therefore, any ethical norms proposed as guidelines for sexual expression, while they certainly must include the ethical norms proper to all interpersonal relationships, must also go beyond these norms to deal explicitly with the sexual aspects of such relationships.

This insistence on including sex-specific norms as part of any adequate sexual ethic is not a trivial matter. Loving one another is truly a substantive activity of human life in all the various ways we do that in meeting one another's needs and bearing one another's burdens. In this loving lies the very substance of our lives as Christian human beings. Such loving is essential to the moral value of all our human relationships. But sex is not essential to, and at times is quite inappropriate and even in conflict with, our loving others. Consequently, we need more than just norms which guide the ethical aspects of all interpersonal relationships. We also require sex-specific guidelines for our sexual behavior, and it is precisely such guidelines which the fourth position on the morality of homosexuality fails to give us,[51] and even studiously ignores or dismisses as irrelevant. I fault the fourth position, therefore, not so much for being wrong as for being seriously incomplete, even to the point of distorting by negligence the nature of the relationships it proposes to guide. It is quite possible, therefore, that a more complete discussion of sex-specific norms would alter, perhaps even radically, the conclusion of the fourth position that homosexual unions should have equal moral status with heterosexual ones.

SUMMARY

Having completed a critical analysis of the general positions to be found in the current literature on the morality of homosexual acts and relationships, the materials are at hand for the construction of what may be a more adequate moral position. Despite having found shortcomings, to a greater or less degree, in all four positions, there is much to be learned from them and affirmed in them. Any carefully wrought intellectual position can be a good teacher, even if one finds oneself in ultimate disagreement with the teacher. As we turn now to a more positive statement on the morality of homosexual acts and relationships, it is important to recognize and embrace what has already been learned. A brief summary of this learning will be in order here.

The first or traditional position which denies any moral value to homosexual acts and relationships has several merits which must be kept in mind as we proceed. For one thing, it takes seriously the biblical and theological bias against active homosexuality as something not in accord with God's will and refuses to surrender that view simply to satisfy contemporary cultural demands. For a second thing, it offers a position on the morality of sexual behavior that is logically consistent, for the most part, and exquisitely clear, if excessively narrow, in regard to the values human sexuality should serve. Its great weakness is to be found in the absolute character of the moral prohibitions it insists upon without addressing in any serious way the contemporary problematic of homosexual acts and relationships.

The second position, for all its defects as a serious ethical view of human sexual behavior, forces us to face the basic goodness of sex, of physical pleasure and sexual gratification, as important dimensions and vehicles of human development. Its radical failure is its inability, or more properly its refusal, to deal with these realities in a fully human way. If nothing else, the second position reminds us to pay careful attention to our theological understanding of creation, sin, and human sociality.

The third position which tolerates stable homosexual relationships as an acceptable moral compromise with the Christian sexual ideal deserves our attention for both its compassion and its intellectual rigor. It accepts stable homosexual relationships in the interest of promoting a fuller, more humanly rich life for homosexual individuals. Intellectually, it recognizes the limits of the biblical and theological tradition when faced with a new question. For in raising the issue today about the moral validity of loving, caring homosexual relationships, in the light of our contemporary knowledge of human sexuality, we are clearly dealing with a new question which cannot simply be assumed to fall under traditional prohibitions. Its weakness, to my mind, is twofold. When all is said and done, this third position justifies sexual behavior as a means to an end, an end which is only accidentally related to the means it is supposed to justify. It also tends to proceed negatively in its argumentation in that it justifies homosexual acts and relationships by finding nothing in the biblical or theological traditions that would count ultimately and absolutely against such practices. But it fails to articulate any positive Christian or human significance to such acts and relationships.

Finally, the fourth position has two great merits which must be taken very seriously. First, it argues for a single, positive norm for all human sexual acts and relationships, a norm rooted in the common humanity and call to grace of all human beings regardless of sexual orientation. Second, it properly focuses on the quality of the interpersonal relationship of the sexual partners as the key moral consideration in all human relationships. If sexual acts and relationships do not foster the quality of the interpersonal relationship of the partners, it matters little whether the acts are homosexual or heterosexual in nature, or whether they are aimed at procreation or personal gratification or the quieting of concupiscence or some other end.

The weakness of the fourth position, as has been indicated at length, is its neglect of the specifically sexual character of the acts and relationships it would evaluate. In neglecting this important dimension, it either ignores or denies the revelatory character of our human sexual natures. Since it shares this neglect or denial with the second position, and to a much lesser extent with the third position,[52] I would like to conclude the present chapter with a brief, but important consideration about the physical and biological complementarity of male and female sexuality.

COMPLEMENTARITY

A number of people, who commented upon the argument being advanced in the present work while it was in the process of development, suggested that more attention should be paid to the complementary nature of human sexuality. One person, in particular, claimed to see no difference morally between heterosexual intercourse and homosexual intercourse for the two-in-one flesh unity of the sexual partners. More crudely but accurately put, what difference does it make morally which organ is pushed into which orifice?

There is, I think, no simple and easy answer to that question, and, however crudely expressed, it is an important question. The traditional insistence upon procreative possibility as the sole justifying reason for all sexual activity had a ready and clear answer for the difference it made. If we make the change from procreative possibility to a committed, faithful shared life and love as the essential meaning and purpose of human sexual activity, the answer becomes much more difficult. Clearly a wider range of sexual expression, once morally forbidden by the norm of procreative purpose, now becomes morally open to married couples as actions or dimensions within their total sexual relationship. The question, then, must be raised whether the biological and physical complementarity of male and female sexuality is without any moral signifi-cance whatsoever.[53]

None of the four positions discussed thus far have answered this question in any satisfactory way. The first position assumes that this biological complementarity is decisive morally in an abso-lute way.[54] The second and fourth positions dismiss this comple-mentarity as morally irrelevant. The third position finds it to be of great significance in determining the sexual ideal, but not of abso-lute decisiveness for moral judgment about all acts and relation-ships. In developing my own position for the reader's consider-ation in the following chapter, this issue of complementarity will be one of the major considerations to be addressed.

NOTES

1. Kosnik, *Human Sexuality,* pp. 200–206. Malloy, *Homosexuality and the Christian Way of Life,* seems to me to advance a somewhat distinc-tive argument based on the notion of a way of life to which I am deeply indebted; however, both the argument in the text and my conclusions differ in significant ways from Malloy.

2. For Orthodoxy see Stanley Samuel Harakas, *Toward Transfig-ured Life: The Theoria of Eastern Orthodox Ethics* (Minneapolis: Light and Life Publishing Company, 1983), p. 263; for Protestant views see James B. Nelson, *Between Two Gardens: Reflections on Sexuality and Religious Experience* (New York: The Pilgrim Press, 1983), pp. 65–95.

3. The conviction that actions derive their entire moral meaning from the intention of the moral agents is not uncommon. A clear example of this can be found in the statement released by the National Office of Dignity (November 1, 1986), in response to the Vatican letter on "The Pastoral Care of Homosexual Persons," entitled *Dignity Response to the Vatican's Statement on Homosexuality.* In that press release one finds a sentence such as, "How are we to interpret a document which demeans our very existence by calling us 'disordered' and our loving expressions 'morally evil' but does not discuss providing pastoral care for thousands of our brothers who are dying of AIDS?" The question is well taken, but the document in question does not call homosexual people disordered, and many actions proceeding from a subjectively loving intention can be im-moral because the love is not rightly ordered, even while it is loving.

4. The existence of unconscious thoughts and motivations, the hu-man capacity for rationalization and self-deception, the social condition-

ing of our ideas and values, all help to ground the possibility of such an explanation which is undoubtedly applicable in many situations. They do not, of course, establish its truth as a universal fact.

5. The essence of the first position being discussed in the text is that homosexual actions are objectively wrong. To establish the possibility or even the likelihood that such actions are chosen because of some subjective defect in the moral agent says nothing about the objective status of such acts. The position described in the text really takes the objective wrongness of such acts for granted and so begs the whole question.

6. Marie Marshall Fortune, *Sexual Violence: The Unmentionable Sin* (New York: The Pilgrim Press, 1983), pp. 14–41.

7. *Intrinsece malum* means intrinsically evil; it suggests that an action is evil of its very nature so that it can never be a proper moral choice. *Peccatum mortale ex genere suo* means that an action is a mortal sin on the basis of the kind of act it is. This latter claim is much harsher in that it includes the subjective intentions of the moral agent in the judgment, or assumes that the action was done with sufficient freedom and thought. Contemporary moralists have called the intelligibility of both notions into question. My colleague at Duquesne, George Worgul, pointed out to me that both *Persona Humana* and "The Pastoral Care of Homosexual Persons" avoid calling any sexual acts *peccatum mortale ex genere suo,* or *intrinsece malum,* though they came very close to the latter idea.

8. In the modern age authority has been given a bad name and is often equated with authoritarianism which is an unfortunate mistake. William W. Meissner, *The Assault on Authority* (Maryknoll: Orbis Books, 1971); Jeffrey Stout, *The Flight From Authority* (Notre Dame/London: University of Notre Dame Press, 1981). Authority is a reasonable business; authoritarianism is a matter of imposing one's will on others without reasonable defense.

9. "The Pastoral Care of Human Persons" is a good example of this more burdensome rule for homosexual individuals. See paragraphs 14 and 15 in particular, *Origins* 16, 22, p. 382.

10. *Persona Humana,* 8, calls homosexuality either an innate instinct or a pathological constitution. It refers to the personal difficulties and inability to fit into society of homosexual individuals. Finally, it describes homosexual individuals as people who suffer from this anomaly. Kosnik, *Human Sexuality,* p. 305. The letter, "The Pastoral Care of Homosexual Persons," 7, *Origins* 16, p. 380, is even harsher in its judgment, calling the homosexual orientation "a disordered sexual inclination which is essentially self-indulgent."

11. Ara Dostourian, "Gayness: A Radical Christian Approach," in

Louie Crew (ed.), *The Gay Academic* (Palm Springs: ETC Publications, 1978), pp. 355–379. Also see Kosnik, *Human Sexuality*, pp. 207–208.

12. Rustum and Della M. Roy, "The Autonomy of Sensuality: The Final Solution of Sex Ethics," in Gordon and Libby (eds.), *Sexuality Today and Tomorrow*, p. 327; their sex manual is *Honest Sex* (New York: New American Library, 1968).

13. The literature on sin is enormous. A few useful works are cited here. Charles E. Curran, "Sin," *Directions in Fundamental Moral Theology* (Notre Dame: University of Notre Dame Press, 1985), pp. 99–118; James Gaffney, *Sin Reconsidered* (New York/Ramsey: Paulist Press, 1983); Fairlie, "Lust or Luxuria," in *The Seven Deadly Sins Today*, pp. 175–190; Eugene H. Maly, *Sin—Biblical Perspectives* (Dayton: Pflaum/Standard, 1973); Brian O. McDermott, S.J., "The Theology of Original Sin: Recent Developments," *Theological Studies* 38, 3 (September 1977), pp. 478–512.

14. David Reuben, *Everything You Always Wanted To Know About Sex** (New York: Bantam Books, 1970), p. 124.

15. Kelly, "Sexuality and Concupiscence in Augustine," makes the point that sexual desiring in and of itself its not disordered, a point I shall return to later. The point being made in the text is that it is rarely an easy matter to tell the difference between lust and sexual desire.

16. The second position described in the text invokes social regulation of sexual behaviors only to protect individual rights as it understands them. Consequently, legitimate social intrusions into sexual matters really have nothing to do with sexuality, except in the case of children.

17. A brief explanation of the different kinds of normative ideals and their application to the human situation can be found in John H. Wright, "An End to the Birth Control Controversy?" *America* (March 7, 1981), pp. 175–178. Since I will adopt the language of "normative ideal" in the following chapters, a brief word of explanation is in order. By a normative ideal I mean to suggest an ideal which human beings ought to try to realize in their actions, and which also obliges them to do what they can to change either the world or themselves so as to correspond more fully to the ideal. An ideal is not a moral rule. Do not commit adultery is a moral rule, but it can hardly be said to be a normative ideal for human sexual behavior. Normative ideals do, of course, lead to the articulation of moral rules, which must be understood in light of the ideal.

18. An example of the moral requirement to work to change external conditions so that a normative ideal can be realized would be the demand to abolish laws and institutions which foster racial discrimination. Only after such changes in the external circumstances of life are made can the ideals of brotherhood and sisterhood, or freedom, equality and justice for

all, be seriously attempted. On a more theoretical level, efforts to change circumstances are equivalent to working to remove virtual impediments from people's lives. See Hanigan, *As I Have Loved You,* pp. 54–57.

19. There is little, if any, solid evidence to support the claims made by some religious groups that conversion also changes a person's sexual orientation, either radically and at once or slowly over a period of time. Conversion is a religious and moral experience, not an experience of magic. Conversion can be equated with the removal of actual impediments from people's lives in order to make normative ideals capable of realization. We can only aid others in this task; we can never do it for them, and so conversion is always a personal act and an achievement of grace. Nevertheless, conversion does make new things possible for the converted person and it cannot be ignored in discussions of sexual morality and human possibility. On conversion see Walter E. Conn (ed.), *Conversion* (New York: Alba House, 1978); Charles E. Curran, "Conversion: The Central Moral Message of Jesus," *A New Look at Christian Morality* (Notre Dame: Fides Publishers, 1970), pp. 25–71; James P. Hanigan, "Conversion and Christian Ethics," *Theology Today* 40, 1 (April 1983), pp. 23–35.

20. Kosnik, *Human Sexuality,* p. 203; paraphrasing the leading exponent of this position, Charles E. Curran, "Dialogue with the Homophile Movement: The Morality of Homosexuality," *Catholic Moral Theology in Dialogue* (Notre Dame: Fides Publishers, 1972), p. 217. See also Charles E. Curran, "Moral Theology, Psychiatry and Homosexuality," *Transition and Tradition in Moral Theology* (Notre Dame/London: University of Notre Dame Press, 1979), pp. 59–80; and "Moral Theology and Homosexuality," *Critical Concerns in Moral Theology* (Notre Dame: University of Notre Dame Press, 1984), pp. 73–98.

21. Kosnik, *Human Sexuality,* p. 215.

22. One of the points consistently overlooked in the literature is who it is who makes the judgment that homosexual individuals are incapable of celibacy. Kosnik, *Human Sexuality,* p. 214, suggests that the data of empirical science answers the question, a highly unlikely prospect. Clearly, one would never know whether such a possibility was within reach unless one tried to live it for some length of time.

23. Charles E. Curran, "Father Curran's Positions," *Origins* 15, 41 (March 27, 1986), p. 669. "This position obviously does not accept or condone homosexual acts without personal commitment."

24. See the articles in Nugent (ed.), *A Challenge to Love.* All but two argue the morality of homosexual acts on the basis of the quality of the

relationship. See especially Margaret A. Farley, "An Ethic for Same-Sex Relations,", pp. 93–106, and Fortune, *Sexual Violence,* pp. 42–112.

25. Farley, p. 105, gives a handy summary of this argument.

26. Kosnik, *Human Sexuality,* pp. 92–95.

27. My colleague, David F. Kelly, has made this argument in conversations with me.

28. Daniel Maguire, "The Morality of Homosexual Marriage," in Nugent (ed.), *A Challenge to Love,* pp. 118–134.

29. Mackin, *What Is Marriage?* pp. 80–126.

30. *Code of Canon Law: Text and Commentary,* Canons 1057, 1058.

31. *Ibid.,* p. 743; the right is not absolute, as the text will explain and the code recognizes.

32. Hollenbach, *Claims in Conflict,* pp. 14–15.

33. By actively impeded I mean to indicate intentions and actions that are directed to interfering with or negating the right. One is not obliged to cooperate actively with another in the pursuit of such goods. The refusal to cooperate could be understood as a kind of passive impeding.

34. Schillebeeckx, *Marriage,* pp. 256–257.

35. Lest the words in the text be misunderstood, a word of explanation is in order here. Strictly speaking, a right entails a claim upon another to provide what is due to the one asserting the right. Since there is no one upon whom a claim for sexual satisfaction, happiness or fulfillment can be made, we have no positive right to these goods. We have the right to pursue them, but that is all.

36. I refer the reader back to note 22. I point out that the claim made in the text is an assumption—hence the words "may possibly be." Human beings are often surprised at what they are capable of once they set their minds and hearts on a specific course of action. It should also be noted that it is not beyond the realm of Christian possibility that we will be asked to forego what appears to be a satisfying degree of humanity in our lives in order to take up the cross and follow Christ. Louis Monden, S. J., *Sin, Liberty and Law* (New York: Sheed and Ward, 1965), p. 117, quotes Karl Rahner very ably to this point. See note 10 at the end of Chapter V below for the text of Rahner's quotation.

37. The burden of proof that there are additional moral conditions limiting human sexual behavior beyond free mutual consent is clearly upon those who would make the claim. The Christian tradition, of course, has argued that there are additional conditions, among them the fitness of the subjects to enter such a relationship, the common good, and so on.

38. Ontically good ends refer to ends that are worthy choices of

human decision making before particular circumstances and consequences are considered. So, for example, sexual pleasure is an ontically good end, but it is not morally good for everyone, always, under all conditions. See Louis Janssens, "Ontic Evil and Moral Evil," *Louvain Studies* IV, 2 (Fall 1972), pp. 115–156.

39. In *Humanae Vitae*. 12, Paul VI described the connection in this way. "Indeed, by its intimate structure, the conjugal act, while most closely uniting husband and wife, capacitates them for the generation of new lives, according to laws inscribed in the very being of man and of woman." Gremillion, *The Gospel of Peace and Justice,* p. 433. What these laws could be other than biological ones is hard to understand. The connection between love-making and life-giving is certainly biologically dependent, but it is rooted morally in the nature of committed love, not in biology.

40. In the section which follows I am indebted largely to Peter Bertocci, *Sex, Love, and the Person* (Kansas City: Sheed Andrews and McMeel, 1967).

41. James T. Burtchaell, *Philemon's Problems: The Daily Dilemma of the Christian* (Chicago: ACTA, 1973), pp. 78–80, gives a good example of the dehumanizing character of sex simply for procreation. The Catholic moral tradition's opposition to surrogate motherhood and artificial insemination by donor reflects the same opposition to using one's body simply as a means to an end, even where the end is procreation.

42. Many of the moral difficulties we have in regard to sexual behavior have nothing or very little to do with the fact of sex being involved. Often we are faced with lying, manipulation, injustice or various forms of coercion. The problem with sexual coercion is that it is coercion, not that it is sexual, although when it is sexual it strikes rather fundamentally at the dignity of the human person in a way that other forms of coercion might not.

43. The clearest and most forceful defender of the proposition that the end, and only the end, justifies the means from a Christian perspective is Joseph Fletcher, *Situation Ethics* (Philadelphia: Westminster Press, 1966), pp. 120–133.

44. That sexual behavior can be intrinsically dehumanizing and so unloving is clear to us in situations where the individuality of one's sexual partner is of no account. One wants a body, not a person. This is the case with prostitution, with so-called impersonal sex and with a variety of other sexual activities.

45. Intrinsic goods, such as friendship, which involve us in relationships with other people, bring with them their own moral obligations and

responsibilities, even while we value them for no other purpose beyond themselves. But the good of pleasure need not involve us with other people. For sex to be valued simply in this way involves ignoring or depersonalizing one's sexual partner. Hence, in practice to value sex as an end in itself is little different than valuing it simply as a means as far as other people are concerned.

46. In this accounting of sexual activity, sex is simply a skill, no different than learning to play the piano or to play basketball. But even these activities call for personal love and self-dedication if one's skill is to get beyond the merely mechanical. The flaw in this way of valuing sex is really a flaw in one's understanding of what it is to be a human being.

47. William H. Masters and Virginia E. Johnson, *The Pleasure Bond: A New Look at Sexuality and Commitment* (Boston/Toronto: Little, Brown and Company, 1970); James B. Nelson, *Embodiment: An Approach to Sexuality and Christian Theology* (Minneapolis: Augsburg Publishing House, 1978), pp. 87–93, is one of the very few theologians who attend to this important aspect of human sexuality.

48. Masters and Johnson, *The Pleasure Bond,* p. 47.

49. Rollo May, *Love and Will* (New York: W.W. Norton & Company, Inc., 1969), pp. 37–63.

50. James P. Hanigan, *What Are They Saying About Sexual Morality?* pp. 116–120.

51. Richard A. McCormick, S.J., *Notes on Moral Theology 1965–1980* (Lanham: University Press of America, 1980), p. 739; Daniel C. Maguire, "Of Sex and Ethical Methodology," in Dennis Doherty (ed.), *New Dimensions in Human Sexuality* (Garden City: Doubleday and Company, Inc., 1979), pp. 138–139; Curran, *Critical Concerns in Moral Theology,* p. 90.

52. Curran, *Critical Concerns in Moral Theology,* pp. 94–95, briefly notes the significance of the complementarity of the sexes as a contributing factor to the sexual ideal.

53. By physical complementarity I mean the structural and systemic receptivity of the female vagina for the male sexual organ. By biological complementarity I refer to the mutual contribution of male and female to the procreation of new life. In raising the question of the significance of these modes of complementarity, we are entering into the complexities of the natural law method of moral reasoning. See Josef Fuchs, S.J., *Natural Law: A Theological Investigation* (New York: Sheed and Ward, 1965); Grisez, *The Way of the Lord Jesus,* pp. 173–204; Michael B. Crowe, *The Changing Profile of Natural Law* (The Hague: Nijhoff, 1977); Charles E. Curran, "Natural Law," *Directions in Fundamental Moral Theology* (Notre

Dame: University of Notre Dame Press, 1985), pp. 119–172. I am much less impressed by the revisionist effort in Anthony Battaglia, *Toward a Reformulation of Natural Law* (New York: Seabury Press, 1981).

54. See Chapter II, note 34. Despite many disclaimers that *Humanae Vitae* proposes arguments that are a form of biologism, i.e., a system of thought in which biological laws become moral norms, it is hard to know what else to call a system in which biological complementarity is given decisive moral significance. Physical and biological nature have moral significance in that they provide us with indispensable knowledge of reality in regard to human possibilities and tendencies, and so to properly human goods. But they do not provide us directly with moral norms. Biologism provides a truncated view of *human* nature.

Four

SEXUALITY AND VOCATION

In the present chapter I intend to argue that human sexuality is a basic pointer to the vocation or calling every person receives from God to live a life of love in the particular circumstances of one's world. The specific form we give to our sexuality, that is to say, the way of life from which our sexual behaviors derive their meaning, is to be understood as a concrete specification of that vocation, a specification made necessary not by sin but by human finitude.[1] Hence, it is essential to say something about the notion of a vocation at the outset.

THE MEANING OF VOCATION

A vocation or a calling is something one both receives and does. It is both a gift and a task, a freely offered invitation either to be rejected or to be freely accepted by acting upon it.[2] As a gift received, it implies a giver who has freely initiated the call, someone, therefore, to whom a response must be made whether or not we appreciate the call. In Christian understanding, of course, that someone is God. As a task, it implies a mission to be accomplished, a being sent forth into the world with a message to deliver, an office to be executed, a task to be performed. Consequently, a vocation and the mission it entails have a social dimension of their very nature. One is called by God out of the community and sent back to the community to serve it in some way. While a vocation, then, is an intensely personal matter of profound religious significance, it is also a social reality with important ethical implications of noteworthy consequence to the community, for the community mediates, tests, and confirms the authenticity of the calling as well as being challenged and served by it.[3]

It has been a perduring conviction of Christian faith, though one not always manifest in its law and practice,[4] as well as one of its unique contributions to the fund of human wisdom, that the ideal for human sexual activity, in its most complete, self-giving expression in sexual intercourse, is that it be the ritual sign of a publicly acknowledged, mutually committed and fully shared life. More simply put, sex finds its full moral significance in its capacity to ritualize and confirm a life fully shared in love[5] and embraced as a vocation.[6] The very act of sexual intercourse between a male and a female embodies, symbolizes and celebrates this significance[7]—the two leaving father and mother, cleaving to one another and becoming one flesh in an act that has both personal and social import. Like all authentic rituals, the act of sex is sacramental in the sense that it effects what it symbolizes. It makes real and present here and now the very reality it points to beyond itself, a life shared in faithful love. At the same time, the sacramental act is a pledge and a promise; the couple commit themselves in the act to strive to realize this unity in love more fully in the future even as they participate in and celebrate that realization here and now.

Sexual intercourse makes the two one flesh, both ritually[8] in the act of love-making in which the two are really, albeit temporarily, joined together as one, and substantially in the fruits of the act which are the new or renewed bonds of shared love between the couple and the new child to be who is flesh of their flesh and bone of their bone. The new life and love to be created and to be shared in marriage must not be understood in the first place as the new child to be and the parental love extended to him or her. Rather, this new life and new love must first be seen as the new common life and love of the married couple themselves, which in Christian understanding is but their participation in the divine love-life. It is marriage which is the sacrament, the sign of Christ's union with his Church, not the birth of children or the establishment of a family.[9]

But for this life in love to be authentically human, as Christian faith understands the human, it must image God's love.[10] That is to say, it must be diffusive of itself, or it must always have an orientation to extend its internal life of love beyond itself. The new, shared love of the couple must not only be prepared to serve others when and as occasion arises for such service; that is a moral demand made on every individual Christian believer in virtue of the vocation received in baptism. Married love must also itself be a service to others, a gift of itself for the building-up of the community.[11] Hence, marriage is properly entered into as a vocation, a way of life that is itself a calling to discipleship and service, and not simply as a vehicle for personal fulfillment (though it may surely also be such a vehicle in both the moral and psychological senses of self-fulfillment). Marriage, understood as a vocation, is already a concern for others, and not merely an inter-personal relationship to which a concern for others may or may not be added.

Sexual intercourse, then, can have an integral goodness apart from procreative intent and possibility to the extent that it does intend and effect the confirmation of a life shared in love, but it cannot have this integral goodness if it lacks or deliberately denies its own intrinsic orientation to service or refuses to make its contribution to the common good. The most ordinary and obvious way a couple makes this contribution to the common good is, of course, through the gift of children to the human community,[12] which is why the *willingness,* not the intention, to bear and raise children (the openness to the good of procreation)[13] is a requisite condition for marriage. It is also why the practices of contraceptive intercourse and contraceptive sterilization are never morally indifferent actions or matters of purely private preference, since the decision to conceive or not to conceive a child bears so directly on the couple's calling to serve the community.[14] But where conception is either biologically impossible or morally irresponsible, sexual intimacy still remains the integral symbol of a life shared in love as a service to the community.

A WAY OF LIFE

Can homosexual expressions and unions do this and be this symbolic realization of a vocation? That question leads us to the third and final additional consideration mentioned earlier, the notion of a way of life. When a man or a woman chooses a life of consecrated celibacy for the sake of the kingdom of God, he or she does not simply choose to forego engaging in genital sexual activity. The choice of celibacy, properly understood and embraced, is not a choice not to do something,[15] though it certainly involves the sacrifice of one ontic good for the sake of another, as all categorical choices do.[16] Rather, in making such a choice, a person enters upon a way of life, most commonly a way of life that is shared with others who have made a similar choice. The chosen way of life structures and makes coherent a whole range of feelings, thoughts, purposes and behaviors which flow from and are found to be entailed by, or at the least helpful to, that way of life and which become essential components of the person's self-identity and vocation.

In this context of a way of life it becomes clear that some things are compatible with the way of life and some are not. Deep personal friendships with members of the same and the opposite sex, for example, may be found compatible with the celibate life; sexual intimacy with them is not. Some of the things that are not compatible with this way of life may be proper and morally appropriate for other people in other ways of life. The choice of celibacy, then, does provide a direction for one's sexual identity and energies precisely as a way of life, a way of life that involves both shared fraternal and sororal love in community, and which seeks and finds fulfillment only in spiritual life-giving and life-nurturing with and for others. A selfish celibate life, that is to say, celibacy chosen for reasons of personal taste or convenience, so as to escape the trials and tribulations of sex, commitment and interpersonal love,[17] is quite simply a moral contradiction and a negation of the very way of life one has chosen.

Single people, either heterosexual or homosexual, who have not yet made a commitment to a stable, permanent way of life, be that way the path of marriage, consecrated celibacy, or the single life in the world,[18] or who have had their original choice negated by circumstances such as death or divorce or release from vows, also enter upon a way of life, albeit one that is temporary in its essential thrust.[19] In pairs or in larger groups such people enter upon the rituals of dating and courtship, exploring the possibilities of a more lasting, more intimate relationship with another human being.

Despite its temporary character, this way of life, too, structures a whole range of attitudes, feelings, purposes and behaviors which flow from the way of life. Some actions and relationships which may be compatible with other ways of life are found to be incompatible and morally inappropriate for this way. Other actions which would be inappropriate for other ways of life are highly proper for this one. So, for instance, sexual fidelity and exclusivity are appropriate to marriage, but a variety of dating partners is altogether appropriate for single people. Passionate sexual expression and sexual intercourse are appropriate rituals for those already living the commitment of marriage, but they are premature and inauthentic rituals for those not yet so committed. Less passionate signs of sexual expression such as holding hands, kissing, and so on may well be appropriate to some courting relationships, whereas they are not compatible or wise for committed celibates. In short, the morality of one's sexual acts and expressions needs to be evaluated in the context of the way of life of which they are but a part, and with a view to how they contribute to and enhance that way of life which is itself but a concrete specification, temporary or permanent, of one's Christian way of life.

An analogy may be drawn here between the Christian way of life, considered as a whole, and the way of life marked out by one's sexual condition and choice, which is but a particular specification of that larger whole. The initial choice of the Christian believer is not a choice to do or avoid this or that action. It is a choice of a way of life, a choice to follow Jesus in response to the call of the Spirit. It is only in the context of that overall choice that particular decisions about this or that action, this or that relationship can be weighed and settled. In asking questions such as "Do Christians marry?" (1 Cor 7:1-4), "Do Christians take their complaints against one another to courts of law?" (1 Cor 6:1-2), "Do Christians eat meat offered to idols?" (Rom 14:1-6), and "Do Christians pay taxes?" (Rom 13:5-7), it is not the specific issue as such, but the way of life denoted by the word Christian that is the primary consideration. To be quite sure, the details and complexities of the specific issues ought not to be ignored. But they can only be ordered and evaluated against the understanding and values contained in the notion of the Christian way of life.

As a result, our judgments about particular moral issues are often decided by our more generic understanding of what it means to be a Christian[20] rather than by how we read the meaning and consequences of a particular form of behavior. This has its most graphic illustration in the unsettled differences among Christian people about the moral permissibility of Christian participation in war and other forms of violent resistance to evil.[21] What is at stake in arguments over whether a pacifist or a just war stance is more appropriate to Christian life is not a weighing of the consequences of non-violent resistance to evil vis-à-vis violent resistance in a particular case. Nor is it simply a question of which choice promises to be more effective in realizing the demands of peace, justice and good order, though these considerations are certainly relevant to the question.[22] What is at stake is which form of life best embodies the love for neighbor that Christian discipleship requires. It is the over-arching meaning of the Christian way of life that is at issue and not merely the morality of this act or that act in this or that situation.

VOCATION AND A WAY OF LIFE

What I am trying to suggest here is that our sexuality and the choices we make as to how to live as sexual beings themselves shape a way of life that is part of the larger Christian way of life. More accurately, perhaps, our sexual choices specify concretely how we propose to give a coherent form to our Christian lives as sexual human beings, and some kind of specific choice is inescapable, even if it is one arrived at by default in the absence of any other real possibility. Since Christian living involves service as a response to the call of grace, our sexual choices must be seen as vocations, as ways of life in which and through which this service is to be performed.

Traditionally, despite some criticism of celibacy from some Christian denominations,[23] we have recognized the life of consecrated celibacy as a worthy way, indeed, for the sake of accuracy, as the more excellent way,[24] for a sexual human being so graced to embody the Christian way of life. That way of life enables both a life dedicated to the quest for profound personal communion with God in prayer and prayer for God's people, as well as a way of life of unconditional availability and service to one's fellow pilgrims. It need not be [25] a frustration of one's sexuality but a sublimation of sexual energy into activities of love and service to others. Because it is a way of life that has public significance, it requires a public commitment, and hence, as a public way of life, it is also capable of serving as a sign or a witness to the eschatological reign of God as well as to the incarnational love of the Word made flesh and dwelling among us.

The single life as a stable, permanent life choice has rarely been given the attention it deserves, and so it has been accorded little or no status as a possible Christian vocation. Rightly or wrongly, it was usually assumed that people remained single out of necessity, or chance, or selfishness, or sexual indifference, rather than as a matter of deliberate and graced decision.[26] The single life was most often regarded as a temporary, transitional stage which was not, and insofar as it is temporary should not be, seen as a vocational specification of one's Christian existence, since it was, as a matter of psychological and moral intentionality, transitional. Or it was regarded as a fateful necessity due to circumstances of birth, family or social condition. But in either case, the single life was never given the attention it deserved by theologians or pastors nor has its meaning been explored as it deserves to be.[27]

Despite this neglect historically, however, there is no theological reason to doubt that the choice to live as a single person in the world in order to serve the human community, be that community particularized as a family, a school, a parish, an occupational community or some other real group of people, can be an authentic call of grace in which one finds one's particularized identity as a disciple of the Lord. Like other vocational choices, this choice, too, is mediated to the individual through a whole host of particular persons and circumstances external to the self as well as by one's own talents, by one's physical and psychological attributes, and by one's personal qualities of taste, temperament and character. Again like other vocational choices, this choice also focuses one's sexual energies and identity in a particular way and marks out what is and is not appropriate sexual behavior in the context of this particular specification of the Christian way of life. Because such a choice does not require formal public acknowledgement and a distinctive social space[28] in which to be exercised, it does not have the capacity as a way of life or a vocation to serve as sign or a witness, though the individual making the choice may well prove to be a highly distinctive Christian witness in his or her own personal life.

The single life in the world, deliberately chosen as one's response to the call of the Spirit and as a basic condition of one's service to the world, also lacks the established community support, the public sense of permanent fidelity, and the social acceptance of the culture which the religious vocation enjoys from the outset to varying degrees. While these lacks may well make the vocation more difficult to comprehend and to live, and the obligations intrinsic to the vocation more difficult to specify in general terms, they do not negate its present reality or its very real possibility for those people for whom marriage, for one reason or another, is impossible or unsuitable, and consecrated celibacy in community is unrealistic or not attractive. Informal community networks of like-minded and similarly-situated friends can be developed; the sense of permanency can be grown into; cultural acceptance can be challenged to broaden its horizons of understanding and valuation. Indeed, these tasks may very well be a fundamental part of the service the single vocation in the world both enables and entails.[29] In any case, this vocational choice should not be lightly dismissed for either heterosexual or homosexual persons.

Heterosexual marriage in both its ritual and substantive aspects has also been traditionally recognized as a vocation. The sexually exclusive and faithful union of the couple serves as a symbolic sign of Christ's union with his Church, even as it sustains and nourishes the common life in love of the couple, contributes children to the human community, and becomes the established focus for the basic social unit of society, the family. Sex in marriage, then, is not simply a matter of personal or inter-personal gratification and celebration, but it also enables the married couple to carry out their vocation as sexual Christian people. Marriage as a social institution with significant social consequences also requires public acknowledgement and social space for its living, the latter most often realized, in the quaint expression of an old tradition, by the sharing of bed and board.

VOCATION AND HOMOSEXUAL RELATIONSHIPS

Homosexual relationships, because they lack the capability of serving the community through the gift of children, and because they were also thought to lack the ritual capability of becoming two-in-one-flesh signs of Christ's union with his Church, have been assumed in the Christian tradition to be inner-directed, selfish, non-vocational ways of life.[30] If we break the cyclical biological link between sex and procreation as definitively essential to the moral evaluation of sexual relationships, as I have argued we must logically do in light of the developing tradition, and have actually already done in our implicit and explicit moral judgments about some sexual practices, then we must ask whether homosexual unions can and sometimes should be understood to be graced callings oriented to the service of God's people.[31] If they can be properly so understood, then they should be accorded equal normative status with heterosexual unions as the Christian sexual ideal for sexually active people.[32] If they are not to be rightly so understood, then they must be judged to be incompatible with the Christian way of life. It is the latter position I intend to argue here by way of conclusion to this chapter.

In making the following argument, it seems only prudent to ward off some possible misunderstandings at the outset. I have no wish, and no grounds in faith or in reason, to deny the possibility of humanly tender, caring, loving, dedicated homosexual relationships that are substantially characterized by all the value characteristics appropriate to morally good inter-personal relationships, as those are articulated, for example, in the book, *Human Sexuality*.[33] Nor do I have any wish or reason to question that the parties to such relationships can also be outgoing in their care for and service to the human community in a variety of interesting and valuable ways. Finally, I have no reason to doubt the testimony of others to the actual existence of such homosexual couples, however few or many they may be. What I do wish to dispute is that such admissions, taken in conjunction with all that has been said to this point, settle the issue of the morality of homosexual acts and unions from a Catholic Christian theological perspective.

Let me suggest that, in addition to the moral characteristics of all sound inter-personal relationships, the following values, to be taken as moral norms, should also characterize sexual relationships in Christian self-understanding.[34] The list, not intended to be exhaustive, would include the following characteristics: the practice of sexual exclusivity and fidelity;[35] the acceptance of sexual activity and pleasure as a gift of God for which one expresses gratitude and respect both to God and one's sexual partner but which one never claims as a right;[36] the acceptance of full responsibility prior to sexual activity for the consequences of one's sexual acts;[37] the recognition of sexual activity as a fundamental aspect of one's vocational calling, having both personal and social significance for the living of that vocation, so that the act of sex is itself an exercise and realization of one's vocational calling. To express this last norm in a different way, to love one's sexual partner sexually must at the same time be to love God by carrying out the divine will for their lives together, so that such an action contributes to the sanctification of the couple. The act also has social import in that the couple's life together, precisely as a sexual union, has been acknowledged and blessed by the Christian community and received as an essential form of their service to the Church and the world.[38]

The fact that many church communities, and almost all historically, have refused to acknowledge and bless homosexual unions and receive them as an appropriate form of Christian service[39] cannot tell definitively against such unions today, since the very point at issue is whether the Church should acknowledge and bless such unions. It does, however, contribute to the presumptive bias against them, a bias that is stronger or weaker depending on the theological weight individual churches give to tradition.[40] But in light of the value-norms enumerated above, it becomes clear what must be established about homosexual relationships if they are to overcome the presumptive bias and receive acknowledgement and blessing. The argument to be pursued here is that, in the light of our present knowledge about human sexuality and of the experience of homosexuals themselves in trying to live as faithful Christians, that bias cannot presently be overcome.

In scrutinizing the list of values in the second previous paragraph, it is clear that there are no insuperable, theoretical obstacles to homosexual unions being sexually faithful and exclusive, nor to homosexual people accepting sex as a gift for which to be grateful, nor to their accepting social responsibility for any consequences of their sexual activity.[41] The heart of the matter, then, rests with the claim that sexual activity must be an essential aspect of the exercise and realization of their vocational calling and have social as well as personal import. Homosexual relations, I would suggest, miss the mark on both counts.

Homosexual individuals are not called to a two-in-one flesh unity because they cannot become such a unity. They can become a two-in-one flesh unity neither ritually in the act of sexual intercourse, nor substantially, either in the new shared life in love of unity and difference that is male and female, or in the new life that is flesh of their flesh and bone of their bone. There are three claims made in that sweeping and debatable assertion which I will treat in reverse order.

The third claim in the above assertion is the clearest and the most obviously true. A homosexual couple simply cannot realize the two-in-one flesh unity that is the new child, the biological result of fertile heterosexual intercourse. As I have previously argued, this inability to procreate does not seem to me to be of definitive significance in ruling out homosexual acts and relationships. But that does not mean it is inconsequential and of no moral relevance to the issue. For the sexual union of human beings finds part of its Christian, human meaning in the procreative power of a freely shared, embodied love to produce a new reality, one that participates in and is yet different from the reality of the two partners. There are good reasons for sanctioning sexual unions that lack or do not deliberately intend this procreative possibility, but those reasons are never adequate to negate the importance of this possibility, nor to override the deliberate refusal of openness to the possibility that is manifested by one's choosing to act sexually in certain ways. To accept a homosexual union as of equal moral worth with a heterosexual union[42] would be to sanction and bless just such a negation and refusal.

The second claim asserts the impossibility of a homosexual couple becoming a two-in-one flesh unity substantially in a shared life in love of unity and difference. Homosexual partners can, of course, become very intimate friends and they can share, among other things, the mutual pleasuring of sex. But their oneness is and remains the oneness of friends to which unity sexual activity is not essential and is often a distraction.[43] If sex is, in fact, essential to their friendship, the moral value of the friendship is called into serious question, for it brings into doubt the unconditional nature of their being for one another as friends.[44] The unity of friends certainly has features of unity and difference, but that difference is not sexual and so it is not in their sexual relationship that they manifest this unity and difference. Furthermore, friendships can be broken or simply wither away without moral fault on the part of either friend. But such is not the case with the sexual relationship called marriage.[45] In entering marriage, persons assume obligations and responsibilities which are not merely legal in nature, and which they do not have simply in virtue of being friends. Of course, in marriage both friendship and sexual attraction can wither and die, on the assumption that they were both present in the first place. But the marital relationship itself cannot do so without moral fault, however hard it might be to pinpoint the fault.[46]

Finally, the homosexual couple cannot become a two-in-one flesh unity ritually in the act of sexual intercourse. They can only try to imitate or simulate the authentic ritual of sexual love.[47] To develop and substantiate this claim, a closer look at ritual activity is called for.

RITUAL AUTHENTICITY

All kinds of ritual acts can be inauthentic for any number of specific reasons, but generally it can be said that ritual acts fail to realize their authentic meaning for one of three reasons. First, they can fail in authenticity because they are done as if they were magic acts that automatically achieve their end without the serious and truthful investment of human subjectivity. Both heterosexual and homosexual acts can suffer from this defect. Its most common manifestation is the belief that engaging in sex will make one's partner love and care for oneself or will cause one to care for the other. Other signs of this same illusion that ritual acts are magic can be seen in such things as the belief that sex will abolish one's sense of loneliness, that sex will put meaning into one's life, or that having a sexual partner proves one's attractiveness and worthiness. There is nothing unique to homosexual relationships in regard to this particular failing in authenticity of the ritual that is sex.

Ritual acts can also lack authenticity when they are done in a careless, boring or inattentive way, i.e., when they are done badly or in a routine manner as a matter of obligation. Clearly, once again, heterosexual and homosexual acts are both prone to this common human failing, one that permits of a wide range of degree. Such boring and routine practice of ritual activity can easily beset the act of sex, especially in relationships of some lasting duration. As a result the failure in authenticity that is boredom easily leads to a perception of sex as magic, as in "the magic has gone out of our relationship," and the temptation to seek a new sexual partner. The more honest cause of this lack of authenticity is inattentiveness to the relationship itself which sexual behavior ritualizes. Hence, boredom as a reason for the inauthentic ritual also points to the third and most fundamental reason for the failure in authentic ritual, hypocrisy.

Ritual acts often lack authenticity because they are carried out hypocritically, which hypocrisy is sometimes conscious and sometimes not. That is to say, there is no reality, or no experience of the reality which the ritual act is symbolizing and making present. This can be a common failing of human sexual acts, both heterosexual and homosexual acts, where there is no shared life in love, or where there is no intention or purpose to give oneself and receive the other in his or her totality. What the sexual act ritualizes, the mutual and total self-giving and receiving of the partners, is either not a reality or is not intended and valued as a reality to be realized in an ever deeper fashion. Hence the ritual act becomes so much empty show, an act of passing amusement which lacks the power to transform lives.

But the failure that is hypocrisy can run more deeply than the pretense that actions mean something to us that they do not, in fact, mean. And this is where homosexual acts inevitably fail to meet the test of authentic ritual. For ritual acts make present the reality that they symbolize precisely by ritually enacting that reality. The ritual act, and the materials or elements used in the ritual action, must have the capacity to symbolize the reality they would make present. Otherwise, we are only pretending, or simulating, or play-acting in our ritual behavior. It is at this point that the complementarity of human sexuality becomes such a crucial consideration.

The unity ritualized and enacted in sexual behavior is a two-in-one flesh unity, a unity that has its created basis in the physical and biological complementarity of male and female. There are various ways human beings can imitate, or play at imaging this unity, but apart from the actual basis in reality of male and female sexual union, these ways are only pretense or imaginative simulations of the real thing. To say that they are imaginative simulations is not to judge their moral worth out of hand, but merely to point out that such actions are not authentic rituals of a two-in-one flesh unity. To think they are is only to deceive ourselves. Such imaginative simulations may well have their own purpose and their own justification, but they cannot lay claim to being the real thing. Hence, whatever else may be said in favor of homosexual acts and relationships, they cannot be understood as exercises and realizations of the inter-personal, vocational meaning of sexuality.

It is also difficult to see how or why any sexual activity or relationship other than the vocation of marriage would be a basic element in the social mission or service that is intrinsic to any Christian vocational calling. It is interesting to read Paul and some of the early Church Fathers on this question, especially since they were so disposed to see celibacy as such an evident sign of the new life and freedom received in Christ.[48] Paul, for one example, tolerates marriage as preferable to burning up with sexual passion (1 Cor 7:9). He praises periodic abstinence from sexual relations for married couples so they may devote themselves to prayer, but wisely suggests it only be for a short time and by mutual consent lest one or the other be tempted to infidelity (1 Cor 7:5-6). Yet he also acknowledges marriage as a gift (1 Cor 7:7) and sees in the relationship a clue, a sign of the greater mystery of Christ's union with his Church (Eph 5:31-32). He vaguely sees that the marital relationship is one of mutual sanctification in a way that friendships are not (1 Cor 7:14).[49] In short, it is a special calling to which the sexual relationship is intrinsic.

The same points can be made through the mode of questioning. When a married couple engages in sexual intercourse freely and lovingly, they are ritually enacting the meaning of their relationship; they are, in fact, re-creating, enhancing and celebrating that meaning. What meaning are homosexual couples creating, enhancing and celebrating? To what call of grace are they responding? Surely it is not enough to simply say they are responding to the call to love one another, since sexual activity is not intrinsic to such a call. When married couples engage in sexual intercourse and realize the substantial goods of their actions, they are exercising and realizing both the personal and social meaning of their calling, to be for one another—this is my body given for you—and thereby to establish and secure that center of life and love around which family develops and grows and serves society. Their sexual relationship is fundamentally essential to carrying out the vocation. While homosexual couples can certainly mirror some of these characteristics in their life together, why is sexual activity essential to their efforts? Their sexual activity undoubtedly has personal or private significance to them, but what is its social import? In what way does it edify the community, or sustain its unity, or add to its numbers? Friends who are not also sexual partners can be mutually sustaining and supportive of one another and find in their friendship stimulus, a support, and even a purpose for a shared service to the world. What would genital sexual activity add to the intrinsic meaning of such a calling?

It would, then, be my contention that only the vocation of marriage shapes a way of life in which free and complete sexual expression is an essential component and can realize both its personal and social significance; and that this realization requires that marriage be heterosexual. I would further contend that individuals who find themselves to have an irreversible homosexual orientation, something not lightly to be assumed, rightly read that condition as an invitation to Christian discipleship either as a single person in service to the world or in a life of consecrated celibacy, as those vocations have been sketched out above. I do not know, nor do I know how to determine beyond question, whether homosexuality is to be understood psychologically as a pathology or as a natural and normal sexual difference. I do know that, theologically, God's grace can be found at work in the homosexual condition and that it must be taken seriously as one indication of the concrete form one's vocational call to holiness and service should take.

The above argument is not proposed as conclusive beyond all question or doubt. There are many points that are not sufficiently developed, many claims that require further substantiation. The final chapters will touch on a few of these incomplete reflections. If the present argument has any merit at all, it seems to me that merit lies in rooting our sexual lives in the more fundamental structure of the Christian life, the following of the Lord Jesus who reveals to us the creative, redeeming, sanctifying Triune God. This following of Christ, which urges as its most central commandment that we love one another as he has loved us, does not place a major emphasis on sexual fulfillment and sexual happiness as essential components of discipleship, and certainly does not see sexual expression as essential to the love it commands. It surely does not gainsay these goods as good, nor does it deny their capacity to contribute powerfully to the human ability to love God and neighbor. But they are among the goods that are peripheral to the seeking of the kingdom of God and so must find their concrete worth in our lives in terms of how they advance our quest for the kingdom. That is the context in which I have tried to place a Christian sexual ethic.

Whether or not our predecessors in the faith were as ignorant and as inhibited in sexual matters as they have often been accused,[50] some of them, at least, do seem to have been aware of the central importance of loving God above all things. If one takes that as a starting point, then the central question we must put to all created realities is how they help us advance in this quest. It is not sufficient to argue that one does not see the harm in this or that particular practice or relationship. With Paul we must recognize that while there may be no forbidden things, not everything does good (1 Cor 6:12). In holding up an ideal of sexuality and sexual behavior, the Church has the responsibility of affirming the positive power of the ideal in its fullness. For sexual behavior, this fullness is found in the challenge, the joy and the sorrow of the committed fidelity and stability of heterosexual marital love.

NOTES

1. In this chapter and the chapters to follow it is essential that the difference between sin and finitude be clear. Both sin and finitude, as notions, imply limits to human life and human possibilities. As realities we experience, sin and finitude impose limits on human life and its possibilities. But sin is evil and so the limitations that arise from sin are undue limitations. In the face of such limits we properly declare them to be unfair and see in them violations of justice that are opposed to the reign of God. Finitude, on the other hand, is not evil, especially if we are committed to a Creator God who made everything very good. The fact, therefore, that human beings must choose this rather than that, adventure upon one way of life rather than another, is not itself an evil nor a matter of injustice. Put negatively, the fact that we cannot have it all is not a consequence of sin, but of the fact that we are creatures, finite and so limited of our very nature. Indeed, the desire to have it all is a manifestation of the most fundamental of all sins, idolatry, inasmuch as it expresses a desire to be the Creator rather than an acceptance of self as a creature of God. Of course, this desire to be God is quite different than the desire to realize one's potential to the fullest, although self-fulfillment or self-realization as a direct and primary goal of one's earthly existence certainly borders on idolatry.

2. The basic Christian vocation in which all more specific callings are rooted is, of course, received in baptism. Like all callings, it is something received, not something self-initiated. Because it is received, it is not altogether under our own control in its demands and responsibilities. A great deal of nonsense about the appropriateness of baptizing children or infants could be eliminated if we recognize that one may actually be called without having at that moment the psychological capacity to recognize and acknowledge the call for what it is. Of course at some point in life the decision must be made consciously as to whether or not to respond freely to the call. The baptized are heirs of Christ, just as infants may be the heirs of their parents or grandparents. The call is real enough, just as the inheritance is real enough, whether the heir can recognize and appreciate it for what it is. Consequently, any calling, any invitation brings with it its own demands for a response and for a response appropriate to the invitation or call. Enda McDonagh, *Invitation and Response: Essays in Christian Moral Theology* (New York: Sheed and Ward, 1972), has articulated the whole of the Christian life in these terms, as have other theologians. The foundations for this approach to moral theology are to be found in H. Richard Niebuhr's classic work *The Reponsible Self: An Essay in Chris-*

tian Philosophy, ed. James M. Gustafson (New York/Evanston/London: Harper & Row, Publishers, 1963).

3. Apart from community no sense of vocation is possible. See Hanigan, *As I Have Loved You,* pp. 79-87.

4. Theodore Mackin, S.J., *Marriage in the Catholic Church: Divorce and Remarriage* (New York/Ramsey: Paulist Press, 1984), pp. 5-19, summarizes this claim which is then detailed at length in later pages.

5. *Gaudium et Spes,* 49, in Gremillion, *The Gospel of Peace and Justice,* p. 285.

6. To say that marriage is a vocation, or is embraced as a vocation, is to say among other things that the parties to the marriage do not create the terms and conditions of their union entirely by their own will. Rather they accept a pre-structured call, within which they work out their common life together. The more traditional way of speaking of this pre-structured call is to say that God is the author of marriage (*Gaudium et Spes,* 48) or that marriage has been divinely instituted. The acceptance of some basic conditions as essential to marriage, e.g., sexual fidelity, permanence, openness to children, are minimal signs of the recognition of marriage as a vocation. Most married couples will grow into a sense of the vocational significance of their marriage rather than fully grasping it at the outset.

7. Andre Guindon, *The Sexual Language* (Ottawa: The University of Ottawa Press, 1977), p. 423.

8. Burtchaell, *Philemon's Problem,* pp. 130-133; Hanigan, *What Are They Saying About Sexual Morality?* pp. 116-120. The important point to understand about ritual acts, as far as sexual activity is concerned, is that they are actions which try to capture, in a real way, but never in all its fullness, a meaning, a reality which is prior to and more important than the ritual act itself. The ritual act really does make present this meaning or this reality. In the case of sexual acts, the two are made one flesh. But the sexual act itself, which is, in fact, a joining of bodies, ritualizes the unity of persons, the unity of heart and mind and purpose and life of the couple, and not simply the joining of bodies. Where this prior meaning, this antecedent reality does not exist, ritual acts will be so much empty and hypocritical show, as false protestations of love and affection testify, or will smack of magic, as indicated by the common expectation that having sex will earn or win the love of one's sexual partner. The failures of ritual activity to be authentic are discussed in more detail later in this chapter.

9. Despite the dynamisms inherent in marital love for children and family, the sacramental sign of Christ's union with his Church is the union of the couple, not the family. I am suggesting that there is consider-

able theological and ethical significance to this fact to which we must be attentive.

10. Mott, *Biblical Ethics and Social Change,* pp. 39-42.

11. I Cor 12–14; Paul points out in these chapters that all spiritual gifts, among which we count the vocation to marriage, while of personal benefit to the recipients, are also intended for and are to be used for the benefit of the community, for the common good, for the building up of the body of Christ. Apart from this orientation, the gifts have little claim to being gifts of the Holy Spirit.

12. *Gaudium et Spes,* 50, in Gremillion, *The Gospel of Peace and Justice,* pp. 286-287. Children are not simply blessings and responsibilities for the parents alone. They are blessings and responsibilities for the whole human community, as we recognize in the community responsibility for education, legal protection, welfare laws and countless other ways.

13. *Code of Canon Law: Text and Commentary,* Canon 1101, pp. 784-786.

14. In and of itself, the willingness to bear children does not exclude all contraceptive intercourse or any possibility of contraceptive sterilization. For such practices to be excluded absolutely, the intrinsic malice of such actions must first be established. What can be established about such actions is that they can never be justified on purely private grounds, since marriage and children have the inescapable social dimension to which we have repeatedly referred. Such decisions touch upon the very nature of the vocation one has accepted. Consequently, one can scarcely expect the teaching office of the Church to fulfill its responsibility either by simply abandoning the decision about conception to the private consciences of individuals or by simply affirming the moral acceptability of contraceptive practices.

15. George H. Frein (ed.), *Celibacy: The Necessary Option* (New York: Herder and Herder, 1968); Mary Anne Huddleston, I.H.M. (ed.), *Celibate Love: Encounter in Three Dimensions* (New York/Ramsey: Paulist Press, 1984).

16. A categorical choice is a choice to do this action or live this way of life rather than to do something else. Categorical choices are by their nature limiting or excluding choices. See O'Connell, *Principles for a Catholic Morality,* pp. 61-63.

17. John S. Dunne, *The Way of All the Earth: Experiments in Truth and Religion* (New York: The Macmillan Company; London: Collier-Macmillan Ltd., 1972), pp. 16-24.

18. The single way of life in the world has been recognized by the Church in the form of secular institutes; *Code of Canon Law: Text and Commentary,* Canons 710-730. But many people choose the single way of

life without formal membership in any group and without vows. The forms, therefore, that the single vocation can assume are various.

19. People who are single, as a matter of fact, but who are open to or actively seeking a life-partner are involved in a way of life, but that way of life is both intentionally and structurally transitional and so temporary of its very nature. It may, of course, turn out to be permanent insofar as no suitable life-partner is found, but it is never embraced as a permanent state of life.

20. Hollenbach, *Nuclear Ethics,* p. 24, makes this point as regards war. Richard A. McCormick, S.J., "To Save or Let Die: The Dilemma of Modern Medicine," in Tom L. Beauchamp and LeRoy Walters (eds.), *Contemporary Issues in Bioethics* (Belmont: Wadsworth Publishing Company, Inc., 1978), pp. 334-337, makes the same point in regard to the protection of life. Stanley Hauerwas, *Vision and Virtue,* pp. 68-89, makes the same point in a theoretical way, as he does in all his works.

21. Hanigan, "War and Peace: Christian Choices," pp. 21-24.

22. John Garvey, "Murderous Evil: Does Nonviolence Offer a Solution?" *Commonweal* CXII, 6 (September 20, 1985), pp. 485-487, points out the need to consider actual consequences in regard to the question of non-violence.

23. Max L. Stackhouse, *Creeds, Society, and Human Rights: A Study in Three Cultures* (Grand Rapids: William B. Eerdmans Publishing Company, 1984), p. 97.

24. Strictly speaking, it is the life of the three vows of poverty, chastity and obedience, known traditionally in Roman Catholicism as the religious life, that is considered to be "the more excellent way." I have sketched the meaning of this claim in Hanigan, *As I Have Loved You,* pp. 193-195. What needs to be stressed about this way of speaking is that the Church does not suggest that the religious life or a life of celibacy is "the more excellent way" subjectively. As we use the terms today, therefore, the claim tends to appear either meaningless or outrageous.

25. McIsaac, *Freud and Original Sin,* p. 83.

26. There is an interesting parallel between the vows of poverty and chastity and the brute experiences of material and sexual deprivation. An essential aspect of the virtue of the vows lies in the voluntary acceptance of a way of life as a vehicle of service made possible by grace. To be forced to live in poverty or to be forced to live a life of celibacy by the forces of necessity or human tyranny lacks the virtue which can lend redemptive power to these ways of life. In more general terms, it is the voluntary acceptance of suffering as an inescapable condition of a particular mission

or way of life that makes suffering redemptive. See Hanigan, *Martin Luther King, Jr. and the Foundations of Nonviolence,* pp. 263-276.

27. Susan A. Muto, *Celebrating the Single Life* (Garden City: Doubleday and Company, 1982), represents an important corrective to the neglect of the single vocation.

28. For the notion of social space and its political and human significance see Hannah Arendt, *On Revolution* (New York: The Viking Press, 1965), pp. 22-41. To say that the single vocation does not require a distinctive social space does not mean that such a space might not be highly desirable. To create a distinctive social space, however, does require some kind of public commitment and rule which is often antithetical to the choice of the single life.

29. For a way of life to have moral status precisely as a way of life, it must enable certain human possibilities of growth and entail certain duties or obligations which also promote human responsibility. Benedict J. Groeschel, O.F.M. Cap., *The Courage To Be Chaste* (New York/Mahwah: Paulist Press, 1985), pp. 77-84, has some interesting suggestions in this regard.

30. "The Pastoral Care of Homosexual Persons," 3, *Origins,* 16, p. 379.

31. I would remind the reader that the question here is not whether homosexual individuals can be understood to have a graced calling to the service of God's people, but whether homosexual unions, precisely as sexual, can be so understood.

32. By sexually active people I mean those individuals who are in relationships in which genital sexual expression is an accepted and fundamental aspect of the relationship or who are seeking to enter into such a relationship. Expressed negatively, I mean those people who have not chosen either a life of consecrated celibacy or deliberate singleness in the world.

33. Kosnik, *Human Sexuality,* pp. 92-95.

34. Hauerwas, *Vision and Virtue,* p. 89, expresses the relationship between self-understanding and norms in the following way. " . . . even though moral principles are not sufficient in themselves for our moral existence, neither are stories sufficient if they do not generate principles that are morally significant." The present paragraph is attempting to suggest some significant moral norms whose meaning and basis is to be found in the Christian story, though, unlike Hauerwas, I think they are morally defensible on other grounds as well.

35. If human sexual relationships find their deepest meaning as signs

of Christ's union with his Church (Eph 5:22-31), then fidelity and exclusivity in those relationships are called for. Adultery, prostitution, and promiscuity become forms of idolatry or infidelity to one's calling.

36. In canonical terms, people who marry incur a *debitum,* a debt. They owe, as it were, conjugal intercourse to their spouses. I do not wish to deny, by what is written in the text, the canonical point being made by the use of such language. Marriage does entail the willingness, the consensual agreement to share sexual intercourse, and to this extent it can be said to be an obligation of marriage and so also a right. But this right to intercourse is a generic right. In practice, the giving and receiving of selves in sexual intercourse is always the renewal of the gift of self, and never concretely a right one can claim here and now against the free consent of one's sexual mate. If one limits one's thinking to canonical categories, marital rape is an impossibility. But morally and existentially it is far too often a sad fact.

37. This norm may appear to be less rooted in the Christian story than the previous ones. However, a reflection on the love of a Creator God who assumed the responsibility for the consequences of the sins of his creatures, the fruits of his love, by sending his Son to die for their redemption, may serve to root responsibility for the consequences of our actions more fully in Christian self-understanding. I also hasten to point out that responsibility for something is by no means the same as being guilty of something.

38. Since marriage is a vocation, it must be tested and received by the community. That is the import of the insistence upon a public ceremony and one reason for the historic opposition of the Church to clandestine marriages. See Schillebeeckx, *Marriage,* p. 317.

39. I do not mean to suggest that this is the reason why church communities refused to bless homosexual unions. But whatever the reasons for the refusal may have been, and they were largely centered on the lack of procreative possibility in such unions and so their apparent "unnaturalness," the outcome was that such unions were perceived to lack vocational significance.

40. There are both theological and practical reasons for giving some normative weight to tradition to some degree. If Jesus, the Risen Christ, remains present to and in his Church through the power of the Spirit, then what the community of believers has affirmed and lived before us must be taken with considerable seriousness. Practically speaking, tradition serves as a useful challenge and corrective to our being caught up uncritically in the spirit of the present time. Finally, it is an illusion to think we can escape from the history that has shaped our understanding. See Jaroslav

Pelikan, *The Vindication of Tradition* (New Haven: Yale University Press, 1984), pp. 3-20.

41. With the recently discovered AIDS virus and its connection to homosexual behavior, a distinct challenge is posed to active homosexuals as to what social responsibility for the consequences of their actions might mean.

42. The judgment in the text about the moral worth of a relationship does not refer to the actual moral worth of any specific homosexual relationship relative to that of any specific heterosexual relationship. There are certainly many actual heterosexual relationships that are morally inferior in many ways to actual homosexual ones. The judgment is concerned only with the objective status of the way of life.

43. Friendship is based upon shared or mutual interests, interests which are in principle shareable by others than merely the two friends so that friendship of its very nature is not an exclusive relationship. Friendship turns us together outward toward the world. Sex turns us together toward one another. *Philia,* or the love of friendship, and *eros,* or sexual love, need not be rivals or enemies of one another, but they are different affectional realities whose integration is not an easy task. That is one reason why marriage is not an easy relationship.

44. More than any other human relationship, true friendship is unconditional in nature, but both the shared interests on which the friendship is based and the non-exclusive nature of friendship put limits on what friends may ask of one another. To make sex a condition of friendship is to violate the very nature of the relationship. It seems to me, therefore, that Gregory Baum, "Catholic Homosexuals," *Commonweal* (February 15, 1974), p. 481, begs the question when he writes, "We have the religious witness of Christians and Catholics that homosexuality grounds responsible sharing and sustained friendship." That may well be the case. But do homosexual acts ground such friendship and are they essential to sustaining it?

45. Friendships can wither away and die without moral fault because there may be no moral obligation to sustain an interest in what served as the basis of friendship in the first place. But marriage is a vocation, a calling accepted as a gift with specific moral responsibilities, among which is the obligation to try not to let the relationship wither and die.

46. Nor does it seem particularly necessary to try to do so, nor to point a finger at one's partner in blame for the failure of the relationship. The Eastern Orthodox liturgy for remarriage after divorce is both instructive and suggestive in this regard. It involves an extensive confession of sin for the failure of the first marriage, understanding sin not so much as an action or a series of actions, as a pattern of indifference or insensitivity or

neglect. See Paul Ramsey, "Liturgy and Ethics," *The Journal of Religious Ethics* 7, 2 (Fall 1979), pp. 152-160.

47. Guindon, *The Sexual Language,* pp. 83-109, 413-424.

48. Louis Bouyer, *Introduction to Spirituality,* trans. Mary Perkins Ryan (Collegeville: Liturgical Press, 1961), pp. 135-136.

49. In 1 Corinthians 7:14 Paul says, "This is because the unbelieving husband is made one with the saints through his wife, and the unbelieving wife is made one with the saints through her husband." And he argues in the next verse that the children of such a union are also made holy. This is not a magical view, since Paul allows the unwilling non-believer to depart and considers the marital bond dissolved if he or she does so. Friendships, too, may be holy and sanctifying, but marriage is holy in a more fundamental and thoroughgoing way.

50. Keane, *Sexual Morality: A Catholic Perspective,* pp. 4-13; Eric Fuchs, *Sexual Desire and Love: Origins and History of the Christian Ethic of Sexuality and Marriage,* trans. Marsha Daigle (Cambridge: James Clarke & Co; New York: The Seabury Press, 1983), pp. 84-171.

Five

SEX AND THE
VIRTUE OF CHASTITY

There are any number of additional remarks that could, and undoubtedly need to be, made at the conclusion of this study. In the interests of brevity and clarity of focus, I intend to restrict the remarks in these final chapters to three areas of concern. Those areas are sex and the virtue of chastity, sex in relation to sin and human freedom, and our limited human knowledge of God's will. First, some additional comments about sex and the human virtue of chastity should help to clarify and confirm the point of view being advanced in this work.

THE MEANING OF CHASTITY

The virtue pertaining to the proper conduct of our sexual lives has traditionally been called the virtue of chastity.[1] The word chastity is commonly misused today in our society to mean abstinence from—and even distaste for—all sexual contacts and relations. As a result the virtue is understood to have an essentially negative meaning and is not widely held in high repute. Indeed, it is frequently the object of disparaging remarks and off-color humor. Chastity is often understood to imply a fear of or complete indifference to sexual feelings and experience. Chaste people are often portrayed as naively innocent and immature, or are regarded as equivalent to sexually inhibited or repressed individuals who need psychological and social liberation. Such individuals can hardly be held up as models of human wholeness and as figures to be emulated.

This negative reading of chastity is unfortunate, if understandable, for it blinds us to an important human virtue.[2] As a virtue, chastity is a disposition or stable habit of the self, a structured and learned aspect of one's character, which inclines the human person without coercion to act in chaste ways. Like all human virtues, chastity must be understood as an enabling, human strength that affords human beings an enhanced capacity for self-determination and self-control. In the case of the virtue of chastity, it inclines them to the free and responsible use of their sexual energies and powers. More generally, the virtue of chastity enables the integration of one's sexuality into one's overall way of life as a healthy and contributing factor.

To be chaste, then, is not to be prudish or sexually repressed, nor does chastity mean that one regards sex as essentially flawed or dirty, or as somehow incompatible with God's grace and holiness. Still less is the chaste person the sexually ignorant or unaware individual. On the contrary, the truly chaste person has a high esteem for human sexuality and for the possibilities of growing in love through sexual expression. To be chaste does not mean one is oblivious to sexual attraction and desire, nor does it mean that one never experiences sexual temptation. Chastity is a human virtue, not a virtue which turns human beings into angels.[3]

Like all human virtues, chastity is rooted in and based upon natural human tendencies or inclinations, not imposed upon these inclinations as some alien and coercive force.[4] Virtues are the guides, not the jailers of our nature. The tendencies upon which virtues are built are called natural because they are pre-voluntary or given orientations of the self which point the way toward human fulfillment and wholeness. They are tendencies of the self which human freedom does not create but can only nurture and guide, or attempt to ignore and frustrate. The natural inclinations or tendencies upon which the virtue of chastity is based are most notably the human inclinations to the enjoyment of physical pleasure, to touch and be touched, to experience tenderness and warmth, to be acknowledged and valued by other human beings for what we are rather than for specific achievements, to share intimately with them and to see that intimacy give rise to new life. More simply and fundamentally, the natural inclination upon which chastity is built is the human desire to love and be loved without limit. The moral virtue of chastity both norms and enables these inclinations so that they can be realized in humanly healthy, non-destructive and holy ways. Quite simply put, the virtue of chastity informs and enables the humanness of our loving one another as sexual persons.

To act in accord with the virtue of chastity may well require a degree of sacrifice and self-restraint.[5] It will entail at times the moral necessity of saying no to certain ontic goods which in other situations or under different circumstances would be acceptable objects of moral choice. Chastity may, for example, require the faithful wife, while away from home on business, to deny herself an evening of warmth and pleasure with a willing and attractive male colleague, thus foregoing the very real ontic goods of sexual pleasure, human companionship and shared intimacy. The virtue may demand that the celibate spiritual adviser who finds himself strongly attracted sexually to an advisee refer his client to another spiritual director, foregoing the ontic goods of shared sexual pleasure and close personal friendship.

But while the virtue of chastity does often require foregoing certain ontic goods, it does not entail causing or allowing ontic evil, nor does it deprive oneself or other human beings of what is due them in virtue of their human dignity.[6] The chaste person is not less human for being chaste, nor does he or she deprive others of a measure of their humanity, no matter what sacrifices the virtue of chastity may require. The chaste person is not less but more human in the sense of being freer and more self-determining. The chaste person is more able to act toward other people on the basis of freely chosen values which have integrated the biological and psychological demands of nature, rather than merely react to them on the basis of biological instinct or psychological compulsion.

SEXUALITY AND SIN

Given the range of possible sexual vocations indicated above and the conditions of chastity appropriate to each, it is clear that sexuality cannot be erased from one's vocational existence. But sex, or explicit sexual activity in its various forms, is another matter. Sex simply cannot be regarded as an activity essential to human personal well-being and holiness. Sex is surely not a biological appetite comparable to the human needs for food and drink,[7] nor a psychological need similar to the needs for affection and meaning. Sex is not rightly regarded, nor is it commonly experienced, as a natural concomitant of all warmly affectionate, inter-personal relationships, though a greater or less degree of sexual attraction may well be part of many such relationships. No sensible and observant philosophy, and still less Christian theology, can regard sex as an unsullied biological urge of no great human significance or consequence. Hence, there exists the inescapable human quest for the meaning of sexual activity, the need for moral guidelines for such activity, and the human self-discipline required to pursue this meaning and follow these guidelines. In short, human beings need the virtue of chastity for personal and social well-being.

Human sexuality moves us to attend to, care for, and seek personal intimacy with others. Sexual desires and longing have their place in this quest for intimacy, as does the external expression of these desires. But both personal and historical experience testify to the need for sexual passion and desire to be socially regulated[8] and personally disciplined. That is to say, there is both a social and a personal responsibility to structure human life in ways that will enable human beings to give chaste expression to their sexual desires and longings (which is not equivalent to non-sexual or inhibited sexual expression). The habitual inclination and ability to act in this disciplined and responsible way is the substance of the virtue of chastity.

Apart from a living faith in a providential God whose own analogously sexual passion is for eternal communion with his people, sexual expressions and activities can take on any idiosyncratic meaning people wish to give to them. In such a situation only strictly consequentialist norms dealing with the extrinsic consequences of sexual behavior can be employed to judge moral responsibility in sexual matters. The popular and negative way such norms are expressed is that any sexual activity is morally proper as long as no one gets hurt. The more sophisticated and positive approach is to argue that it is the relational significance of sexual acts that serves as the norm of their moral quality. Such norms are certainly not wrong, but they are seriously incomplete.

What I have been trying to urge throughout this study is that Christian faith and moral theology do, and should, employ a different sort of moral calculus, even while attending carefully to the foreseeable consequences of human acts. A Christian moral calculus must also reckon from the demands of vocational fidelity to a determination of appropriate behavior, and not merely calculate the likelihood of certain behaviors to enable or fulfill human hopes and aspirations.[9] A Christian moral calculus must reckon with the kind of persons we are and are called to become by God's grace, and not consider only the external circumstances which will enhance human life and well-being. There are times and reasons for Christian believers to take up the cross to follow Christ, to forego certain human pleasures and satisfactions because they rival or impede greater goods, to accept the limitations and restrictions that a specific way of life imposes on them, and to find in these demands of discipleship positive human fulfillment and the very meaning of life itself.[10]

The right to marry, for instance, designates as morally right in a general sense a specific vocational choice; it does not ground or warrant a right to have sex with any particular person at any particular time. The marriage vows themselves, which accept the other for better or worse, recognize that marriage itself may face circumstances in which sex is either impossible or morally inappropriate, but the vocation is not thereby cancelled nor the vocational demand for fidelity abrogated. One theoretical and practical mistake, it seems to me, that many advocates of artificial contraception repeatedly make in defending a married couple's right to practice contraceptive intercourse is to insist on the impossible sacrifice which sexual abstinence requires. To argue for the importance of a couple's continuing sexual activity, when a new pregnancy would not be responsible, on such grounds as sex is needed to prevent infidelity, to forestall the possibility of marital indifference or hostility, or to avoid some other marital ill, is to make a good practical argument. Such an argument is not without prudential, and so moral, relevance, since prudence is an essential moral virtue. But it is an auxiliary and secondary consideration at best,[11] and runs the risk of ignoring or denying the fact that at times married couples are called upon, even in their sexual lives, to take up the cross.

The chief reason why married couples, for whom a new child would at this time be a morally irresponsible choice for any number of valid reasons, may practice contraceptive intercourse[12] is that sexual intercourse is an essential expression of their vocational calling apart from considerations of procreative purpose or possibility. The fact that sex is nice, pleasurable, fun, even at times ecstatic, and often very helpful to their psychological union, underlines its character as gift, but does not argue for its moral or human necessity at any particular time or place. The virtue of chastity, then, must be understood as the free, learned ability to live sexually one's calling in the most appropriate ways in a variety of circumstances. The freedom granted us in Christ finds its realization sexually in the virtue of chastity, and not in so-called free sex, or in the abandonment of sexual moral principles and norms, or in the repression of and ignorance about sexuality. This freedom also negates all ideas of sexual activity as in any way personally necessary to living a fully human and Christian life.[13]

CHASTITY AND CONSECRATED CELIBACY

Historically, the importance of chastity as a virtue in the Christian life came to be symbolized in the choice of consecrated celibacy or virginity,[14] though the practice of chastity was hardly restricted to those making such a choice. The new life of faith given in Christ and animated by the Holy Spirit had as one of its clearest manifestations, after martyrdom of course, the ability of Christian men and women to control and direct their sexual desires and energies in the service of God. One interesting consequence of this new life in Christ was the conviction that it was now possible for men and women to be friends and soul-mates, to see one another as persons and not merely as objects of sexual desire and pleasure.[15] Three things about this symbolic enactment of the virtue are often overlooked.

The life of consecrated celibacy is not chosen for its own sake, but for the sake of the kingdom of God (Mt 19:12; 1 Cor 7:32-35).

Such a choice is, therefore, not a rejection or a negation of the human value of sexual expression, but it does relativize the value of sex. In bearing witness to the over-riding worth of the kingdom, the life of consecrated celibacy serves as a reminder to every way of life that it is the search for the kingdom of God that is to come first in our lives (Mt 6:33), not the pursuit of sexual satisfaction and fulfillment. In offering such a radical witness to the kingdom, consecrated celibacy further reminds us that even God's good gifts, among which we must count sex, can become obstacles to the pursuit and service of God.[16] The greater the gift, the greater its potential for both good and evil, for leading us toward or away from God. If it is true that the Christian tradition has overemphasized the dangers to the neglect of the possibilities inherent in the gift of sex,[17] that is no reason to ignore or downplay the dangers. They remain very real and present.

The second thing often overlooked about the symbolic enactment of chastity is that it is a special calling, a way of life dependent upon the grace of God. As a way of life it is held in high esteem because it is such a strong testimony to grace, a sign of the efficacious presence and activity of God among us, though certainly not the only sign. But this dependence upon God for a chaste, celibate life is no less for any other Christian sexual way of life. Marriage, for instance, is not a license for unchastity, but an invitation to a different way of living chastely. Hence temptations to unchastity in whatever way of life are just that, temptations to reject the grace of God and the path of discipleship. Our sexuality and sexual behavior, then, along with everything else human, have been taken up into the divine plan for our salvation as vehicles of sanctification.[18] The virtue of chastity is for everyone both a gift and a demand of grace.

The third aspect of the life of consecrated celibacy we often overlook is that it is a symbolic enactment of a virtue,[19] and so not the reality of the virtue in all its fullness. We have neither right nor reason to expect all consecrated celibates to be perfect models of chastity for us in their personal lives. Their commitment is to try to live the virtue in the personal circumstances of their own lives, not to actually do so. We cannot, therefore, use the failures and difficulties celibates may experience in their lives as an argument against the virtue itself. Their witness lies in their public willingness to try to live this way of life, though obviously their personal failures severely undercut such witness.[20] In addition, what their lives enact is a virtue to be emulated, not a set of behaviors which are ethically normative for others. This last point is of major importance, so let me add an additional word about the relationship between virtue and action.

VIRTUE AND ACTION

As we have seen, a virtue is a settled disposition of the self which inclines the virtuous person to act in accord with the virtue. It is not a guarantee that one will always so act. A person whom we recognize to be trustworthy, for example, is one we expect to keep faith with us. We expect this because experience has shown that he or she consistently does keep faith with us and with others. But such a person may not always keep faith, and the failure to do so may have either of two explanations. The first explanation is that the person is not quite as virtuous as we thought; the enabling strength that is a virtue was not strong enough in a particular situation to resist temptation. Most human beings are familiar with this kind of experience in one form or another. We struggle to be patient, or temperate, or generous, or truthful, and we fail. We know, or think we know, what the virtue demands of us in terms of behavior, but we do not do it. We fail in virtue and rebuke ourselves for not being sufficiently patient, or generous. We reveal that we know the true meaning of a virtue when we confess we were not strong enough to resist the temptation. Our prayer reflects this in that we repent of our failure and weakness and pray for the grace or the strength to be more patient, more generous, and so on.[21]

But there is another possible explanation for the individual's failure to keep faith on a particular occasion. It may not be a failure in virtue at all. It may be that the individual in our example was not clear about what specific behavior was appropriate in a particular set of circumstances, or judged that keeping faith required a different sort of behavior than the one we expected. While experience does bear out the idea that truly virtuous people often have a connatural feel[22] for the proper object of the virtue, this is not always and inevitably the case. Neither the understanding nor the possession of a virtue guarantees an infallible judgment about the behavior appropriate to the virtue in all situations. While a person would be well advised, for example, to get advice about what justice requires in a particular situation from one known to be just, rather than from one known to engage regularly in unfair practices, there is no surety that the virtuous person will know in every case what the just act is to which the virtue of justice inclines.

Consequently, while it may be well be sensible to look to those committed to celibacy for advice on the practical implications of the virtue of chastity, we will be on far more secure ground in seeking wisdom from them about the virtue itself and its relationship to the quest for God, than about the ethical norms and behaviors appropriate to our own particular sexual way of life. If there is a problem with so much of Catholic sexual morality having been developed almost exclusively by a male, celibate clergy, that problem lies in the confusion between ethical norms and practical, spiritual advice,[23] and in the excessive attention devoted to actions rather than to the virtues which should inform actions. In sum, the life of consecrated celibacy bears witness to the importance of the virtue of chastity in the Christian life as an essential condition of both neighbor-love and love for God. It does not provide us, and should not be expected to provide us, with an image or model of the ethical norms and specific behavioral practices appropriate to the conduct of our sexual lives.

To express this important idea in a more concrete fashion, one can learn a good deal about the virtue of chastity from reading, for example, Pope John XXIII's *Journal of a Soul*.[24] But the married man will find little help in living the virtue of chastity in his own situation if he takes the disciplinary practices of a young seminarian, one day to be Pope, as normative in his own life. It is, for one instance, surely an important safeguard to celibate chastity not to express openly and regularly one's sexual feelings and desires to the person who is the object of those desires. Such a practice, however, is not the least bit inappropriate for the married man in regard to his own wife. Marital chastity invites just the opposite kind of behavior. Or again, it is contrary to chastity for the celibate nun to indulge in dreams and plans for romantic evenings with a man for whom she feels sexual attraction. Such behavior, however, is more than appropriate for a married woman in regard to her husband.

To live a chaste life, especially in the midst of a sex-saturated culture, is no easy task. Inevitably, advice about chastity takes on a negative guise, admonishing that one avoid this or that possible danger, suggesting this or that way of dealing with or avoiding sexual temptation. There is, I suspect, no escape from such a strong, negative emphasis, especially when one is first struggling to establish the habit of chastity.[25] But the essence of chastity is positive, affirming a deep reverence and respect for the embodied sanctity of one's self and others, a reverence and respect well captured in Paul's way of referring to the body as a temple of the Holy Spirit (1 Cor 6:19). The single best expression of a sense of the virtue of chastity I have ever heard was captured in a prayer said regularly by a married couple just before they made love. The prayer will be familiar to many readers, but in a context other than the marital bed. Before celebrating their shared life and love in the sexual act, this couple prayed, "Bless us, O Lord, and these thy gifts which we are about to receive from thy bounty, through Christ, our Lord."

For the Christian vision of life, then, sexuality is a gift of God, constituting us as who and what we are, sexual human beings. Its proper appreciation and use requires and is the virtue of chastity. Sex is also a gift of God, a gift given to persons bound together in a unity of life and love, as the above prayer makes clear. It is a gift given to the two of us, not a gift given to individuals for their own amusement or satisfaction, although, being a freely given gift, it remains theirs to do with as they would. The virtue of chastity, therefore, does not mean a failure to appreciate these gifts, but quite the opposite. It means a deep appreciation for and a desire to use sexuality and sex as the gifts they are. It is because these gifts have such a central importance to human life and love that the virtue of chastity is esteemed so highly and judged to be of such great importance in our journey toward the kingdom of God.

SEX AND THE EUCHARIST

To conclude these reflections on sex and the virtue of chastity, let me suggest an analogy between the gift of sex to human beings and the gift of the Eucharist to the Church. This analogy is not at all fanciful or inappropriate since the Eucharist is the body of Christ given for us, the blood of Christ poured out for us, unto the forgiveness of sins and the generation of new life and love. Such words would be most fitting between lovers, if they were spoken with sincerity and truth. There are several points about this analogy which are worthy of our attention for the light they throw on the meaning and value of sex and the virtue of chastity.

In the first place, the Eucharist is a gift to be shared, a gift that is, at one and the same time, a sign, an instrument and a pledge of unity with one another and with God. It is a celebration and confirmation of an already existing unity, not a gift to be sought and cherished in isolation, nor one to be used to smooth over or hide fundamental divisions in faith and love between people. It is also a pledge of a future unity, a pledge that carries with it the obligation to seek reconciliation and unity here and now to the degree that we can. It is a gift of profound personal importance and personal intimacy in strengthening one's personal relationship with the Risen Christ, but also of great social significance and service in building up the unity of the body of Christ.[26]

The renewed Eucharistic practice of the Church following the Second Vatican Council has highlighted and clarified many of these truths. The Eucharistic celebration is not to be held in private, except by way of rare and necessary exception. Inter-communion between Christian denominations is possible where there is a common faith and serious reason for it. But open communion is not a practice to be encouraged or done as a matter of routine, for it fails to take seriously the meaning of the gift. The Eucharist is, to be sure, both a sign and an instrument of unity, but it always presupposes the prior act of repentance and baptism, and so the prior unity of a publicly acknowledged and shared faith. The reception of the Eucharist is preceded not only by the personal confession of one's sinfulness as an expression of one's desire for reconciliation with

God, but also by the symbolic gesture of the kiss of peace as a sign of one's willingness for reconciliation with one's neighbors.[27] All this could be said, *mutatis mutandis,* about the gift of sex, both as God's gift to us and our sharing of the gift with one another.[28]

A second point of similarity between the gift of the Eucharist and the gift of sex can be found in the necessity of each gift to the life of the community each forms. Without the celebration of the Eucharist, the Church is not the Church. "I tell you most solemnly, if you do not eat the flesh of the Son of Man and drink his blood, you will not have life in you" (Jn 6:53). It is in celebrating the Eucharist that the body of Christ gives visible and sacramental expression to its very existence. How often, how regularly the Church must do this can have no fixed rule. Prudence would suggest that it do so often, and current, as well as ancient, practice makes a weekly celebration mandatory where possible. Certainly the Church could live if the Eucharistic celebration became impossible for a length of time due to circumstances beyond its control. But it could not even begin to live without the gift of the Eucharist at all; without the body broken and the blood poured out there is no life for the Church.

The necessity of the Eucharist to the life of the Church, however, is not the same for any one individual in his or her life of faith. Circumstances might well make it necessary or even morally preferable that an individual or group of individuals do without the Eucharistic celebration for an extended period of time. And this necessity could be accepted, the preference gladly embraced, if it were for the sake of the kingdom of God. All this could be said, *mutatis mutandis,* about the gift of sex and the community it forms called marriage.[29]

There is a third point of similarity between the two gifts. One may, but one should not, receive and use them in bad faith. But so freely given is each gift that the responsibility for the serious and respectful use of the gift is entirely one's own. Sex, like the Eucharist, is God's gift to us, but for both gifts we become the ministers of the gift to one another. It is, then, both possible and proper for the community to whom the gift has been entrusted to establish guidelines for the reverent and respectful reception of the gift. It is also appropriate for the community to require certain competencies in the ministers of the gift. That community has, after all, been admonished not to cast pearls before swine (Mt 7:6).

That repentance and reconcilation after serious sin should precede the reception of the Eucharist; that the reception should take place in an appropriate context; that some time of prayerful reflection and abstention from food should come before receiving the sacrament to insure both awareness and attention—these, and other customary guidelines, are not unreasonable. That the ministers of the Eucharist be authorized by the community for their task; that they be recognized as people of faith and good moral practice; that they carry out their ministry with reverence and attention—these and other requirements are not undue restrictions of personal freedom or unreasonable norms. But they are not absolute rules and are not enforced as such. Mainly the function of such norms is to issue an appeal to the individual conscience. Once the appeal has been issued, the gift is given freely and without question to all, short of flagrant public scandal,[30] who come forward to receive it, and the question of bad faith on the part of the minister or recipient of the gift is left to God and the individual. Again the same things, *mutatis mutandis,* could be said about the gift of sex.

These close parallels between the Church and marriage and the gifts of the Eucharist and sex are not to be understood as accidental or extrinsic similarities. They are rooted in the very essence of the realities themselves. Because Christ is the sacrament of the encounter with God,[31] the Church, made alive and nourished by the gift of his body and blood, is the body of Christ and the sacrament of Christ's presence in the world. So the Eucharistic celebration is the primary sacramental act of the Church in which one most fully, albeit sacramentally, encounters the Church and so Christ and so God.

So also, because marriage is the sacramental sign of Christ's union with the Church, it is in the marital union that one encounters the mystery of Christ in the Church. Just as the Church is made alive by the gift of Christ's body and blood, so the marital union is made alive by the mutual gift of the couple of their bodies and lives to one another. Sex is the primary sacramental act of the marital relationship, in which one most fully embodies and encounters, albeit sacramentally, the mystery of marriage, and so of Christ and the Church, and so of God. To complete the inter-relationships, sex in marriage creates the family which is the *ecclesiola in ecclesia*.[32] Just as Christ makes the Church, and so himself, present by the gift of his life for it, so also the married couple make the Church, and so Christ, present in miniature by the gift of their bodies and lives to one another.

It is in this setting that both the meaning and the value of sex and the virtue of chastity need to be placed. It is, then, clearly not procreation which is the linchpin, as it were, of Christian sexual ethics, but the committed fidelity and stability of marriage as the normative context of sexual acts and relationships. It is not one's stance on artificial contraception that is the norm of an orthodox understanding of Christian sexuality, but one's view of the normative ideal of marriage. Given the theological truths that the Church professes as the good news of Jesus Christ, how could it esteem sex and chastity more highly? On what grounds could it settle for less than the normative ideal of human sexuality?

CHASTITY AND HOMOSEXUALITY

What this discussion of the virtue of chastity has to do specifically with the lives and behaviors of homosexual individuals can be expressed in a few simple propositions. Homosexual people, no less and no more than heterosexual individuals, are called to practice and grow into the virtue of chastity. Homosexual people, no less and no more than their heterosexual counterparts, are capable of accepting the challenge to live chaste lives. As the recent pastoral letter on ministry to homosexual people rightly insisted:

> What is at all costs to be avoided is the unfounded and demeaning assumption that the sexual behavior of homosexual persons is always and totally compulsive and therefore inculpable. What is essential is that the fundamental liberty which characterizes the human person and gives him his dignity be recognized as belonging to the homosexual person as well.[33]

Finally, the moral norms for the practice of the virtue of chastity are determined not by one's sexual condition but by one's sexual vocation understood within the wider context of every Christian's call to holiness. The appropriate behavioral safeguards for living the virtue of chastity in one's concrete circumstances must finally be left to the prudential judgment of the individual in dialogue with experienced and wise fellow pilgrims. More than this on a general level it is rash to say.

Because the lived experience of our sexuality and sexual practice seems to depart so often and so widely from the normative ideal, it seems imperative to say something about these departures from the norm. Accordingly, we turn next to some considerations about sex in regard to sin and human freedom.

NOTES

1. Groeschel, *The Courage To Be Chaste,* pp. 12–13, defines chastity in somewhat negative terms as follows: "I use the terms chaste celibacy and chaste single life to mean the avoidance of all voluntary genital and pregenital sexual behavior. They also imply a decision to avoid personal relationships of human affection which are likely to be genitally expressed. . . . Chastity for all Christians means avoiding sexual satisfaction from auto-eroticism or from deviant behavior. It does *not* mean isolation, rejection of human love and friendship, or refraining from certain non-genital behavior related to the expression of one's sexuality. Chastity implies an heroic effort at times to confront the dark and self-centered aspects of one's inner being."

2. For a discussion of virtue in general and its importance in human life see John W. Crossin, O.S.F.S., *What Are They Saying About Virtue?* (New York/Mahwah: Paulist Press, 1985).

3. Groeschel, *The Courage To Be Chaste,* p. 35, alerts us to the historic dangers of human sexual unrealism.

4. Crossin, *What Are They Saying About Virtue?* pp. 6–7, emphasizes the positive side of virtue as the flourishing of human excellences and relates it briefly to both spiritual theology and contemporary psychological and developmental theories.

5. Self-restraint and sacrifice are not unique requirements of the virtue of chastity. All worthy human endeavor entails some degree of self-restraint and the sacrifice of one good in favor of another.

6. Like all the virtues, chastity, too, has associated with it a dimension of the virtue of justice. See Josef Pieper, *Justice,* trans. Lawrence E. Lynch (New York: Pantheon Books, 1955), pp. 40–47.

7. Sexual desire can, of course, be considered as a biological appetite similar in kind to the desires for food and drink. While this way of understanding sexuality has some traditional support and contemporary usefulness, it is, in the long run, more deceptive than helpful. See Hanigan, *What Are They Saying About Sexual Morality?* pp. 69–70.

8. No known human society fails to regulate sexual desire in some way, though the manner and degree of regulation differ greatly. The motives behind such regulation also differ significantly and it is these reasons for regulation, rather than the need for and the fact of regulation, that are matters of human dispute and difference.

9. Hauerwas, "Love's Not All You Need," in *Vision and Virtue,* pp. 111–126, makes a clear case for the view of Christian ethics developed in the text. "The ethic of the Gospel is not a love ethic, but it is an ethic of adherence to this man [Jesus] as he has bound our destiny to his. . . . As an ethic of love the Gospels would be an ethic at our disposal since we could fill in the context of love by our wishes. . . . " (p. 115). Hans Küng, *On Being a Christian,* trans. Edward Quinn (Garden City: Doubleday & Company, Inc., 1976), pp. 534–536, makes the same point in a more abstract way, though he often seems to ignore it in application.

10. To invoke the cross of Christ as a justification for an ethical position is both unwarranted and unfair. The language of the cross, and more specifically of suffering and self-sacrifice, generally functions in Christian ethics as paranetic or exhortatory discourse. Simply put, such language provides motivation for action, not justification for a particular way of acting. Nevertheless, the cross of Christ is not simply a motivational symbol. It also serves as what my colleague, David Kelly, has called a hermeneutic theme, in his *The Emergence of Roman Catholic Medical Ethics in North America,* pp. 436–447, or what, more recently, Josef Fuchs, S.J., "Christian Faith and the Disposing of Human Life," *Theological Studies* 46, 4 (December 1985), pp. 682–683, has called a maieutic hint. Karl Rahner, in responding to what he calls a welfare ethics, has expressed the consequence of the cross for the moral life of the Christian by asking: Must Christians not acknowledge "that the world stands under the *sign of the cross* to which God himself has been nailed? That it follows logically that God's commandment may demand even the death of a person; that there is no bitterness, no tragedy, no despair in the world which would be too high a price for God's eternal promise; that one may do no evil in order to reach the good; that it is an error and a heresy of 'welfare

ethics' to think that the moral good cannot put man in a tragedy which offers no outcome within the limits of this world; that, on the contrary, the Christian must expect, almost as a matter of course, that his Christian existence will bring him sooner or later into a situation in which he must give up everything so as not to lose his soul and that it is not up to man always to keep out of a 'heroic' situation. . . ." Karl Rahner, *Dangers dans le catholicisme d'aujourd'hui,* cited in Monden, *Sin, Liberty and Law,* p. 117.

11. Prudence, like chastity, also suffers from a bad press today, often implying caution, conservatism, even a timid and fearful approach to decision making. But the moral virtue of prudence is simply that virtue which inclines the individual to choose a course of action wisely, that is in a way that is both fitted to the situation and to human dignity. See Josef Pieper, *The Four Cardinal Virtues,* trans. Richard and Clara Winston, *et al.* (New York: Harcourt, Brace and World, 1965), pp. 3–40; for a briefer statement, see Crossin, *What Are They Saying About Virtue?* pp. 14–16.

12. I ask the reader to note carefully the word "may" practice. One of the obvious difficulties in answering the question about the use of artificial means of birth control is that the answer must be dependent on both the reasons of the agents for doing so and the conditions or situation of their lives which make sense out of their reasons. A simple always-or-never answer will not do, as even the official teaching from Rome has recognized in certain cases. See Bernard Häring, *The Law of Christ,* III, pp. 348–356.

13. The most comprehensive and forceful defender of Christian freedom as freedom from necessity is Jacques Ellul. See especially his *The Ethics of Freedom* (Grand Rapids: William B. Eerdmans, 1976); more briefly, "Christian Responsibility for Nature and Freedom," *Cross Currents* XXXV, 1 (Spring 1985), pp. 49–53. Ellul's clearest application of the meaning of freedom from necessity can be found in his *Violence: Reflections from a Christian Perspective,* trans. Cecilia Gaul Kings (New York: The Seabury Press, 1969), pp. 81–145. While the conclusions Ellul draws from his view of freedom are not my own in many cases, the basic idea of freedom as including the human ability to push back the walls of necessity seems quite accurate and useful.

14. Bouyer, *Introduction to Spirituality,* p. 135.

15. Herbert W. Richardson, *Nun, Witch, Playmate: The Americanization of Sex* (New York/ Evanston/San Francisco/London: Harper & Row, Publishers, 1971), pp. 31–36. Andrew M. Greeley, *The New Agenda* (Garden City: Doubleday & Company, Inc., 1973), pp. 137–138.

16. The similarities between sexual experience and the experience of

mystical prayer have often been pointed out. But they are worth some attention here to confirm the point being made in the text. Sexual pleasure and sexual ecstasy are gifts in the same way that ecstatic prayer experiences are gifts. Both experiences can be great blessings and aids to a deepening personal love, either of one's spouse or of God or of both. But one can also fall into the trap of valuing the gifts above the giver, of cherishing the experiences for their own sake rather than the person to whom we relate in and through these experiences. This very real possibility helps to explain why so much of the Catholic spiritual tradition has been suspicious of sexual pleasure and sexual relationships. The tradition has been alert to the very real possibility that human beings fall in love with being in love, instead of loving persons. On the other hand, our fear of such experiences, our unwillingness to give ourselves over to deep, passionate, ecstatic experiences with the beloved, can also block the growth in the personal intimacy of the relationship. This is true, not only for sexual relationships as sex therapists have discovered, but also for our spiritual relationship with God in prayer. See Marilyn May Mallory, *Christian Mysticism: Transcending Techniques* (Amsterdam: Van Gorcum Assen, 1977), pp. 198–220, who argues that Christian mysticism aims at the liberation of eroticism.

17. One of the most outspoken critics of the Christian tradition's overemphasis on the dangers of sexuality is Andrew M. Greeley, who has explored the positive possibilities of sexual experience and grace in a variety of ways, most recently in novels. See Greeley, *Sexual Intimacy* (Chicago: Thomas More Press, 1973).

18. Schillebeeckx, *Marriage,* pp. 110–118.

19. The life of vowed celibacy is a public life inasmuch as the vows are public affirmations of the intent to live in a certain way. This intent is symbolized by the way of life, but entering the way of life does not guarantee the presence of the fullness of the virtue, any more than the wedding vows guarantee the fullness of life and love which marriage symbolizes. Both ways of life are expressions of faith and hope, and as such testimonies to the grace of God. They will come to perfection only in the fullness of the kingdom of God.

20. To take up a vocation is to assume a responsibility for something larger than one's own personal success or failure. Hence one's personal failures in living the vocation have more than personal significance. They actually challenge the faith and hope of others in the power of God's grace to transform lives. This may seem unfair or unwarranted to those people whose view of human life is radically individualistic, but in Christian faith it is both true and fair that we live off one another's faith and hope, as well

as off one another's moral virtues. Hence, the responsibility one has in a public way of life goes beyond one's personal fulfillment or individual happiness, though these remain important clues for the way of life one ought to choose.

21. It should be pointed out that we do not become more virtuous simply by prayer. Unfortunately, what we often want in such prayers is not increased ability to be more patient or chaste, but less temptation or fewer challenges to the strength we do have. Groeschel, *The Courage To Be Chaste*, p. 88.

22. Regan, *New Trends in Moral Theology*, pp. 163–167.

23. For the distinction between ethics and spirituality see James P. Hanigan, "Militant Nonviolence: A Spirituality for the Pursuit of Social Justice," *Horizons* 9, 1 (Spring 1982), pp. 13–16.

24. Pope John XXIII, *Journal of a Soul*, trans. Dorothy White (New York: McGraw-Hill Book Company, 1965), pp. 13–17.

25. Groeschel, *The Courage To Be Chaste*, p. 92, suggests that it takes three months to overcome the pull of a former habit and to begin to establish ease in the new inclination.

26. *Lumen Gentium* (The Dogmatic Constitution on the Church), 7, in Austin Flannery, O.P. (ed.), *Vatican Council II: The Conciliar and Post Conciliar Documents* (Collegeville: The Liturgical Press, 1975), p. 355.

27. The importance of a reconciliation with one's neighbor, which is symbolized in the kiss of peace, before the reception of the Eucharist is a reflection of the biblical injunction in Matthew 5:23–25: "So then, if you are bringing your offering to the altar and there remember that your brother has something against you, leave your offering there before the altar, go and be reconciled with your brother first, and then come back and present your offering." Gustavo Gutierrez, *A Theology of Liberation*, trans. and ed. by Sister Caridad Inda and John Eagleson (Maryknoll: Orbis Books, 1973), pp. 262–279, has explored very well the questions this theological imperative poses for the Church in a divided world.

28. Charles P. Kindregan, *A Theology of Marriage* (Beverly Hills: Benziger, 1975), pp. 81–83, has a brief comparison between sexual love and the Eucharist. He also discusses sexual love as God's gift to human beings, pp. 33–38. The expression *mutatis mutandis* means literally having changed the things that must be changed. Since the comparison between the gift of the Eucharist and the gift of sexual love is a form of explanation through analogy, one must be careful not to look for or expect a literal, point by point comparison. For example, in the present paragraph, the Eucharist does not lose validity when a priest must celebrate it in private, because the priest always acts as a representative of and in the name of the

community. Obviously the same sort of thing cannot be said about a husband enjoying solitary sexual pleasure.

29. Again, to point out but one instance of *mutatis mutandis,* the Church as a whole would not voluntarily choose to forego celebrating the Eucharist for the same kind of reasons a married couple might choose to forego sexual relations. The Church does not celebrate the Eucharistic sacrifice on Good Friday, for instance. But that does not mean that married couples should forego sexual relations on Good Friday as well.

30. Technically, scandal is any action which is likely to become a stumbling block or snare to others, taking them as they actually are, on their journey to faith. The malice of scandal has its roots in the inner attitude of unconcern for how one's own actions will affect the spiritual well-being of others. Public scandal refers to actions taken in the public arena, so that the actions themselves and their context are readily and commonly known. In the case of the Eucharist, to offer the gift publicly to one commonly known to be an active non-believer or an unrepentant sinner is to display an unconcern both for the gift of the Eucharist and for the faith of those in attendance. It would, in biblical language, be to cast pearls before swine (Mt. 7:6). Concrete questions of scandal are extremely complex and difficult. There is a burden on the strong in regard to scandal to respect the faith of the weak, as Paul has admonished us (Rom 14:1–21). For an extended treatment of the nature and kinds of scandal see Häring, *The Law of Christ,* II, pp. 472–494.

31. This expression has been made common by Edward Schillebeeckx, O.P., *Christ the Sacrament of the Encounter with God* (New York: Sheed and Ward, 1963).

32. The Second Vatican Council referred to the family as the domestic Church. The Latin expression in the text means literally the little church in the Church. See *Lumen Gentium,* II, in Flannery, *Vatican Council II: The Conciliar and Post Conciliar Documents,* p. 362.

33. "The Pastoral Care of Homosexual Persons," 11, *Origins* 16, 22, p. 381.

Six

SIN, SEX, AND HUMAN FREEDOM

Despite a strong cultural tendency in much of Western society to equate sin almost exclusively with violations of sexual morality, a practice which unfortunately devalues the importance of both realities and clouds the meaning of both terms, some comments here about sin and sex seem essential. For, while there are many sinful acts that have nothing to do with sex, the deliberate abuse and misuse of our sexuality can properly be called sinful. However important it may be to stress the positive and enabling side of human sexuality, its negative and destructive potential cannot simply be ignored.

SIN AND SEXUAL ACTS

Throughout this entire essay I have deliberately avoided writing a single word that would call homosexual behavior or homosexual relationships sinful. Sin is a very explicit and weighty word. To call an act a sin or a relationship sinful is to say, among other things, that it should cease forthwith no matter what the cost, or, lacking the ability to simply end the sin, one is obliged to withdraw any kind of voluntary cooperation from the sinful deed or relationship. To call an act a sin is not only to judge the ontic worth of a concrete act in specific circumstances, but also to pass judgment on the motivational integrity and psychological capacities of those doing the act. I do not think such judgments are in every case impossible and unwarranted, but they are without foundation when made in general, abstract ways. What conclusions, then, if any, may be drawn from the analyses and arguments in the previous chapters about the sinfulness of homosexual acts and unions?

Homosexual acts and relationships, along with a great number of heterosexual acts and relationships, depart considerably from what has been proposed here as the Christian sexual ideal. Homosexual acts that fall short of the ideal are no more or less sinful for being homosexual acts than are heterosexual acts that fall short of the ideal. Despite Thomas Aquinas to the contrary,[1] homosexual promiscuity is no more morally corrupt or morally deviant than heterosexual promiscuity. Heterosexual prostitution is no less morally perverse than homosexual prostitution. There is simply no reason in faith or experience to regard heterosexual sins against the virtue of chastity as less sinful than homosexual sins against the same virtue. Because of the social and cultural hostility directed toward homosexuals, there is some reason to think that homosexual sins against the virtue of chastity may be frequently less serious.[2]

In rebuttal of the third position on the morality of homosexual acts discussed above, I have argued that the Christian sexual ideal, in one of its specific vocational forms, is objectively possible for every person of Christian faith[3] and no compromise with the ideal is acceptable. In keeping with traditional moral analysis, I would readily agree that any number of subjective and situational factors might, in specific cases, mitigate or abolish an individual's responsibility for falling short of or even acting in contradiction to the normative ideal. Indeed, we all fall short of the ideal at times, whatever the specific form we have chosen to give our sexual lives, without there being any question of committing a serious sin.[4]

Furthermore, Christian believers are not called to live up to or conform to ideals,[5] but to love both God and neighbor. That is to say, the measure of Christian morality and virtue is not how exactly specific actions correspond to objective moral norms, but how fully actions embody, express and serve love for God and neighbor. The exclusive focus on how closely or to what degree acts or relationships conform to some ideal is what breeds legalism,[6] and in sexual matters perverts the virtue of chastity into the vice of prudery, and the virtue of Christian freedom into lascivious license. But the cure for these two dangers is not to abandon the moral ideal altogether, for the ideal is necessary to give intelligibility and direction to our sexual behavior.

The issue of the sinfulness of sexual acts and relationships, therefore, cannot be addressed simply and exclusively by asking whether or not they contravene some ethical norm or ideal. The more pertinent questions, both theologically and pastorally, would be questions such as these: How and in what way do such acts or relationships embody a rejection or a repudiation of the ideal? How and in what way do they enable people to give the ideal concrete and approximate embodiment in their lives and move them closer to a fuller realization of their vocational calling? Serious personal sin, or what has traditionally been called mortal sin, enters the picture, it seems to me, only when there is an outright rejection of the ideal or a deliberate refusal to allow the ideal to function as a critical judge of one's relationships and activities.[7] In the case of homosexual acts and unions, only those acts and relationships embraced with the rationale and intentionality of the second position discussed above certainly entail such a clear rejection of the ideal that they would deserve the name of mortal sin and be grounds for public rejection and personal exclusion from communion with the body of Christ.[8]

What of homosexual individuals who are involved in relationships involving overt homosexual acts on the model and with the intentionality of either the third or fourth positions we discussed above? Are such actions always sinful in a sufficiently meaningful sense of the word that they are morally obligated to cease performing such acts or withdraw altogether from the relationship? While such acts and relationships clearly contravene the ideal, or in more traditional language are objectively disordered, I do not know how such acts and relationships can be judged to be sinful in a general, uninvolved way. But I believe at least two things can be said about such situations that would provide some moral guidance.

The first remark is that such relationships cannot and should not expect to receive public recognition and blessing, nor should the specifically sexual character of such relationships be publicly flaunted. The moral significance of such sexual relationships, and that significance may be considerable,[9] is personal, not social. The sexual acts pertaining to any relationship, while they may have social consequence, are, or should be, private,[10] and their sinfulness (not their failure to correspond to the ideal) is a matter for the judgment of personal conscience informed by the teaching of the Church.[11] Furthermore, the public recognition or public flaunting of such relationships, which is not at all the same thing as an open acknowledgement of one's homosexual orientation, is tantamount to a repudiation of the ideal, a revolutionary act as it were, symbolically designed to overthrow the ideal and to create a new and contradictory meaning for sexual relationships.[12]

The second comment is that the normative ideal of Christian sexuality serves, not primarily as a rule simply to be obeyed, but as a normative challenge to everyone in a sexual relationship, homosexual and heterosexual alike. It demands that we examine our conscience to ask whose good and what good is being sought in and through sexual acts. How does this sexual relationship serve the Church and the world? How does it reflect the primacy in one's life of the quest for the kingdom of God? Does one's sexual life truly enable a free and chaste love for others? It is on the foundation of the moral ideal that more specific moral norms can be developed and in the light of which they are to be understood.

The refusal to allow oneself to be challenged in any way by the ideal, the unwillingness to test repeatedly its wisdom and truthfulness for application in one's own life and relationships is a sign that something is morally amiss in a rather serious and fundamental way. If, however, we take human moral development seriously, as we must,[13] it is clear that the repeated testing of our sexual relationships by the normative ideal will yield different obligations and responsibilities at different stages of our development. Like so much else in our life of faith, the Christian sexual ideal is something we grow into and embody more fully as we experience its truth and its demands in our lives. Our sexual lives in this regard are not any different than our experiences with the demands of justice, or of truthfulness, or of respect for life. We often fall short of the normative ideals pertinent to these dimensions of our lives and only come in time, if ever, to realize the full scope of what these ideals ask of us. This falling short of the ideal sometimes happens without any repudiation or gross neglect of the ideal being involved. At other times we fall short because we reject or choose to ignore what the ideal asks of us. Only in this last instance can we speak of serious sin, and even in this case, only after the concrete circumstances have been understood.

This comment is not in any way intended to undercut the ideal as normative for Christian life, nor to suggest that one's failures to live the ideal are not to be taken seriously as manifestations of the power of sin in one's life. Quite the opposite is the case. What I intend here can, perhaps, best be illuminated by the use of an analogy with another sexual practice which is also a topic of some debate today.

AN ANALOGY

It is clear that masturbation as a sexual practice done for the purpose of achieving sexual release or pleasure[14] contravenes the Christian sexual ideal. In more traditional language, it is a seriously disordered action and an objectively grave evil.[15] To perform such an action knowingly and deliberately for whatever reason was, therefore, traditionally judged to be a mortal sin.[16] On the basis of sound pastoral experience, especially in the confessional, the notion of actual and virtual impediments[17] was applied to the practice of masturbation to acknowledge that masturbation was not always, and perhaps not even often, an act of malice and a repudiation of the divine will. It was recognized that such factors as ignorance, passion, habit, emotional immaturity, physical tiredness or simple inattentiveness often mitigated or even abolished the subjective responsibility of the person performing the act of masturbation. In the language I have been using here, acts of masturbation were not necessarily repudiations of the normative ideal of sexuality,[18] but did fall short of or contradict the ideal.

In the light of this awareness of mitigating factors, people who had fallen into the habit of frequent masturbation were counseled to keep trying to overcome the habit, to keep attending Mass and receiving the Eucharist, and not to cut themselves off from communion with the body of Christ. It was often the case that with growth in emotional maturity, the development of new relationships, and persistent prayer and effort to live up to this ideal, the person would overcome the habit and conform his or her behavior more closely to the ideal.

The traditional analysis of masturbation given above had the merit of preserving the ideal of Christian sexuality as normative even while it found a way to recognize and deal with a particular deviation from the ideal as something less than deadly sin breaking one's relationship with God and communion with the Church. In the renewal efforts in Catholic moral theology, however, this approach to the question of masturbation has been found less than fully satisfactory for a number of reasons with which I agree, but do not need to go into here.[19] It is not simply the above traditional analysis as applied to the possible sinfulness of homosexual acts and relationships which I am proposing here, though where it fits the case of particular individuals, it is certainly appropriate and accurate. Yet there seems to be something overlooked or ignored in this traditional analysis.

HUMAN FREEDOM AND SIN

The true test of all human freedom, including the freedom given in Christ through the gift of the Holy Spirit, lies in one's ability to act in accord with the good.[20] In religious terms, it lies in one's ability to do the will of God. This test of freedom has two key aspects to it, a subjective aspect and an objective aspect. The objective aspect is the good to be done, or the will of God which constitutes the normative ideal of human behavior. The subjective aspect is the human ability to do this will, which implies also the desire to do it along with the desire and the ability to know it. But the key subjective element is the ability to do it, the real capacity to act which is captured in the words "I can."[21] It is clear in our experience that we sometimes know what we should do and even wish to do it, but find ourselves unable to do it. This experience, as St. Paul has expressed it (Rom 7:14–23), is the experience of the power of sin in our lives.

But the power of sin does not affect only our ability to act. It also impairs our desire to know and do the good, and it diminishes and at times even abolishes our ability to know the good. It is the power of sin which makes our hearts hard and indifferent to the good, our eyes blind and unable to see the good. To the degree we are caught up and held in bondage by the power of sin, we need not only forgiveness for our sins, but redemption or liberation from the very power of sin itself. This need is quite clear in regard to the previous example of masturbation. It is one thing to know that this is a practice one should not do; it is a second thing to desire not to do it; it is a third and most crucial thing to have the ability to act in accord with the knowledge and the desire. Only where the ability is present, which presupposes, of course, the presence of both desire and knowledge, is freedom fully realized, the ability to act in accord with the good.

What the application of the notion of impediments to the practice of masturbation recognized is that there are personal and social factors for which one may not be responsible which affect the human ability to desire, know and do the good. To the extent and degree that these factors are present in a person's life, they may diminish personal responsibility for his or her actions, so that such actions are, in traditional language, only venial sins or imperfections, despite being seriously disordered acts or clear violations of a normative ideal. But the presence of impediments does not make a disordered action rightly ordered, nor does it make ideal an action which contradicts the ideal. Still less does the presence of impediments abolish or render void the power of sin in that person's life. Quite the opposite is the case; the impediments manifest the presence of that power, either as the power of sin in us or in the world.[22] For whatever reason, the ability to act in accord with the good is lacking. The individual may not need forgiveness for sins so much as he or she needs liberation from sin. This situation of needing liberation from the power of sin, as I understand it, is what we meant traditionally by describing someone as being in a state of sin.

SIN, FREEDOM, AND HOMOSEXUALITY

If we apply this analysis of sin and freedom to the question of homosexual acts and relationships, the first thing to be asked is whether a homosexual orientation is a manifestation of the power of sin in a person's life, while a heterosexual orientation is not. To repeat for the sake of clarity, it is not a question of whether a homosexual orientation is sinful or not; it isn't, any more than a propensity to chemical addiction is sinful. But is it a manifestation of the power of sin so that it weakens or negates one's ability to desire, know and act in accord with the normative sexual ideal? Is a homosexual orientation as such an excusing impediment which mitigates or abolishes the homosexual's responsibility for the sinfulness of homosexual acts?[23]

The answer to that question must, I think, be no, though it could be such an impediment in a particular case when joined with other factors.[24] The fact that there are people with an abiding homosexual orientation who, nonetheless, knowingly and willingly embrace the normative ideal of Christian sexuality and live chaste lives as consecrated celibates or as single people in the world confirms this negative answer. It is, then, not one's sexual orientation nor the mere presence of sexual attraction and desire in one's life that is a manifestation of the power of sin. The power of sin manifests itself in our sexual lives, not in sexual desire itself, but in both the unruliness and the imperiousness of our sexual desires.[25]

The imperiousness of sexual desire refers to the experience of wanting sexual pleasure and release in one form or another so insistently that one can think of little else, and in subtle, often unconscious ways one begins to take steps to bring about the desired end. The imperiousness of sexual desire makes chastity unthinkable and unattractive. In the grip of sexual passion it is difficult to know the good, to want the good, to do the good, for the good of sexual satisfaction has become one's god for the moment. This is one way that all human beings, homosexual or heterosexual, are tempted sexually. Married people, no less than single people, can be and are tempted in this way, even in relation to their own spouses, which is why they often can be inconsiderate of the feelings and desires of their sexual partners and imperious in their sexual demands upon them. In the face of the imperiousness of sexual desire, homosexual chastity and heterosexual chastity, single chastity and marital chastity, are all equally difficult.[26]

The unruliness of sexual desire, on the other hand, points to the experience of wanting to express affection sexually toward individuals with whom such expression is inappropriate or in ways that are inappropriate. Of course, this distinction between imperiousness and unruliness is largely analytical, since most sexual temptations will involve both aspects to some degree. But such is not always the case. The desire, for example, to share sexual pleasure with one's spouse can be imperious without being unruly. The desire to express one's love for one's fiancé or fiancée through some form of sexual expression may not be unruly in the sense I am using the word here. But the desire might well be or become imperious and lead also to unruly expressions of sexual affection. Or again, the desire of a teacher to express affection sexually toward a student may not be imperious, but it is an unruly desire, since sexual expression between teacher and student is always inappropriate.[27] The unruliness of sexual desire may not make chastity as a virtue unthinkable or undesirable in general, but it does make it difficult in a particular case to know and desire and do what is good. And it is at this point that we must come to grips with homosexual desire.

Are homosexual desires unruly of their very nature and so manifestations of the power of sin in a person's life? Are they always to be counted as temptations which threaten and weaken our knowledge, desire and ability to do the good, so that to yield to them willingly is a sin? From an epistemological viewpoint, this, it seems to me, is the central question in the whole discussion of homosexual acts and sin. For that reason, let me repeat and summarize briefly what has led us to this question.

It is not the fact of sexual attraction and sexual desire, but their often imperious and unruly character that raises the question of the power of sin in regard to human sexuality. The power of sin manifests itself in human life subjectively[28] in the way it affects the human ability to know, desire and so ultimately to do the good. We have seen how the imperiousness of sexual desire, be the desire heterosexual or homosexual, does, in fact, threaten to, and sometimes actually does, take over human freedom. Hence, we properly understand it in the first case as a temptation to be resisted, in the second case as a power from which we need to be liberated. Part of the enabling strength of the virtue of chastity is the human control over sexual desire, so that it does not negate our ability to know, desire and love the good. The chaste person is not unfamiliar with the imperiousness of sexual desire; he or she has mastered this false emperor, knows the imposter for what it is and has the desire and ability to resist its demands. In respect to the imperiousness of sexual desire, both homosexual and heterosexual individuals are in the same situation.[29]

We have also seen what it means to call sexual desire unruly. Sexual desires can be directed toward persons, animals, or objects which are not appropriate to such desires for a great variety of reasons. Sexual desires can also seek satisfaction with appropriate objects of sexual desire in ways that are humanly inappropriate.[30] If such desires are not also imperious, they are not nearly so destructive of human freedom, but as temptations to act in ways we know we should not act or desire not to act, they are clearly manifestations of the power of sin in our lives. At the least they threaten our knowledge of the good and our desire to do the good, by creating in us a rival desire, for the satisfaction of which we may soon be seeking justifying reasons. Again, the virtue of chastity enables the human person to direct his or her sexual desires and energies to appropriate objects in appropriate ways. The chaste person is not unfamiliar with unruly sexual desires, but recognizes them for what they are, temptations, and so finds the desire and ability to resist them.

It is in this context, then, that we have come to ask whether homosexual desires are, of their very nature, unruly. To repeat once again, this is not a question about the sinfulness of homosexual desires as such.[31] It is a question of whether such desires are a manifestation of the power of sin in us, and so are necessarily to be understood as temptations which morally we are obliged to resist.

If we recall the earlier discussion of the four ways of morally evaluating homosexual acts and relationships, the first and third positions we examined saw such desires to be, to some degree, ontically flawed. In the case of the first position, such desires were considered to be unnatural or objectively disordered because they contravened the divinely created purpose for human sexuality, namely procreation. The third position viewed homosexual desires as ontically flawed inasmuch as they moved people to aspire to a relationship that was less than ideal. The second and fourth positions, on the other hand, accepted such desires as of equal ontic worth with heterosexual ones. The kinship between the first and third positions and that between the second and fourth positions is to be found in their shared answer to the present question,[32] despite the different directions they each proceed to take on the basis of the answer.

If it were possible to affirm with any certitude that a homosexual orientation was, in fact, a physical, psychological, moral or spiritual aberration, the charge of ontically flawed in regard to homosexual desire would be justified. But we have seen that such a sure and general judgment is not warranted by what we know about homosexuality from any of our sources. It seems wisest, then, to proceed on the basis that such desires are not of their very nature unruly, and so cannot be understood simply as temptations to be resisted. But how can such an answer fit with the position adopted in this book on the morality of homosexual acts and relationships? And what does it mean for the sinfulness of such acts?

SEX AND DESIRE

One distinction which should help to clarify my answer to these questions is the distinction between sexual desire and a desire for sex. If the account of the virtue of chastity given in the previous chapter is correct, as I believe it is, then the drive behind human sexual desire is a drive toward personal intimacy and friendship. This desire for personal intimacy manifests itself in human life as the power of *eros*,[33] that human longing to possess and be possessed by the object of one's desire and longing, the desire to become one with one's beloved. While sexual union may be the most obvious sign and common consequence of erotic desire, it is by no means the only one. Such human longings as the desire for mystical union with God, the desire for truth, for beauty, for justice, for the unity of family and friends, are all fueled by erotic desire. This is quite different than the desire for sex, which may or may not be integrated into one's larger desire for personal communion with others.

Now it must be readily admitted that it is not always, if ever, easy to distinguish sexual desire from the desire for sex in one's own life. It must also be acknowledged that sexual intimacy often seems an intuitively natural aspect of one's sexual desiring and an important confirmation and realization of the desire for oneness. In the light of the claims I have made about the meaning of sexual behavior, it would be astonishing if such were not the case. Consequently, sexual desire and the desire for sex are commonly experienced psychologically as a single desire, a fact which merely confirms the sacramental or symbolic significance of sexual intercourse discussed earlier.

But human experience also testifies to the desire for sex apart from any desire for personal union with the other, and to the often illusory and always unstable nature of erotic desire which can so readily pass or so quickly change the focus of its attention once the specifically sexual aspect of the desire has been satisfied.[34] The theological way of dealing with such common human experiences is to insist that *eros* must be integrated with *agape* and brought under its discipline and guidance.[35] As a matter of practical importance, those who seek a stable and lasting relationship as the concrete expression of their desire for oneness are well advised to cultivate and integrate that form of human affection known as *philia* into their relationship.

For the vast majority of heterosexual individuals, the desire for personal intimacy and oneness is directed toward and realized in a relationship with a member of the opposite sex. For homosexual individuals, this same desire for intimacy and oneness will usually be directed toward and realized in a relationship with a member of the same sex. I see nothing that should lead us to a moral preference for one form of the desire over the other, nothing that would ground a moral preference for one way of realizing the desire over the other. To the contrary, it seems a healthy feature of human life to have intimate personal relationships between men and men, and between women and women, as well as between women and men.[36] In their own way, single people and committed celibates, who have integrated their sexuality and vocation in healthy ways, bear witness to this same possibility of loving members of one's own sex in an emotionally warm and humanly tender fashion as well as members of the opposite sex.

The desire to have sex, however, is another matter. The desire itself is natural to all animal natures, including human nature, but it clearly must be integrated into one's life project in a human way. That is to say, one must humanly inquire into the meaning of sexual activity, or, as was said earlier in criticism of the fourth moral position, develop sex-specific guidelines for human sexual behavior. It is not that the desire to have sex is of itself somehow wrong or ontically flawed. Sexual pleasure is one of God's gifts and so ontically good. But it is not an independent good, one that stands apart, as it were, from human character and human relationships and the human quest for God. Like all other finite goods, sexual pleasure is sometimes appropriately sought and sometimes not. Whether or not an individual will judge it to be morally appropriate to act upon the desire to have sex will depend upon the moral meaning one attaches to this form of human behavior, and so upon the normative ideal of sex one proposes.

SEX AND ONTIC GOOD

Because sexual pleasure is an ontic good, the desire to have sex is at root always a desire for a good. If the act of sex proves to be indeed pleasurable, as it often does, and if it involves a shared pleasure, a bond of gratitude and affection is developed between the sexual partners. If there are no untoward consequences of the act, as, for example, an unwanted pregnancy or a violation of another relationship, the sexual experience itself inevitably appears as a good experience, one that not only brings pleasure, but fosters feelings and sentiments toward oneself and others that are highly moral and deeply humanizing.[37] For this reason, even if one somehow becomes convinced that the act itself was morally wrong and so repents one's moral failing, it is difficult to repent for having had and enjoyed the experience itself since it seems so right and was obviously productive of good.

In looking back over one's sexual experiences, there may be some in which manipulation and deceit played a part, or in which coercion of a physical, social or psychological nature was used. Such actions and relationships are rightly matters for repentance. But in repenting of such acts and relationships, it is not the sexual pleasure and shared intimacy for which one repents, but the deceit, the manipulation, or the coercion. Those past sexual experiences which resulted from free and mutual consent, which were accompanied by a degree of mutual trust and respect, and which clearly had no negative social consequences, linger in the mind as happy and instructive experiences, for which one would be an ingrate to repent. It is little wonder that a sexual ethic which unequivocally deems such experiences to be morally destitute and deserving of damnation appears prudish or inhuman. Such an ethic certainly seems to manifest either a fear of or lack of appreciation for one of God's good and ennobling gifts.

This description of sexual experience cannot, I think, be denied. For sex is one of God's good gifts, sexual pleasure is an ontic good, and shared sexual experience that is not exploitative is productive of sentiments of gratitude and affection, as well as being instructive about ourselves and our relatedness to others.[38] All this is just as true about homosexual experiences as about heterosexual ones. Are such experiences to be counted as sin simply because they do not correspond to some ideal of human sexuality?

Like all of God's good gifts to his people, sex and sexual pleasure do not become evil because they are abused or misused. Moral evil does not transform an ontic good into an ontic evil, and so it is altogether proper that one remember with a degree of fondness and gratitude sexual experiences that one may now judge to have been morally flawed. The converse of this experience is also true. Moral goodness does not transform an ontic evil into an ontic good. One may well remember with sorrow and regret actions or experiences that one now judges to have been morally correct. The police officer who killed a would-be assassin, the teacher who expelled an unruly student, the wife who left an abusive husband, the Savior who died on a cross, all acted in ways that were morally correct, but their morally correct behavior does not turn the ontic evil they have caused or allowed to exist into ontic good. Such actions are remembered with regret and sorrow, just as the decision to perform them was faced in the same way and the actions were undertaken with reluctance. But the sorrow and regret are directed at their ontic quality, not their moral quality. When we inquire, therefore, into the morally correct forms of sexual behavior, it is neither wise nor truthful to deny the presence of ontic goodness in certain forms of morally inappropriate sexual behavior.

Sexual desire, therefore, is always desire for an ontic good. But the morality of our desires is not determined simply by the ontic goodness of what we desire, but by the moral intentionality with which we invest the desire and the corresponding capacity of our actions to embody and realize this intentionality in a concrete situation. In a number of the revisionist efforts currently underway in Catholic moral theology, moral evil is frequently defined as deliberately to cause or allow ontic evil to exist in the world without a proportionate reason.[39] Using this definition of sin or moral evil, theologians have applied it to such cases as contraceptive intercourse, masturbation, homosexual relations, divorce and remarriage, and contraceptive sterilization.[40] In all of these cases they recognize the presence of ontic evil in one form or another. All of the cases except divorce and remarriage involve the ontic evil, it is said, of the absence of the procreative good, or, more concretely, the absence of a procreative possibility in sexual behavior. Divorce involves the dissolution of an inter-personal union, and remarriage spells the end of that union in a decisive way, hence losing the goods of fidelity and the sacrament. Whether and to what degree such actions are morally justified is said to depend upon the presence or absence of a proportionate reason for causing or allowing the ontic evil to exist in the world in this situation.[41]

While I am generally sympathetic to this style of moral reasoning, I find it extremely confused and confusing when applied to matters of sexual behavior. For one thing, an ontic evil must be understood not simply as the absence of a good, but as the absence of a good that is in some sense due.[42] To illustrate the point simply, I have no talent for singing. Now a fine singing voice is an ontic good, but its absence in me is not an ontic evil, for there is no meaningful sense in which it can be said to be due me as something essential to my human well-being or anyone else's. A beautiful sunset is an ontic good. But the fact that there does not happen to be one outside my window as I write is hardly an ontic evil.

In regard to the goods associated with human sexuality, children are unquestionably ontic goods, and one of the basic ontic goods resulting at times from sexual behavior. But the ontic good that is the procreative result of an act of sexual intercourse does not mean the act was morally good, despite the presence of this ontic good.[43] So also, the absence of a child in a sexual relationship is not in itself an ontic evil, for children are not due goods but freely given gifts of God to whom we have no strict right. A childless marriage, for instance, is not necessarily marred by the existence of an ontic evil, though the absence of children may be a profound psychological disappointment to the couple and result in some other kind of ontic evil. There may indeed be ontic evil present in a childless marriage in terms of a physical or psychological disability in one or the other of the partners which makes conception impossible. But this ontic evil does not pertain so much to the relationship as to the physical well-being of the person afflicted by the evil. Furthermore, the Church itself teaches that there are times and situations when the ontic good of children would not be responsibly sought in marriage. Hence, the absence of procreative possibility in such cases, either on a temporary or a permanent basis, would not necessarily be an ontic defect in the relationship.

In the light of the previous analysis, it would be my contention that couples, whose situation meets the moral conditions for avoiding pregnancy,[44] neither cause nor allow an ontic evil to exist in the world by practicing contraceptive intercourse.[45] The negative significance of insisting upon the presence of certain conditions for the moral suitability of avoiding contraception is to ensure that the couple not deny their willingness to fulfill their vocational responsibility.[46] The positive significance of the demand that the requisite conditions for avoiding pregnancy be present is not to ensure a proportionate reason for causing or allowing an ontic evil, but precisely to ensure that they do not cause or allow such an evil at all. The ontic evil caused or allowed by irresponsible parenting is not, of course, the new child so conceived, but the economic or psychological or physical strains on marital and family life the pregnancy brings with it. By the same token, then, the ontic evil in homosexual relationships, if there is any, is not to be found in the absence of a procreative good or a procreative possibility. In what sense could such a good be said to be due in such a relationship? Where, then, if anywhere, is such an ontic evil to be found?

It is at this point I must ask the reader to reflect again upon the arguments and norms developed in Chapter IV. The gist of the argument was that sexuality and sexual behavior must be understood in terms of, and integrated into, our more fundamental vocation to follow Christ in loving service to the neighbor. Our sexual behavior realizes its full ontic and moral worth as an expression and embodiment of our vocational intentionality. The ontic evil caused or allowed in sexual acts that are morally wrong is to be found precisely in the absence of such vocational integrity. It is for this reason that it is simply impossible to declare all homosexual actions and unions gravely sinful of their very nature,[47] though they lack the objective capacity to embody fully such vocational integrity and so to correspond to what may, subjectively, be a proper vocational intentionality. For such acts and relationships may very well include not merely the desire for sex but also the desire for interpersonal communion and intimacy as both a sign and service of one's Christian discipleship. Such acts and relationships do not correspond to the normative ideal,[48] but they may be, in the lives of particular homosexual couples, steps toward the ideal and toward a fuller understanding and acceptance of one's sexuality as part of one's Christian vocation.[49] Whether these acts are positive steps toward the ideal is a matter that must be left to the consciences of individuals in serious consultation with an able spiritual guide, whose task is not to judge sins, but to remind us that the ideal continues to call us beyond where we presently are.

To conclude these reflections on sin and sex, it may be helpful to recall that the Roman Catholic Church has traditionally insisted that in matters sexual there is no such thing as parvity of matter. This had the unfortunate pastoral result of causing teachers, preachers and confessors to treat all deviations from the normative sexual ideal as mortal sins, though compassionate confessors would often look for impediments that mitigated or abolished subjective culpability. One understandable reaction of many theologians and pastors and faithful Catholics in general to this clear excess was to suggest that too much attention had been paid to sexual behavior and sexual morality. There are more urgent and more weighty issues for Christians to be concerned about than who is sleeping with whom. More recently, the excessive emphasis on the mortal gravity of all sexual sins has led to analyses of the traditional teaching on sexual morality in political and socio-cultural terms.[50] Such analyses often find the teaching to be a subtle instrument of control and domination, designed to preserve both male superiority in the Church and society and the domination of a clerical, celibate caste within the Church.

Whatever merit there may be to these criticisms of the traditional teaching, it is still worth attending to the basic claim about the importance of what human beings think and do about sex. There is no parvity of matter in sexual things in the sense that what we do sexually is not a minor matter. It matters a great deal, for the kinds of persons we are, for the kinds of relationships we establish, for the kinds of values which support and guide the social order, and most of all for our ability to love God and neighbor without conditions. Negatively expressed, lust is not a minor enemy of human life; it is, in traditional language, a deadly sin.[51] To be mastered by it is fatal, especially if one recalls the words attributed to Jesus by the evangelists. "For at the resurrection men and women do not marry; no, they are like the angels in heaven" (Mt 22:30; Mk 12:26; Lk 20:34–36). To the degree, then, that having sex with those one loves, or even with one's sole life partner, is a personally indispensable necessity and condition of the relationship and of our willingness and ability to love the other, it would seem clear that we are unfit for the kingdom of God and fall short of the normative ideal. That is the eschatological context in which we must think about the possible significance of our own sexual behavior, be it homosexual or heterosexual.

But are all homosexual acts and relationships sins, and grave or mortal sins at that? The answer, quite simply and directly, is no. Are homosexual acts, then, fit objects of deliberate moral choice? Again, the answer is no. The moral meaning and worth of all such choices can not be answered in the abstract. The good news of the Gospel of Jesus Christ is a proclamation and promise of high human possibility. The Church, in service to its Lord, can be expected to do no more or less than teach the Christian sexual ideal in all its fullness. The degree to which our actions miss the mark of this ideal and the degree of our responsibility for that failure are questions to be answered concretely in the internal fora of conscience and the confessional. The degree to which we simply find ourselves unable to desire and hit the mark is a manifestation of how strongly we need to be liberated from the power of sin. The degree to which we knowingly and deliberately act in ways which take us ever farther from the mark suggests our need for serious repentance and forgiveness.

NOTES

1. Thomas Aquinas, *Summa Theologiae,* IIa IIae, q. 154, arts. 11 and 12. Thomas considered homosexual acts to be more serious sins than improper heterosexual acts because they were against both nature and right reason. Using the same rationale, he considered them to be more seriously disordered actions than adultery and rape. This kind of dichotomy between acts against nature and acts against right reason collapses in looking at the consequences of evaluating acts in this way.

2. The reason for thinking homosexual acts may be frequently less serious than heterosexual sins is the social distortion and coercion that the homosexual individual experiences. Such distortion often inhibits human freedom and so may mitigate human responsibility for one's actions.

3. I do not wish to enter here the debate about whether or not there is a specifically Christian ethic and so whether the Christian sexual ideal is objectively possible only for Christians in virtue of their faith or is objectively possible for all human beings in virtue of their humanity. I am content in the present context to settle for the more restrictive claim without further trying to explain or defend it. For a discussion of the issue of the specificity of Christian ethics see Charles E. Curran and Richard A. McCormick, S.J. (eds.), *Readings in Moral Theology No. 2: The Distinctiveness of Christian Ethics* (New York/Ramsey: Paulist Press, 1980), and Vincent MacNamara, *Faith and Ethics: Recent Roman Catholicism* (Dublin: Gill and Macmillan; Washington, D.C.: Georgetown University Press, 1985).

4. The Roman Catholic Church has traditionally taught that all violations of the virtue of chastity are objectively serious disorders. I am going to disagree, in a certain sense, with this teaching later in the chapter. I only wish to point out here that the normative sexual ideal, which is positive, not negative in its thrust, is something we can and do fall short of without sin. The husband, for example, who neglects to express his love

for his wife on special occasions is falling short of the ideal, but it is unlikely that he is in every instance sinning seriously in doing so.

5. It is always worth recalling that the Christian way of life involves following a person, not trying to realize impersonal ideals.

6. Legalism is a difficult term to define. Used pejoratively, as it is in the text, legalism can be described as adherence to the letter of the law even in spite of its spirit. What legalism means to some Christian ethicians can be seen in Fletcher, *Situation Ethics,* pp. 18–22. A more balanced view of ethical traditions which take the form of law, and which ought not to be called legalism, can be found in Wayne G. Boulton, *Is Legalism a Heresy? The Legacy of the Pharisees in Christian Ethics* (New York/Ramsey: Paulist Press, 1982).

7. In making this suggestion, I am trying to indicate what the notion of fundamental option means specifically in sexual matters. For the notion of fundamental option see Josef Fuchs, S.J., *Human Values and Christian Morality* (London/Dublin: Gill and Macmillan, 1971), pp. 92–111, and *Personal Responsibility and Christian Morality* (Dublin: Gill and Macmillan; Washington D.C.: Georgetown University Press, 1983), pp. 53–83; also Franz Bockle, *Fundamental Moral Theology* (New York: Pueblo Publishing Company, 1980), pp. 105–110. Eugene J. Cooper, "The Notion of Sin in Light of the Theory of Fundamental Option," *Louvain Studies* IX, 4 (Fall 1983), pp. 363–382, explores the practical implications of fundamental option for the meaning of specific sins.

8. To reject in such a radical fashion a Christian moral ideal would be a personal rejection of the Christian community. Personal honesty would demand that one exclude oneself from communion. If one were known by the community to have made such a rejection, then public exclusion from the community, the rejection of communion with the individual in question, would be no more than the truthful acknowledgement of a known fact. Such exclusion need not mean personal hostility and social intolerance toward the individual, though regrettably it often is accompanied by such unholy attitudes.

9. Many authors have pointed out that for homosexuals to move from sexual promiscuity to a stable and caring sexual relationship is a distinct moral advance. That seems quite true and is what the text is acknowledging. But so also is it a moral advance for a person of uncontrollable temper to go from beating up the persons who incur his wrath to merely abusing them verbally. This latter type behavior can be considered a moral advance, but it still contravenes the moral ideal.

10. Sexual activity is or at least ought to be inter-personal, and so not for public display. So sexual acts are private acts, acts that are not on display

for the amusement or judgment of the community. Hence, concrete sexual actions must be evaluated in their moral quality by the individuals who engage in them. That does not mean that the community's moral standards and general evaluations have no part to play in the evaluation.

11. Conscience is a personal, subjective reality, but it also has a social and objective dimension to it, which, if ignored, can hardly be considered conscientious. See Hanigan, *As I Have Loved You,* pp. 131–142.

12. A magazine like *Playboy* is a useful symbolic illustration of the public flaunting and challenge to a traditional ideal. *Playboy* is revolutionary in that it wishes to overthrow one understanding of human sexuality in favor of another and contradictory ideal. To insist upon public recognition of a sexual act or relationship which contradicts an ideal, and to do so by publicly flaunting the act or relationship, is a similar symbolic and revolutionary action.

13. While moral development is, of course, a subjective process, it is susceptible to objective study and description. Consequently, we objectively recognize that moral norms and rules not only mean different things to different people relative to their development, but that their reasons for doing or avoiding certain actions are socially rooted and limiting. Hence, what can be objectively required of such people morally is also limited by their development. Useful summaries of developmental theory can be found in Crossin, *What Are They Saying About Virtue?* pp. 53–104, and Ronald Duska and Mariellen Whelan, *Moral Development: A Guide to Piaget and Kohlberg* (New York/Paramus/Toronto: Paulist Press, 1975). More substantial, scholarly treatments can be found in Walter Conn, *Conscience: Development and Transcendence* (Birmingham: Religious Education Press, 1981) and Donald E. Miller, *The Wing-Footed Wanderer: Conscience and Transcendence* (Nashville: Abingdon Press, 1977).

14. There are a variety of reasons for masturbation, not all of which obviously contradict the ideal. Kosnik, *Human Sexuality,* pp. 219–229.

15. *Persona Humana,* 8–10, uses such language as grave moral disorder, serious depravity, intrinsically and seriously disordered act. The document can speak this way because it is convinced that "the authentic exigencies of human nature . . . manifest the existence of immutable laws inscribed in the constitutive elements of human nature and which are revealed to be identical in all beings endowed with reason" (4), Kosnik, *Human Sexuality,* p. 301.

16. For a disordered action to also be a mortal sin required sufficient reflection and free consent. That is to say, not only objective gravity was necessary but also certain subjective conditions were essential for mortal

sin. Burtchaell, *Philemon's Problem,* pp. 78–83, has shown the inadequacy of this understanding of mortal sin.

17. For the notion of impediments see O'Connell, *Principles for a Catholic Morality,* pp. 74–76, and Hanigan, *As I Have Loved You,* pp. 54–57. Simply expressed, actual impediments are those factors in a given situation which stand in the way of human knowledge and free choice. Virtual or habitual impediments are those factors in the character of a person which do the same.

18. Again this is an attempt to apply fundamental option theory to the issue of masturbation. What seems clear, at the very least, is that many people who masturbate are not even implicitly rejecting the good of human sexuality or even preferring the good to the Giver and Creator of the good. But, as *Persona Humana,* 9, Kosnik, *Human Sexuality,* p. 307, points out, none of this can be simply assumed to be the case.

19. Charles E. Curran, "Masturbation and Objectively Grave Matter," in *A New Look at Christian Morality* (Notre Dame: Fides Publishers, 1970), pp. 201–221; Keane, *Sexual Morality,* pp. 58–70.

20. Mortimer J. Adler, *The Idea of Freedom: A Dialectical Examination of the Conceptions of Freedom* (Garden City: Doubleday and Company, Inc., 1958), p. 586, has pointed out five different conceptions of freedom in Western thought. The notion operative in the text he calls "the acquired freedom of self-perfection" which he defines as "a freedom which is possessed only by those men who, through acquired virtue or wisdom, are able to will or live as they ought in conformity to the moral law or an ideal befitting human nature" (p. 608). Without denying the important circumstantial dimensions to human freedom, it is the ability to act in ways appropriate to one's own conscientious convictions that is seen here to be the central element in freedom.

21. "I may do" refers to having the opportunity to act; "I must do" refers to being under some necessity to act; "I ought to do" refers to being under some obligation to act; "I want to do"refers to the emotive desire to act; "I can do" refers to the ability, the strength, the virtue to act. See Hanigan, *As I Have Loved You,* pp. 57–62.

22. Piet Schoonenberg, *Man and Sin: A Theological View* (Notre Dame: University of Notre Dame Press, 1965), deals admirably with sin as a power in the world which also affects us as individuals. To recognize the power of sin in one's life, either in oneself or in the world, is not the same as saying I have sinned.

23. In more colloquial language the question may be put this way: Can homosexual individuals help doing what they do? A popular myth

seems to suggest they cannot help themselves, but if that were the case, why does the same myth pour such moral outrage upon homosexual individuals?

24. The other factors would be the existence of other actual or virtual impediments such as social ostracism, psychological deprivation of affection and so on.

25. Kelly, *The Annual of the Society of Christian Ethics: 1983*, pp. 107–110, has shown the consequence of attributing the power of sin to sexual desire itself. One difficulty Christian theologians have with any kind of human desire is that desire is of its nature self-regarding and so seems to contradict the demand for pure or disinterested love. This view is, I suggest, based upon an inadequate theology and anthropology. See Robert Merrihew Adams, "Pure Love," and John Giles Milhaven, "Response to *Pure Love* by Robert Merrihew Adams," *The Journal of Religious Ethics* 8, 1 (Spring 1980), pp. 83–99 and 101–104.

26. The imperiousness of sexual desire shows itself precisely in its demand for satisfaction regardless of human reason and purpose. As such it raises the question of right, and claims a right to satisfaction on the basis of its own demand for satisfaction. Hence, the object, the occasion, the receptivity of the other are logically irrelevant to its demand. This puts everyone who is faced by the imperiousness of sexual desire in the same boat.

27. Fortune, *Sexual Violence,* p. 110, makes the point that such relationships are morally inappropriate because the power-discrepancy between the two parties to the relationship makes mutual consent a virtual impossibility. Freedom and free consent are possible only between those who are roughly equal. Once the teacher-student relationship is over, the power difference ends and a sexual relationship may become appropriate.

28. The power of sin affects human life both subjectively and objectively, and the relationship between the subjective and objective effects of sin is one of dialectic or reciprocal influence. Nevertheless, it is the traditional Christian claim that the more basic element is the subjective one, so that conversion, a transformation of subjectivity, is the foundational Christian reality. For conversion, see Chapter III, note 19.

29. The imperiousness of sexual desire most radically challenges the human desire and ability to know and desire the good. Hence, it tempts us not to care what we should do, or lures us into indifference in regard to the whole matter of moral goodness.

30. Bestiality is a good example of sexual desire directed toward and satisfied by an inappropriate object. So also is incest. Sado-masochistic

sexual activities are examples of sexual desire seeking satisfaction in humanly inappropriate ways. So also are certain types of sexual fetishism and voyeurism.

31. Desires are not sinful as such. Desires of any kind may be morally culpable insofar as they have been deliberately generated and/or fostered (e.g., by deliberate exposure to pornography for just such a purpose), or, once present unbidden, are deliberately nourished and sustained. To be morally wrong, of course, such desires must also be unruly, or run the likely risk of becoming imperious. Not all sexual fantasies and daydreams would qualify, therefore, as sinful under such norms.

32. The present question, to repeat, is whether homosexual desires are manifestations of the power of sin. Both the first and third positions say yes insofar as they find such desires ontically flawed, albeit to a different degree. The second and fourth positions say no because they find such desires ontically good, but situationally limited in different ways.

33. Paul Tillich, *Systematic Theology,* I (Chicago: University of Chicago Press, 1951), pp. 277–282; Hanigan, *As I Have Loved You,* pp. 148–149.

34. The deceptive nature of sexual desire often shows itself once the desire has been satisfied. What appeared psychologically to be a desire for personal union reveals itself after the fact as a desire for sexual gratification, since no desire for personal intimacy of any kind persists after desire has been satisfied. This deception is not always a matter of conscious or deliberate hypocrisy. *Eros* is unstable of its very nature and cannot be the sole support of a stable and lasting relationship.

35. This, if I understand it, is the thrust of the argument for chastity in *Persona Humana,* 11–12, in Kosnik, *Human Sexuality,* pp. 309–312. *Agape,* or the love of God poured out in human hearts, is not so much a ruling norm as a ruling virtue. God is to be loved above all things and all other human loves are to be taken up into and transformed by that love. It is not so much a matter of suppressing or subordinating *eros* to *agape,* as integrating erotic love and desire into a larger and higher love.

36. Groeschel, *The Courage To Be Chaste,* pp. 106–107. The ability to form close, intimate friendships is often severely inhibited by one's culture. In our American culture, women seem to have more freedom to form close friendships with other women than men have to form friendships with men. Vowed celibacy gives celibates a great social freedom in this regard.

37. To describe anything as humanizing can be easily misunderstood. I mean specifically that good sexual experiences have the capacity to foster in human beings sentiments and feelings that enhance and develop specifically

human capacities. They can make us more self-aware, more in control of our own desires and goals, more compassionate with others, more alert to our need for human companionship and the essential sociality of human nature. More profoundly, such experiences can foster in us a faith and hope for the ultimate goodness of human life.

38. The biblical expression for sexual intercourse is to know the other. See Schillebeeckx, *Marriage,* pp. 12–24, for some of the implications of this knowing.

39. Richard A. McCormick, S.J., "Ambiguity in Moral Choice," and "A Commentary on the Commentaries," in Richard A. McCormick and Paul Ramsey (eds.), *Doing Evil to Achieve Good* (Chicago: Loyola University Press, 1978), pp. 7–53, 193–267; Keane, *Sexual Morality,* pp. 46–51; Edward V. Vacek, S.J., "Proportionalism: One View of the Debate," *Theological Studies* 46, 2 (June 1985), pp. 287–314.

40. For contraception see Keane, *Sexual Morality,* pp. 121–128; Kosnik, *Human Sexuality,* pp. 114–128; for masturbation, see Keane, pp. 58–70; Kosnik, pp. 219–229; for homosexuality, Keane, pp. 84–90; Kosnik, pp. 186–218; for divorce and remarriage, Keane, pp. 140–148; Charles E. Curran, "Divorce in the Light of a Revised Moral Theology," *Ongoing Revision in Moral Theology* (Notre Dame: Fides/Claretian, 1975), pp. 66–106; for sterilization, Keane, pp. 128–134; Kosnick, pp. 128–136, Richard A. McComick, S.J., *Notes on Moral Theology 1965–1980* (Lanham: University Press of America, 1981), and *Notes on Moral Theology 1981–1984* (Lanham: University Press of America, 1985), discusses these issues repeatedly and offers his own evaluation of the arguments from the perspective of proportionate reason.

41. Louis Janssens, "Ontic Evil and Moral Evil," *Louvain Studies* IV, 2 (Fall 1972), pp. 115–156, is the seminal article on ontic evil. Paul Quay, S.J., "The Disvalue of Ontic Evil," *Theological Studies* 46, 2 (June 1985), pp. 262–286 questions the understanding of ontic evil current among many Catholic moralists. Richard A. McCormick, S.J., "Notes on Moral Theology: 1985," *Theological Studies* 47, 1 (March 1986), pp. 85–88, responds to Quay.

42. The reason for insisting that ontic evil involves the absence of a due good is precisely so that one may distinguish evil from human finitude: Curran, *Critical Concerns in Moral Theology,* pp. 95–96. As McCormick points out in his reply to Quay (note 41 above), p. 86, it is also necessary to distinguish *malum naturae,* an evil of nature, from ontic evils which "refer to harms, lacks, pain, deprivations etc. that occur in or as a result of human agency." Ontic evils, therefore, precisely defined, are evils caused or allowed by human beings. Ontic goods, however, are not

similarly restricted to human agency, a fact that can make the whole discussion very confusing.

43. Children are always ontic goods. Their being is good. But children may be the result of a moral evil, e.g., rape, incest, irresponsible marital intercourse. Since one may not commit a moral evil in order to achieve a good, it is hard to see why children could ever be a due good. Procreative possibility, that is to say, normal biological function in male and female sexual beings, is an ontic good, but so also are economic security, psychological well-being and so on. Why does the former have a moral priority, or even an ontic priority, except as an abstraction?

44. To repeat what has already been said, the decision to avoid conception in marriage must be based on objective, as well as subjective, criteria.

45. The absence of procreative possibility in and of itself is not necessarily an ontic evil. Presumably it can also be due to natural biological processes. While the absence of procreative possibility may be caused by human agency, e.g., in using contraceptives, its absence in every case is not thereby an ontic evil, considered from a human and relational standpoint, and not merely from a biological and individualistic perspective.

46. The ontic evil in question would not be the child but the conditions which would render care of the child and the marriage unduly burdensome.

47. For an action to be sinful, in the strong sense of that term, there must be some flaw in the intentionality of the human agent, some degree of malevolence or bad will, some intentional preference for a lesser good over a higher good, or at least indifference to the claim of the higher good. As the argument has been sketched in the text, it is impossible to establish this condition for every homosexual act and relationship. Such acts and relationships may be chosen, in fact, as consonant with one's understanding of the demands of vocational integrity at this moment.

48. All deviations from the normative ideal are objectively grave disorders in reference to that ideal. Whether they are also gravely disordered in reference to the individual's moving toward or away from the ideal is another story. The traditional view of sexual morality looked at actions in the former way. I am suggesting that we do better to look at actions in the latter way, not merely as a matter of spiritual direction, but also as a requirement of moral theology. See Philip Keane, S.S., "The Objective Moral Order: Reflections on Recent Research," *Theological Studies* 43, 2 (June 1982), pp. 260–278.

49. Tad W. Guzie, *Jesus and the Eucharist* (New York/Paramus/ Toronto: Paulist Press, 1974), pp. 128–144.

50. Michel Foucault, *The History of Sexuality,* trans. Robert Hurley (New York: Pantheon Books, 1978); Margaret Farley, "Sources of Sexual Inequality in the History of Christian Thought," *The Journal of Religion* 56, 2 (April 1976); Germaine Greer, *Sex and Destiny: The Politics of Human Fertility* (San Francisco: Harper & Row, Publishers, 1984); Rosemary Radford Ruether (ed.), *Religion and Sexism: Images of Women in the Jewish and Christian Traditions* (New York: Simon and Schuster, 1974); Demosthenes Savramis, *The Satanizing of Woman: Religion Versus Sexuality,* trans. Martin Ebon (Garden City: Doubleday & Company, Inc., 1974).

51. Fairlie, *The Seven Deadly Sins Today,* pp. 175–190; the deadliness of lust, as a power destroying human freedom and leading to both human and spiritual death, may be hard to take seriously in the modern age, in part because it rarely shows itself in its pure form. It is tied closely to greed, pride, envy and anger and feeds these other deadly sins. It is not so much through an analysis of one's theological ideas as through an analysis of one's spirituality that we come to understand the deadly nature of lust. Sandra M. Schneiders, I.H.M., *Women and the Word: The Gender of God in the New Testament and the Spirituality of Women* (New York/ Mahwah: Paulist Press, 1986), pp. 6–7, has an excellent discussion of this difference in terms of our relationship to God in prayer.

Seven

GOD'S WILL AND HUMAN KNOWLEDGE

In writing or speaking theologically, any person takes a very great risk of claiming to know more about God and the divine will than can, in fact, be known. All honest efforts to speak of God eventually lead the person of faith, if not always the theologian, to silent adoration. Theology that is well done begins and ends in reverent respect for the mystery it seeks to understand, and is shaped in significant ways by the piety that informs its search.[1] It is fitting, then, to conclude this study of the relationship of human sexuality and morality to the quest for the kingdom of God with some words on our limited knowledge of God's will.

CONSCIENCE

Although what can be known of God is perfectly plain in the things he has made (Rom 1:19), and despite the fact that the mystery of God's plan has been revealed to us in Christ (Eph 1:9), we human beings have no grounds to claim any extensive and detailed knowledge of God's will or comprehensive understanding of the divine ways. This is even more true in moral matters when we come down to specific cases and must assess what is to be done in the midst of confusing and conflicting motivations and a welter of unclear circumstances and possible consequences. It is not by accident, then, that personal conscience, which is a subjective norm of morality, functions practically and rightly as the ultimate norm of morality.[2] Conscience is the only authority that can have the last word in moral matters because only conscience can judge the subjective sincerity of one's judgments and decisions; only conscience can testify to one's personal sense of moral integrity before God. As the fathers of the Second Vatican Council put it, "Conscience is the most secret core and sanctuary of a man. There he is alone with God, whose voice echoes in his depths. In a wonderful manner conscience reveals that law which is fulfilled by love of God and neighbor."[3]

But, despite its lofty dignity and extensive authority, personal conscience cannot pretend to know objectively in every case that this decision or this action corresponds to God's will beyond all question. Epistemologically, as well as theologically, we all live at the mercy of God. Recognizing one's own fallibility, the limits of one's own perspective and life experiences, and the very real human capacity for rationalization and self-deception, the person of conscience opens his or her mind and heart to the accumulated wisdom and experience of those people who share the same faith, the same values, the same goals, and, indeed, to the insights of all who are his or her fellow pilgrims in the journey of life.[4] Simply put, the person of conscience recognizes the basic need for the formation of his or her conscience and so for what theology calls the social and ecclesial dimensions of conscience.

In this factual necessity for the social formation of conscience[5] lies the experiential basis for the theological importance of the tradition and the teaching authority of the Church.[6] We need our fellow pilgrims, both past and present, as mediators and guides for our knowledge of God's will. It is not a matter of attending to this tradition and teaching authority blindly or uncritically; nor does such attention require that anyone ignore the wisdom of traditions other than one's own. But the tradition which has grounded and handed on truth and salvation for one's life, and which has shaped one's personal identity,[7] as well as the teaching authority graced with the responsibility of preserving and transmitting the same good news, has a special, normative status. What each says about God and the human response to God has an authority that must, in conscience, be reckoned with in a special way.

What does this authoritative tradition tell us about the God and Father of our Lord Jesus Christ and our sexuality? Among other things it tells us that sexuality and sex are the good gifts of an all-holy God to the creatures made in the divine image and likeness. It tells us that our sexuality, our created existence as male and female, is to be joyfully received and taken seriously as a basic clue to God's plan and purpose for human beings. It also informs us that one's experience and knowledge of God are not dependent upon the experience of sex so that sexual activity, in and of itself, is without eschatological significance,[8] though in the proper context the experience of sex may mediate the experience of the divine love and purpose to us. In addition, the tradition tells us that interpersonal love and friendship are relationships of great theological and moral significance, but that they are possible without sex and precarious in the extreme if sex is, or is allowed to become, the central aspect of them. For, in proclaiming the good news of sexuality, the tradition also reminds us that all human life, including the sexual dimension of it, has been deeply and tragically marred and weakened by sin, and we ignore this truth at our peril.

Finally, this normative tradition speaks a human meaning for sexual relationships, a meaning that involves a high calling and a serious responsibility, for such relationships are intended to image and mediate God's passionate and faithful love in the world for the people the divine love has created; sexual relationships are to be signs of the union of Christ and his Church. It can hardly be a matter of surprise, in the light of such convictions, that heterosexual marriage, faithful, exclusive, and indissoluble by human action, is held up as the normative context in which the ideal of sexual behavior is to be lived.

If there are exceptions to this normative ideal, which are also in full accord with God's will, I, for one, have no way of knowing beyond any doubt,[9] any more than I know beyond doubt when or in precisely what way the relationship called marriage truly comes into existence.[10] Nor can I see any way in which the Church as a whole could know of, and, therefore, publicly acknowledge such exceptions. At the same time, I do not know, and I do not see how anyone else can claim to know, beyond any possibility of doubt, that there cannot be any exceptions in sexual behavior and relationships, which contravene the ideal as we presently understand it, but are, nonetheless, in accord with the will of God. Acting as a social body institutionally organized and publicly responsible, it is neither unfair nor unreasonable for the Church to ask the individual conscience to bear the burden of any exception to the normative ideal as presently understood and taught, as is presently the case with birth control,[11] and to acknowledge, in public behavior at least, the normative ideal it proclaims.[12]

In the present theological and ecclesiastical milieu, there are three difficulties related to the position on our knowledge of God's will, which I have tried to sketch in the preceding paragraphs, that require some attention. Those difficulties center around demands for a radical autonomy of conscience,[13] for absolute certitude in religious and moral matters,[14] and for a more independent authority for theologians in the formulation of Church teaching.[15] I venture some brief comments on each of the three demands as they bear on the issue of homosexual acts and relationships.

A carefully constructed theological view of conscience denies the radical autonomy of the individual conscience, even while it acknowledges personal conscience as the final, practical authority in moral matters.[16] In its most profound meaning, conscience is no less than a person's deepest and most complete degree of self-awareness, the sense of who and what one is as this concrete human person.[17] Understood in this more comprehensive and more adequate sense, conscience is seen more clearly to be radically social and communal as well as personal and individual. Who and what one is includes such aspects as one's national, religious, sexual, professional, racial and familial identity, as well as those characteristics of taste, talent and temperament unique to the individual. The conscientious person cannot fail to acknowledge the constraints placed upon his or her knowledge by one's own finite abilities, as well as by the cultural, historical and social perspectives which both enable and limit one's knowing of the world.

Because of these recognizable limitations, because of the power of sin in our lives, and because conscience's loyalty is always to the truth, claims to a radical autonomy of conscience must be rejected as unconscientious. This is even more the case for Christians who acknowledge both the Bible and the Church community as normative mediators of God's will. A Christian conscience which simply denies or ignores the biblical witnesss to the work and will of God or which refuses to be informed by the faith of the Church is simply neither Christian nor conscientious. In practice, then, the conscience of the Christian is formed and tested in dialogue with both Scripture and the believing community, a dialogue which is conducted with a strong presumptive bias in favor of the community. In previous chapters I have indicated how this presumptive bias works in regard to the morality of homosexual acts and relationships.[18]

At the same time that the Christian faith rejects the radical autonomy of personal conscience, it affirms the ultimate authority of conscience, even to the extent of speaking of conscience as the voice of God.[19] Such language is functionally correct, albeit imprecise and dangerous. Functionally, personal conscience is the final authority in moral matters because conscience alone can judge what appears to be right and true to the person and demanded by one's own sense of personal integrity. But that judgment, while it may function with the practical authority of God's will for the individual's life and behavior, is not to be ontologically identified with God's will. The judgment of conscience is a human act and it always remains a human judgment, a human word which we may only hope corresponds to God's word. It must be left to God to read the secrets of the human mind and heart, to pass judgment on the sincerity and truthfulness with which we sought the divine will, and to confirm or deny whether we belong to Christ (Mt 7:21–22). For this reason, conscience or conscientiousness is rightly understood more as a process than as an established or given reality.[20] And as a process it requires that we continually submit our thoughts, attitudes and judgments to the light, both to the light of the Holy Spirit in prayer and to the light of common faith and reason in dialogue with the believing community and the world.

One important implication of this view of conscience is that the judgment of conscience is not a judgment simply about what serves individual well-being or personal fulfillment. It is a judgment about what serves the community and the common good, what builds up the body of Christ (1 Cor 6:12–20; 14:20–26), or, in more contemporary language, what contributes to the transformation of the world and the liberation of the human race from every form of oppression.[21] Such a view of conscience insists that the social dimension of human life receive serious and fundamental attention, and not be treated merely as an accidental or secondary consideration. This is one reason why I have continually asked about the vocational significance of sexual relationships, including homosexual ones. That no one else is hurt by what two people do sexually in the privacy of their home is hardly sufficient for either the Christian normative ideal or for the Christian conscience.

On the other hand, personal conscience ought not to be simply swallowed up by the prevailing community sense of right and wrong,[22] or even by the generic moral judgments of official Church teachers and theologians. There can be a dimension of the prophetic in every judgment of personal conscience, a challenge and a witness from the individual to the community in regard to the freedom and integrity of the Christian life. The discernment of what is prophetic[23] and what is simply stubborn obstinacy is notoriously difficult. Final judgments in this regard often await the unfolding of history and, ultimately, the judgment of God. Nevertheless, because of this prophetic possibility, there is room in the Christian community for conscientious dissent, for a judgment of conscience that differs from the accepted and prevailing norms of the community. And however unfair and burdensome it may seem to the prophet, it is both sociologically and theologically the case that the burden of proof for the dissenting view rests upon the prophet.[24]

We should notice, however, that prophetic dissent is not concerned to overthrow foundations; it is not revolutionary in the strict sense of the term. Prophetic dissent is protestant;[25] it involves a protest against less than adequate ways of understanding and living the Gospel, and so is a call for renewal and reformation. As a protest, the prophetic voice will not ignore or deny the roots and the tradition of the faith, but appeal to them to support its challenge. Revolutionary dissent, on the other hand, is similar to a call for conversion[26] in that it seeks to initiate a new sense of identity and insertion into a different community based on a new foundation. In prophetic dissent it is not a doctrine, or a moral teaching, or even an ecclesial practice that is itself directly challenged or rejected for its own sake. Rather, the fuller meaning and deeper implications of the central core of the traditional faith are perceived to call for something new. Prophetic dissent from certain of the Church's sexual teachings, for instance, may find that the understanding of God's gift of sexuality has not been sufficiently appreciated, its implications not fully explored, its applications too narrowly and too rigidly construed. It may be that homosexual relationships do have a vocational significance that has been overlooked or misunderstood, and it is this significance that the dissenting conscience invites the Church community to consider and recognize. This is a considerably different thing than simply affirming that the ecclesial community has no business proposing norms for human sexual behavior or has been altogether wrong in the meaning it has ascribed to human sexuality.

One practical consequence of this view of conscience is that heterosexual Christians and homosexual Christians need one another as partners in dialogue to share insights into the quest for God and the kingdom of God relevant to sexuality and chastity. Above all, perhaps, it is time to pay more serious and deliberate attention to the single person's vocation in the world as something more significant and challenging to the community of the faithful than mere regrettable necessity. It has been a profound mistake to treat homosexual individuals as moral outcasts or unmentionable anomalies, just as it would now be a mistake to treat them as privileged witnesses to the faith or experts on sexual morality. Groups such as Dignity[27] have an important and proper role to play in fostering the spiritual growth of homosexual Christians, but it is also time that they be integrated more fully into the life of the Church and that a more extensive sharing of spiritual insight into how to live our varied sexual vocations take place.

RELIGIOUS AND MORAL CERTITUDE

Closely related to demands for the radical autonomy of personal conscience are demands or expectations for unchallengeable certitude in religious and moral matters. If advocates of the radical autonomy of personal conscience are generally found on the left of the political and ecclesial spectrum these days, advocates of absolute moral and religious certainty can usually be found on the right. But the two camps are really not very far apart. Both find it difficult to live in the world God has made and allowed to develop as it has. For several centuries claims to absolute certitude have been a boast and a barrier in the Catholic and Orthodox communities. The Second Vatican Council put an end to some of the boasting[28] and partially removed the barrier for many Roman Catholics, but no council can be expected to achieve its goals fully. The impetus toward an unattainable certitude in religious and moral matters remains, and some of the barriers still stand.

If we recall the three theological virtues which define the human relationship to God, we will realize the inappropriateness of all claims and demands for absolute religious and moral certitude. The three theological virtues are faith, hope and love. They are called theological virtues because God is the direct object or end to which the virtues incline us. Faith is in God, hope rests upon God, love finds its fulfillment in God. We have faith because we do not know or know only imperfectly (1 Cor 13:12); we have hope because we do not yet possess (Phil 3:10–16); we experience love as longing because our deepest yearnings to love and be loved cannot be fully satisfied by finite beings (Col 3:1–4). More than this in the present life we do not and cannot have.

Furthermore, we understand these virtues to be gifts of grace, not the result of our own achievements of which we can boast nor our own possessions which we can fully control or hand on at will to others. As St. Paul reminded his young flock at Corinth, we carry our treasure in earthen vessels and not in secure and unassailable fortresses (2 Cor 4:7). These virtues themselves are not clearly comprehended by us in all their depth and richness, for they participate in the very mystery to which they direct us.

The lack of absolute certitude in religious and moral matters does not mean that we have been abandoned to a total relativism or to the absence of any secure anchor or focus in life. It does mean that faith, hope, and love, and the very real knowledge based on or derived from them, have only an eschatological fulfillment. All that we experience in this life can either confirm or challenge our faith, our hope, and our love. Persons, events, things can all be mediators of God's goodness and glory to us, and give us grounds for the reasonableness of our faith, hope and love. They can just as readily be stumbling blocks which mock and threaten our faith, hope and love. But none of these things is God and we must not permit these mediators to assume the place of God in our lives. Hence, we cannot be too sure about and too dependent upon any of these finite realities.

Philosophers often refer to the unverifiable nature of religious and moral claims. What, if anything, they ask, could count as a definitive verification or falsification of a religious claim such as God is love and has revealed the divine purpose to us in Christ, or the Church is the sign and instrument of the unity of all human-kind? What could verify or falsify a moral claim such as we ought to love one another or it is wrong to commit adultery? From the apparent impossibility of any verification or falsification of such propositions, many of them draw the conclusion that religious and moral claims have no cognitive status of any kind. Such assertions merely represent expressions of human emotive preference.[29] If the Church, for example, teaches that homosexual behavior is morally wrong when freely chosen, that simply means that the Church, in the person of its official teachers, does not like such behavior for psychological, social or political reasons of its own.[30] Other, less analytically oriented philosophers, will point out that what the Church claims to know in making such an affirmation is at least relative to its own point of view, which point of view itself is relative to the Church's particular place in history and society at a given time. Hence, while religious and moral claims may have some cognitive status on this latter accounting, they are certainly relative truths, not absolute ones.

It is not so much that our claims about God and the divine will are without the possibility of verification or falsification, but that the kind of knowledge involved in knowing God and the divine will can only have an eschatological verification. St. Paul acknowl-edged as much when he wrote to the Corinthians that if Christ were not risen their faith was in vain (1 Cor 15:17–19). Human analogies are often useful in helping us understand our relationship with the divine mystery. One such analogy may prove illuminating here in regard to the certitude we can have in religious and moral matters.

To repose trust in a human friend is an act based upon faith, hope and love. I trust my friend because I love her, have hopes in her regard, and so deem her worthy of my faithfulness. As the friend shows herself in experience to be respectful of that trust, I come more and more to know that I am right to trust her and I become more and more confident and secure in that trust and the affection it breeds. Will my friend ever let me down? Can I trust her in all things without doubt or question? I may think so; I may even do so. But I will never know absolutely and beyond all possibility of doubt until my life or her life ends. Even then, someone may point out that my trust in her was never tested in certain ways, was relative, therefore, to the time and situation in which we both lived, and I cannot be absolutely certain that she would have passed the test of trustworthiness under different circumstances. I acknowledge that all this is theoretically quite true, even while remaining quite secure practically in my knowledge of her trustworthiness.

So also, in our relationship with God, we can be secure in our knowledge of the divine love and goodness without laying claims to some kind of absolute certitude. I am secure, for example, in my knowledge of God's providential care for his creatures without being able to explain every event, every misfortune, which befalls them in human life. I am confident in my knowledge that my marital relationship bears with it a vocational responsibility for fidelity and service, for which I am answerable both to God and the community of faith, without being able to make an irrefutable argument for how I know that it does, or without being absolutely certain of all the obligations and implications that flow from the demand for vocational responsibility. For it is simply the case that the farther we move from generalities to the specifics of life, the less we can lay claim to certitude in a theoretical sense,[31] even though we may have a sense of absolute conviction in conscience about a particular course of action for ourselves. But even this sense of absolute conviction cannot be freed from the limits and vicissitudes of human subjectivity. How this dialectic between the individual and the community, between subjective certainty and objective relativity, between the absolute nature of the divine will and the relative nature of human knowing, works itself out in practice can again be best developed in terms of an example.

A particular individual may be personally convinced that he is called to spend his life in service to the victims of AIDS. This conviction may be a subjectively certain one, beyond any imaginable possibility of doubt or challenge. The individual may be so convinced in conscience about this calling that he is sure it represents the call of God inspired by the Holy Spirit, so that in performing this service he is carrying out the will of God. The Church community cannot and should not judge, positively or negatively, whether this conviction is, in fact, the will of God for this individual. It is rather the role of the community of faith to confirm that such a decision falls within the Church's own understanding of what love and service to the world mean and that such service does, indeed, represent the kind of activity that followers of Jesus take up in discipleship. Even more, the Church community, in the person of a spiritual director or a small community of friends or religious brothers and sisters, can support, confirm, or challenge the individual in regard to the origin and integral motivation of the call, based upon both how well the call serves the community and how it affects the spiritual and human development of the individual. We may believe and hope that, in carrying out this vocation, the individual is doing the will of God. But the ultimate and absolute knowledge that this service is, in fact, God's will for the individual remains beyond us.

This same community of faith can and should challenge, confront, and finally even excommunicate[32] an individual who, for example, teaches and lives out an ideal of sexual promiscuity on the grounds that it is the best way to show gratitude for God's good gift of sexuality. The mission to promulgate and practice this supposed ideal does not fall within the community's understanding of what service in and to the world means for the disciples of Jesus. However strong the subjective conviction of the individual may be in regard to the divine origin of such a mission, the community denies its objective correspondence to the divine will as it has come to know and love that will in its journey of faith through history. All concrete judgments, then, which fly in the face of or challenge the received tradition and understanding of the Church's mission in and to the world need to be heard and evaluated. But the strength or intensity of one's subjective conviction is not a sufficient warrant for affirming that conviction to correspond to God's will, any more than the objective correspondence of a decision to the received tradition is a sufficient warrant.[33]

When I raise the question, then, as I do repeatedly throughout this book, about the vocational significance of homosexual acts and relationships, it is not because I have some kind of absolute certitude about God's will in sexual matters or know beyond a shadow of a doubt that such acts and relationships lack any and all vocational significance. I raise the question with the purpose of inviting dialogue between the subjective convictions of individuals and the objective teaching of the larger community of faith. For it is only in this process that the individual can test, evaluate, and confirm or alter the judgment of conscience. If, in the process of discernment, the individual comes to the conscientious conviction that his or her sexual relationships need have or should have no ecclesial and public significance, he or she has proclaimed a revolution, not registered a protest. The reasons for thinking such a claim represents God's will will have to be drawn from some other normative source of truth held to be higher than and in contradiction to the faith of the Church. In making such an argument, the individual seeks to establish the community of faith on a new foundation, creating in effect a new community. A decision that claims to be conscientious will, at the very least, acknowledge this intent and consequence. The final judgment about whether this new position truly represents the divine will must be left to the final arbiter of all human judgments, God.[34]

THE ROLE OF THEOLOGY

The third problem to be considered in regard to our limited knowledge of God's will centers around the growing insistence among some theologians[35] for a more independent authority in the formulation of Church teaching. While this particular issue may seem to be of immediate interest only to professional theologians and church authorities, its implications touch us all and its complications illuminate the question of our knowledge of God's will. Consequently, it does seem to merit some attention here.

Christian theology is in the service of the Church and is an intrinsic element of the mission of the Church in the world. While there are some theologians calling themselves Christian theologians who would dispute this view of the theological task, most Catholic and Protestant theologians would not. But there is a prior conviction, common alike to theologians and the Church as a whole, on which the theological mission also rests. Both the Church and theology are called to the service of the truth, and the pursuit of truth, which is the explicit, professional task of the theologian, serves the Church precisely because it is the Church's mission to serve and proclaim the truth.[36] Freedom of theological inquiry, therefore, which is an essential condition for pursuing truth, cannot be rightly denied. In general terms the appropriateness of such free inquiry is widely acknowledged and even encouraged.[37] What seems to have become a matter of some dispute and misunderstanding is the degree of respect and reverence theologians owe to the received tradition of the faith and the interpretations of the tradition proposed by the official teaching office of the Church.[38] Concretely, the issues at stake center around what to make of the arguments and views of theologians which dissent from the teaching of the received tradition and the present magisterium.

It is no secret that more than a few theologians today are convinced that homosexual acts and relationships can be, under certain specifiable conditions, morally appropriate ways for Christian individuals to express their sexuality, as we have seen. In proposing these views and arguments, are the theologians proposing a rebellious alternative to the faith of the Church or are they simply registering a protest against an unduly narrow and restrictive understanding of the Christian meaning of human sexuality? If the former is the case, it is clear that the community of faith must disown such views and, if circumstances warrant it, disenfranchise such theologians.[39] But since almost no theologians would wish to make such an intentionally rebellious claim for their views, how are we to assess these dissenting views and how is the community of the faithful to deal with them?

One could suggest a number of possible ways to deal with dissenting views. They might be submitted to a majority vote of members of the theological community. Such a solution, however, appears to be both practically unworkable and theoretically unsound. Practically, just who belongs to the theological community and who does not would provoke an unending debate more difficult than any present dispute. More substantially, however, the question of truth cannot be decided by a majority vote. Voting is an expression of both opinion and purpose. It has its place in human communities, but that place is not to decide matters of fact or truth, and it is truth that is at stake in properly theological disputes.[40]

A second suggestion would be to leave dissenting views to the sense of the faithful for them to pick and choose which views suit them. In a way this will be the actual situation no matter what other solution one chooses, since individuals will think what they will and act as they decide to act no matter what authority teaches. But to settle for this solution is to abandon pastoral responsibility. The faithful look to their pastoral leaders, and rightly, for guidance in matters of faith and morals and justly expect more from them than a supermarket of opinions. Popularity with consumers is hardly a norm for what is normative in faith and morals for the Christian life.

A third possible solution, one often suggested and practiced in the recent past, is for the dissenting views of theologians to be submitted to the judgment of the magisterium for their conformity to the received tradition. If this course of action is followed, without allowing ample time and opportunity for considerable theological reflection and debate, it would appear that the whole point of the theological enterprise becomes irrelevant. If the practice of doing theology were simply reduced to submitting one's views and proposals to the judgment of the magisterium for their conformity to received tradition, theology would lose all rationale except as the practice of defensive apologetics. It would become, in short time, an ideological and closed system of thought in which no real development could occur.[41]

As a service to the Church and as an intrinsic part of the Church's mission to the world, the work of theologians has several purposes. I do not suggest that I cover all the purposes here, but I will attempt to highlight some of the main ones. One purpose of theological work is to raise questions, either new questions arising for the first time in the modern world, e.g., the question of the use and possession of nuclear weapons, or old questions which contemporary knowledge and circumstances have raised anew for the community of faith. In the present context of this book I have suggested that the religious and moral meaning of human sexuality in general, and the moral status of homosexuality in particular, is such a question. It is the theologian's task to explain the significance of the question, the urgency about finding a solution, and above all why the Gospel urges this upon us at this time. The work being done by liberation theologians, especially in South America today, with its over-riding concern for justice in the world,[42] serves as a most fitting model for this theological purpose.

It is not sufficient, however, for theologians simply to raise questions. A second purpose of theological work is to examine and clarify the issues raised by the questions, to suggest possible answers to the questions, and to advance reasons and arguments for or against proposed solutions. In doing this work, theologians are likely to challenge both the consciences of their fellow Christians and the values of their culture. That is why theology can be a dangerous, even a subversive activity.[43] But challenge and subversion are not the main point of theological work. Theology is concerned with the integrity of the faith and the truthfulness of the Christian vision and practice. Again, in the context of this book, how Christian people understand and live out their sexuality is not a matter of indifference to them or to the Church and the world. The extent of sexual abuse, sexual frustration, sexual confusion and sexual irresponsibility in society makes that very clear. American culture argues increasingly, both in its laws and through its vehicles of public communication, that human sexuality is a private matter, and sexual behavior a morally indifferent one. The Christian understanding of sexuality must dispute these claims, precisely, I have argued, on the grounds of human sexuality's vocational significance.

A third purpose of theological work is to evaluate the compatibility and coherence of its proposals, and of present Church teaching and practice, with the biblical and theological tradition in which they should be rooted. In the course of doing this work of evaluation, arguments will inevitably arise over whether certain proposals are, in fact, revolutionary, or more properly reformist and developmental. Some seemingly revolutionary proposals may not truly be revolutionary in relationship to the faith, though they may have revolutionary consequences for the participation of Christians in the political and social ordering of society. Such an outcome is again well illustrated by the insistence of liberation theology upon solidarity with the oppressed and the preferential option for the poor.[44] Other theological proposals may have a noticeable impact upon the visible life and structure of the Church itself without being revolutionary. Certainly proposals for a married clergy, for a more collegial exercise of authority in the Church, or even for the ordination of women are reformist, not revolutionary, in their main thrust.

One reason the present work has argued the case that it has against the acceptance of homosexual acts and relationships as compatible with the Christian understanding of sex is that I have failed to find the coherence and compatibility of such proposals with the normative biblical and theological tradition. The arguments justifying such acts and relationships seem to stand apart from this tradition. To accept homosexual relationships and behavior on an equal moral footing with the heterosexual relationship of marriage appears to be a revolutionary proposal in the sense that its acceptance requires a foundation other than the Christian truth. I fail to see it as a development of or deeper insight into the Christian meaning of sexuality. It appears to me, for the reasons already presented, a rejection of that meaning in favor of a different, and culturally dominant, understanding of human life and destiny.

CONDITIONS AND CONFLICTS

But theologians are only human and few among them would claim to be infallible. For the theological enterprise to be able to contribute to the mission of the Church, certain conditions surrounding its practice seem to be essential. One such condition is the free theological inquiry already mentioned, an inquiry that can proceed free of fear of reprisal or penalty. A second condition, closely related to free inquiry, is free and open debate among theologians in which their arguments and scholarship can be evaluated and corrected where necessary. A third condition is the availability of their positions and arguments to the faithful at large and the reaction of the faithful to their proposals. Theologians have no monopoly upon theological insight and wisdom. Many faithful people, steeped in virtue and grace, know God and the divine ways far better than theologians. Hence, the sense that theological positions make to the faithful cannot be ignored.[45] Nevertheless, it must be added that no one should base a decision of conscience upon the fact that one or more theologians, or a majority of one's fellow believers, hold a particular position.[46] Only if, and to the degree that, one is convinced of the truth of a particular position does the individual have grounds for any conscientious decision.

Within the Roman Catholic tradition of faith the official teaching office, in the persons of Pope, council and bishops, has a special role to play in the whole process of teaching and conscientious decision-making. They have, in virtue of their offices, a responsibility, a pastoral responsibility, for the soundness of teaching in regard to matters of both faith and morals. Fortunately or unfortunately, few bishops have either the time or the competence to weigh and judge theological arguments. Furthermore, their office is, by its very nature, resistant to anything that appears to be novel or liable to sow confusion and controversy among the faithful. There is, therefore, a strong structural inclination in the episcopal office to disown and silence theological opinion prematurely in the interests of peace and unity among the faithful.[47] To act upon this inclination is, at times, more than merely unfortunate; it can be unfair and ultimately a disservice to the Church. But it is understandable in light of the likely tension and even conflict between the direct responsibilities of the pastoral office and the immediate responsibility of theologians. A brief discussion of this difference in responsibilities will serve as a fitting summary and conclusion of the present work.

Theologians are charged with the task of seeking the truth and of trying to articulate that truth in all its complexity. Moral theologians, in particular, who must deal with concrete issues in the midst of varied and constantly changing circumstances, are reluctant to propose clear and simple answers to general questions of right and wrong behavior. Their answers, as mine have been in this book, are qualified by all kinds of conditions, distinctions and subtle nuances. I do not wish to say, for example, that all practicing homosexual individuals are sinners because of that very fact, because I do not think it is possible for anyone other than God to make that kind of judgment. Nor do I wish to say that homosexual behavior is a perfectly acceptable moral choice for Christian disciples, for I have been unable to find any vocational significance in such behavior. Such a position may be less than neat in its usefulness, but it is the best I can do as I see the truth.

Pastors with direct responsibility for large congregations of people often cannot afford the distinctions and clarifications so necessary to the theologian. To avoid confusion among the people they serve, they are more inclined to say simply that homosexual behavior is a forbidden practice and to engage in it is to sin. Moral theologians, as academic theoreticians, often become absorbed in the exceptions to general rules and devote considerable time and energy to explaining and justifying these exceptions. Pastors, in their role as teachers and guides, most often deal of necessity with the general rules and for good reasons propose them as practical absolutes. On a practical level, in a world where sexual immorality and irresponsibility, especially among younger segments of the population, appear to be rampant, why, pastors may wonder, are theologians concerned to find exceptions to general rules and to qualify, in however limited a fashion, the absolute prohibitions against pre-marital sex, birth control, homosexual behavior, divorce and remarriage, and so on?

The pastoral concern is well taken, but the answer is simple if unsatisfying to pastors. Theologians do these things because they must do them in fidelity to the truth as God has enabled them to see and understand truth. For in the long run, and this, too, is a fundamental part of the Catholic theological tradition, no one can accuse an individual of sin except the individual himself or herself. In the sacrament of reconciliation it is the penitent who is the primary judge and accuser, not the confessor. It is the penitent who weighs personal decisions and behaviors before God, in light of the community's faith and teaching, in the effort to discern how well or badly he or she has responded to God's grace, and, when necessary, to repent of failure and seek forgiveness. Both moral theology and pastoral authority are the servants of this effort at personal conscientiousness, not the dictators or keepers of personal conscience. Competent theologians both teach this and take it for granted in their articulation of complex moral situations and problems. Competent pastors have the far more difficult and important task of educating individuals to assume this personal responsibility even while remaining a focal point of clear authority while these same individuals grow into this responsibility.

The tension between the theological role and the pastoral role reflects the tension we all experience between the dignity and autonomy of the human person and his or her essentially social nature. Both the value of the individual person and the value of the common good demand our respect and allegiance. Pastors and theologians wrestle with both these dimensions, but in different ways. In the present cultural context of western, democratic societies, both pastors and theologians would do well to be aware of how and in what ways that culture's values challenge and repudiate Christian values, and even warp the moral vision and sensibilities of Christian people themselves. Nor are pastors and theologians themselves immune from these cultural influences. A common pastoral response to this challenge is to circle the wagons against the onslaught of the culture and to insist on as much clarity and certitude about the Christian message as they can get away with. This is especially the case where their concern is for the consciences of the weak and easily scandalized among their people, as it may very rightly be. But it is the theologian's immediate responsibility to go out to face the culture, to learn from it as well as to challenge it, to acknowledge both its strengths and weaknesses in the interest, not of a religious rejection of culture, but of its religious transformation.[48] Both roles and tasks are needed in the Church, though they do not and cannot be expected to always live harmoniously with one another. Living within that tension is one of the moral requirements of Christian maturity.

I have tried in this book to articulate the understanding of human sexuality and its vocational significance which I find in the Catholic tradition of Christian faith. I have done so in the conviction that our ecclesial and social attitudes and behaviors toward individuals of a homosexual inclination have often been embarassingly un-Christian and based on false or inadequate views of human sexual-

ity. I have also done this in the conviction that our western culture
has reduced sexuality and sex to a matter of private significance
which centers exclusively upon sexual satisfaction and personal fulfillment. The Christian vision of human sexuality, as I understand it,
denies that that is all there is, or even that that is the most important
thing there is to human sexuality. The normative ideal which the
Church holds up in regard to human sexual behavior is profoundly
social and ecclesial, while never denying the more personal values
intrinsic to sexual relationships. At the same time, the living of the
sexual ideal is intensely personal; it involves a private struggle with
one's self to sort out the forces of love and lust and to learn to control
the latter while nurturing the former. Personal fulfillment and sexual satisfaction are not irrelevant to this struggle, but they are not
the whole story on one's sexual and human journey.

To the degree that the understanding of human sexuality presented here is true, personal conscience will attempt to follow it,
for in doing so it will be faithfully following Christ as best one can.
To the degree it is judged to be false or inadequate to Christian
faith and discipleship, personal conscience will follow the truth as
it is given to see it in the dialogue with the ecclesial community.
For it is only in following the truth, as revealed in Christ, proclaimed in the community of the faithful, and appropriated and
articulated by limited human beings, that human fulfillment and
liberation from all oppressive forces can be found. This is the case
whether one's sexual orientation is homosexual or heterosexual,
and it is the case whatever one's sexual vocation may be.

NOTES

1. Karl Rahner, *Encounters With Silence,* trans. James M. Demske
(Westminster: Newman Press, 1960); James M. Gustafson, *Ethics from a
Theocentric Perspective: I: Theology and Ethics* (Chicago: University of
Chicago Press, 1981), pp. 201–204, discusses how piety shapes theological
investigation, and why he prefers to speak of piety rather than faith. The
term more common in Catholic religious language which corresponds to
piety would be spirituality. See Schneiders, *Women and the Word,* pp. 15–
19.

2. Häring, *The Law of Christ,* I, p. 148; Hanigan, *As I Have Loved
You,* pp. 121–124; O'Connell, *Principles for a Catholic Morality,* p. 92;
R.C. Mortimer, "An Anglo-Catholic View of Conscience," p. 123, and

Hans Schar, "Protestant Problems With Conscience," pp. 91–93, in Nelson (ed.), *Conscience: Theological and Psychological Perspectives.*

3. *Gaudium et Spes* 16, in Gremillion, *The Gospel of Peace and Justice,* p. 255.

4. *Ibid.*: "In fidelity to conscience, Christians are joined with the rest of men in the search for truth, and for the genuine solution to the numerous problems which arise in the life of individuals and from social relationships."

5. The social formation of one's values and so of one's conscience is simply inescapable. Eugene Hillman, "Doing Evil for a Just Cause," *America* 154, 18 (May 10, 1986), pp. 379–382, points this out in regard to conscience as related to military questions. Preston, *Religion and the Persistence of Capitalism,* pp. 71–79, does the same for conscience in relation to the economic ordering of society.

6. O'Connell, *Principles for a Catholic Morality,* pp. 93–95; Hanigan, *As I Have Loved You,* pp. 139–142.

7. Some of the ways in which social groups shape identity are discussed in Hanigan, *As I Have Loved You,* pp. 79–87.

8. Schillebeeckx, *Marriage,* pp. 12–13.

9. Theoretically, it seems to me more accurate to speak of virtually exceptionless moral rules rather than of absolute moral prohibitions, especially if we understand objective moral obligation to include the actual subjective state, developmental as well as circumstantial, of the moral agent. See Donald Evans, "Paul Ramsey on Exceptionless Moral Rules," *Love and Society: Essays in the Ethics of Paul Ramsey,* eds. James Johnson and David Smith. JRE Studies in Religious Ethics I (Missoula: American Academy of Religion and Scholars Press, 1974), pp. 19–46; Keane, *Sexual Morality: A Catholic Perspective,* pp. 50–51.

10. Mackin, *What Is Marriage?* pp. 17–33, provides an excellent introduction to the meaning, the importance and the difficulty of this question.

11. Paul VI, *Humanae Vitae,* 10, in Gremillion, p. 433, puts the burden of the decision to delay birth or avoid it for an indeterminate period on the conscience of the couple, where all agree it properly belongs. Private dissent from the official teaching of what is not certainly an infallible teaching remains a possibility as well, and, again, the burden of proof is properly on the individual conscience of the person who dissents.

12. Scandal is always to be avoided, and, as Paul tells us in Romans 14:1–23, the burden of avoiding scandal weighs more heavily on the consciences of those who are strong in their personal convictions.

13. Donald Evans, "Does Religious Faith Conflict with Moral Free-

dom?" in *Religion and Morality,* eds. Gene Outka and John P. Reider, Jr. (Garden City: Anchor Books, 1973), pp. 348–388; G.L. Bahnsen, *Theonomy in Christian Ethics* (Nutley: Craig Press, 1979); Fuchs, "Autonomous Morality and Morality of Faith," in *Personal Responsibility and Christian Morality,* pp. 84–111.

14. The strange quest for absolute certitude began in the western philosophical tradition with Descartes and at a somewhat earlier period in the theological tradition with Luther. Its clearest cultural manifestation today is the attraction of religious fundamentalism of one kind or another. It seems to me that the quest is fueled theologically by a false understanding of the relationship of faith and reason on either side of the issue.

15. Avery Dulles, *The Resilient Church: The Necessity and Limits of Adaptation* (Garden City: Doubleday & Company, Inc., 1977), pp. 103–112; Charles E. Curran and Richard A. McCormick, S.J. (eds.), *Readings in Moral Theology No. 3: The Magisterium and Morality* (New York/Ramsey: Paulist Press, 1982).

16. God's will is obviously the final authority in moral matters from a religious or faith perspective. Since God's will, however, is not directly and unmediatedly available to human beings, conscience functions as the final authority. Häring, *The Law of Christ,* I, pp. 147–148.

17. Regan, *New Trends in Moral Theology,* pp. 171–173.

18. See Chapter II, note 21, and Chapter III.

19. *Gaudium et Spes,* 16; Haring, *The Law of Christ,* I, pp. 147–148.

20. Conn, *Conscience,* has the best account of conscience as a developmental reality. This is a difficult but rewarding study.

21. Synod of Bishops Second General Assembly, *Justice in the World,* 6, in Gremillion, *The Gospel of Peace and Justice,* p. 514.

22. Burtchaell, *Philemon's Problem,* pp. 93–101.

23. I use prophetic here in the biblical sense of prophet, i.e., as one authorized to speak on behalf of God, but also as one who challenges the prevailing religious teaching and life of the people of God. This latter aspect of the prophet's role means that all teaching is not prophetic. Hence, the magisterium is not and should not be expected to be predominantly prophetic in its exercise. If conscience is, in some sense, the voice of God, it should not be surprising that the judgment of conscience could be prophetic. See Eugene H. Maly, *Prophets of Salvation* (New York: Herder and Herder, 1967), pp. 13–46.

24. Hannah Arendt, *On Violence* (New York: Harcourt, Brace & World, Inc., 1969), pp. 40–44, indicates how sociologically and politically public opinion will inevitably outweigh personal opinion. If the prophetic voice is to be heard at all, space must be created for it; that is to say,

antecedent to the prophet speaking, there must be some vague social willingness to allow for such speech and some social space in which such speech can be heard.

25. Prophetic dissent is protestant in the literal sense of the term; it is a protest against the way things are in favor of the way they should be. It is useful to recall that the father of Protestantism, Martin Luther, sought the reformation of the Church and a correction of abuses in the Church. He was a protestant, not a revolutionary and regarded himself as a Catholic, not a Lutheran, a fact that it took the Second Vatican Council and the current ecumenical movement to make Catholics appreciate.

26. For literature on conversion, see Chapter III, note 19; also Lonergan, *Method in Theology,* pp. 130–131. In conversion we speak of new life, of being born again, of passing from darkness to light. As a result of conversion we are new people, the new Israel, members of a new community. The language of reformation and protest is very different. As a result of prophetic speech, we are renewed or reformed, undertaking a fresh start on an old beginning.

27. Dignity is a nationwide, regionally organized group of homosexual Catholics, formed to support and nuture one another in the faith and to deal with problems affecting the homosexual community. Its national office is located in Washington, D.C. at 1500 Massachusetts Avenue. There are many such groups in the country, most of which still exist on the margins of Church life.

28. Flannery (ed.), *Vatican Council II;* the following documents indicate some of the places in which Roman Catholicism acknowledged its failures and shortcomings in relation to other groups in the world: *Unitatis Redintegratio* (On Ecumenism) 3, p. 455; *Nostra Aetate* 4 (On the Relation of the Church to Non-Christian Religions), pp. 740–741; *Gaudium et Spes* 19, p. 919, in regard to atheism.

29. William K. Frankena, *Perspectives in Morality,* ed. K.E. Goodpaster (Notre Dame/London: University of Notre Dame Press, 1976), pp. 111–119.

30. If one rejects the cognitive status of religious beliefs and moral convictions, there is nothing left but to examine the political, social and psychological origins of these beliefs and convictions. This is a worthy enterprise, but is liable to the genetic fallacy that to establish the origins of an idea is to refute its cognitive content. What one believes might be true, even if one believes it for the wrong reasons.

31. This observation is at least as old as Aristotle, and is too often forgotten or ignored. See J.A.K. Thomson, *The Ethics of Aristotle: The*

Nicomachean Ethics Translated (Baltimore: Penguin Books, 1955), I, 3, pp. 27–28.

32. The scriptural warrants and rationale for excommunication are Matthew 18:15–18 and I Corinthians 5:1–13.

33. Karl Rahner, "On the Question of a Formal Existential Ethics," *Theological Investigations*, II, trans. Karl-H. Kruger (Baltimore: Helicon Press, 1963), pp. 217–234; see also Karl Rahner, *The Dynamic Element in the Church*, trans. W.J. O'Hara (New York: Herder and Herder, 1964).

34. Here are the theological grounds for religious and social toleration of others, not only of opinions and speech, but of actions as well. See *Gaudium et Spes* 16, in Gremillion, p. 255, and *Dignitatis Humanae* (On Religious Freedom) 2–10, Gremillion, pp. 339–344. Here also is the significance of the insistence by Barth, Bonhoeffer, and other neo-orthodox theologians upon the concreteness of the divine command and the claim that God does not issue general orders. See James M. Gustafson, *Christ and the Moral Life* (New York/Evanston/London: Harper & Row, Publishers, 1968), pp. 26–52.

35. Richard A. McCormick, S.J., "Theologians and the Magisterium," in *Readings in Moral Theology No. 3:*, pp. 470–486.

36. Karl Barth, *Protestant Thought: From Rousseau to Ritschl* (New York: Simon and Schuster, A Clarion Book, 1969), p. 299. Theology "should . . . be concerned . . . with truth, with a kind of knowledge which does not have its foundation in some kind of given thing, as such, but in the link of this given thing with the final origin of everything given. If theology does not speak the truth in this sense, then in what sense can it assert that it is speaking of God?"

37. Pope John Paul II, "Address to Catholic Educators," *Origins* 9 (1979), pp. 306–308; for the practical difficulties with such general affirmations see Joseph A. Fitzmeyer, S.J., "John Paul II, Academic Freedom and the Magisterium," *America* 141 (1979), pp. 247–249.

38. Authority in religious and moral matters is not simply a Catholic problem, but it takes on a particular form in Roman Catholicism because of its understanding of the role of the magisterium. Francis A. Sullivan, S.J., *Magisterium: Teaching Authority in the Catholic Church* (New York/Ramsey: Paulist Press, 1983).

39. In principle, it is hard to dispute the right and the need for the Church to disqualify a particular theologian as representative of Catholic theology. In practice, however, it is more difficult to work out fair norms and establish open procedures for carrying out this responsibility.

40. Properly theological disputes are disputes about what is true in

faith. Such disputes must be distinguished from pastoral or practical arguments about the best or wisest way to do things. For example, the argument in the present book is theological in that it concerns the true meaning of human sexuality. If one disagrees with the letter, "The Pastoral Care of Homosexual Persons," one may disagree on theological grounds, i.e., that its view of sexuality is wrong, or on practical grounds, i.e., that its pastoral recommendations are not very practical or sensible. Only the former disagreement is a properly theological dispute.

41. For an alternative to the view proposed in the text, see Grisez, *The Way of the Lord Jesus,* pp. 831–916, especially pp. 901–902.

42. Roger Haight, S.J., *An Alternative Vision: An Interpretation of Liberation Theology* (New York/Mahwah: Paulist Press, 1985).

43. Matthew Lamb, *Solidarity with Victims* (New York: Crossroad, 1983), pp. 100–143.

44. Jon Sobrino, S.J., *The True Church and the Poor,* trans. Matthew J. O'Connell (Maryknoll: Orbis Books, 1984).

45. For the important dialectical interaction of thematic or expert knowledge, in the present case the work of theologians, and non-thematic or the knowledge of lived experience, the sense of the faithful, see Hanigan, *As I Have Loved You,* pp. 137–139.

46. I do not wish to enter into the complexities of probabilism here. For a brief description see Häring, *The Law of Christ,* I, pp. 20–22. One comment will suffice: the fact that some, few, or many theologians hold an opinion is not sufficient grounds for anyone, including the theologians, to act on that opinion. The loyalty of conscience is to the truth. Doubts of conscience are not resolved by recourse to the probable except in matters of interpretation of positive laws. If one must decide on the basis of extrinsic authority, as is sometimes the case, there are always better reasons for following the magisterium than for following one or more theologians.

47. To say that the office has a structural inclination toward silencing novel views is not to say that any particular bishop also has a similar personal inclination. He may or may not, though personally conservative individuals may be more likely to be appointed to the office. Theologians are also subject to structural temptations, most notably to be innovative and controversial so as to get a wider hearing. Again, any particular theologian may or may not be so personally inclined.

48. H. Richard Niebuhr, *Christ and Culture* (New York: Harper & Row, Publishers, 1956); Richard John Neuhaus, *The Naked Public Square: Religion and Democracy in America* (Grand Rapids: William B. Eerdmans, 1984).

EPILOGUE

This book started out with the thesis that homosexuality serves in our time as the test-case for Christian sexual ethics. The test referred to in the thesis was said to have a twofold measure. First, what Christian faith has to say ethically about the meaning and value of human sexuality and sexual behavior must be universally applicable and possible, precisely because the Christian message of salvation proclaims the revelation in Christ of the universal salvific will of God, a will that wishes all human beings to be saved and to come to a knowledge of the truth.[1] Hence, the Christian way of life in all its fullness and ethical rigor is an invitation to all human beings, and the specific ethical requirements of that way of life must be within the realm of possibility for created, fallen and redeemed human nature.[2] In our present socio-historical context, such universality in the sexual realm of human life is best tested by its application to people of a seemingly irreversible homosexual orientation.

The second measure of the test is that Christian sexual ethics itself must be a proclamation of the good news of Jesus Christ, indicating how human sexuality has been taken up into the new life and freedom received in Christ.[3] The meaning and value of human sexuality and sexual behavior, as understood and taught in the community of the Church, must be affirmations of where and how human sexuality realizes its humanizing and sanctifying potentialities. More simply put, Christian sexual ethics should guide human sexuality mainly toward possibilities to be realized rather than toward burdens to be endured.[4] Again, the evangelical quality of any Christian sexual ethic is best measured today by whether it is, indeed, good news for those of homosexual orientation.

The reasons for thinking that the issue of homosexuality is today the kind of issue that makes it the test-case for contemporary sexual ethics, and so an issue in need of fresh, critical examination, were developed in the first chapter and need not be repeated here. But what of the universal and evangelical character of the view of human sexuality argued for in this book? Does the view of sexuality as vocationally significant and of sexual behavior as intrinsic only to the vocation of heterosexual marriage meet the twofold test? Readers of the book will have to make that determination for themselves, but it may not be amiss for the author to indicate why and in what ways he thinks the present work meets the test.

THE UNIVERSAL CHARACTER OF SEXUAL ETHICS

The universal applicability of the sexual ethic proposed in this book is rooted both in the createdness of sexuality by the one, good God and in the universal call to holiness that is the generic description of the Christian vocation.[5] Sexuality of its very nature summons us all into affective relationships of attentiveness and caring with our fellow human beings. Sexuality invites us to enter into the mystery that is the other person, and in the process to find both the mystery that is ourselves and to experience the ultimate mystery that is the ever present source and horizon of all human experience. This is the case no matter what one's sexual orientation. Our sexuality presents us with an inescapable challenge, for we must in some way come to grips with our sexual nature, and with the feelings, desires, curiosity, and hopes we experience as a result of being sexual creatures.

This inescapable challenge faces us all regardless of sexual inclination. It is a challenge that we may experience at times either as more burden than blessing, or as more exciting than threatening. For it is ambiguous, as is all significant human experience.[6] Furthermore, because human life is disordered by sin, our experience of our own sexuality is often an experience of confusion, compulsion, or plain inconvenience, even while it is also an experience of intense aliveness and joy. What I have argued throughout this book is that sexuality, for all its ambiguity and concrete disorder, remains a gift of God pointing each of us toward a role of service to others in the world, and so confronting us with a vocational choice. The key issue or question confronting every human individual is not how to best satisfy one's sexual longings but how to best express one's sexuality in the service of the kingdom of God. In less explicitly religious language, everyone's sexuality and sexual behavior were said to have both personal and social significance, either of which we ignore to our own diminishment.

That understanding of the meaning and value of human sexuality makes no discrimination between homosexual and heterosexual persons. The challenge, the experience and the vocational possibility of sexuality are the same for everyone. Whether such an understanding of sexuality is equally good news for everyone is a more difficult matter. For what constitutes good news for any individual will be judged by one's understanding of what the good is. The four positions on the morality of homosexual relationships and acts reviewed in Chapter III clearly reflected different understandings of the human good and so reached different judgments on which sexual acts are appropriate to the realization of that good. Conformity to God's law as enshrined in the tradition and authority of the Church, the satisfaction of human desires in a context of mutual consent, some degree of satisfying humanity in one's life, the quality of personal relationships, are all human goods, and are all different in content as well as in their appeal to individuals. The good news I find in the understanding of sexuality presented in these pages is that sexuality is a pointer and pathway to holiness and union with God precisely in its capacity to move us into human relationships where respect, caring, and personal transformation become essential if we are to love one another as Jesus has loved us.[7]

While human sexuality faces all of us with the same challenge, experience and vocational possibility, it also makes different vocational choices available and necessary. As was explained at some length in Chapter IV, different sexual behaviors are appropriate to different sexual vocations. The virtue of chastity has a different material content in different sexual ways of life (Chapter V). But this difference in the norms of sexual morality appropriate to different vocations is not based on the difference between male and female, or on the difference between homosexual and heterosexual orientation, and still less on such differences as those of class, race, religion or ethnic origin.[8] Rather the difference in the sexual behaviors morally appropriate to different individuals is rooted in

the differences in their personal and vocational identities, and ultimately, of course, have their foundation in the graces God gives to
each individual.[9] This diversity in vocation, and so in sexual behaviors proper to a particular vocation, does not negate the universal
applicability of the sexual ethic proposed in this book. For all
vocations can be equally paths to holiness for those called to adventure upon them, and the essence of the sexual ethic I have argued
for is vocational fidelity.

THE EVANGELICAL CHARACTER OF SEXUAL ETHICS

But is this sexual ethic good news for those called to vocations
in which overt sexual acts, especially acts of genital intercourse,
are said to be inappropriate? Can the behavioral norms for sexual
activity proposed in the present work meet this test, especially in
the case of homosexuals who would seem condemned to forego
many forms of sexual expression simply in virtue of their sexual
orientation rather than in virtue of their sexual vocation? Let me
acknowledge at once that there are a variety of ways in which this
sexual ethic is not good news, at least in the sense that it is not the
news one wants to hear, had hoped he or she might hear, or,
having heard it, relishes with delight and anticipation. In discussing
sexual pleasure as an ontic good in Chapter VI, I recognized that
certain moral choices are inevitably accompanied by the need to
forego some ontic goods or to accept some ontic evils. It is, then,
understandable that from some perspectives such choices are not
good news and will not be experienced as such. I have neither the
desire nor the ability to propose a sexual ethic that will either hide
or overcome this painful dimension of human existence, inevitable
until the final reign of God is established. If an individual wants to
have sex with someone or anyone, and is told that it would be
wrong, impossible, inappropriate, unwise, or any other negative
and discouraging word, that word will be received as bad news,
unless other wants of the individual have a higher, more compel-
ling priority.

In addition to the problem posed by one's desires and perspective on what counts as good news, it is also helpful to attend to the
experience of those called by God throughout the entire biblical

and ecclesial tradition. To be claimed by God for the service of God's people is a wonderful, awesome, and often painful experience. More than one prophet was dragged kicking and screaming from a comfortable existence to proclaim "thus sayeth the Lord," and the consequences of such proclamation were often painful, even fatal. Jesus had no happy reaction to the prospect of the cross, and what is good news for us was not particularly good news for him from a variety of perspectives. Indeed, the whole message of salvation in Christ, the good news, is necessitated by the bad news that we are sinners incapable of our own salvation. Perhaps more adequately than any other figure of our time, Dorothy Day understood this strange mixture of good news and bad embodied in the love of God as revealed in Christ, a love she called harsh and dreadful.[10] It is for the same reason that Christian life and thought require continuous conversion in order to remain faithful to the Gospel.[11]

These few historical examples make it clear that one's vocation often emerges out of less than desirable social situations or even undesired personal conditions that make the kind of service to which one is called so necessary. In speaking of the Christian life as a vocation, we are not speaking the language of fairness or rights or equal opportunity. The Lord is not an equal opportunity employer in any sense we so rightly demand of human agencies, including the Church. The Christian vocation to holiness always involves taking up the cross, and the cross is always bad news unless it can be recognized as the cross of Christ and so become a vehicle of union with the Lord.

Allowing, then, for the ambiguous character of our human response to the good news of Jesus Christ, the good news embodied in the sexual ethic proposed in these pages seems to me to have the following dimensions. First, it makes personal sexual experience, sexual performance and sexual satisfaction less significant human goods than the current cultural obsession with sexual performance and fulfillment would have us believe. One's worth as a person, one's dignity and attractiveness as a human being are not so deeply tied to one's ability to attract a sexual partner, or to one's capacity to experience orgasm or induce orgasmic experience in one's sexual mate. Nor is the quality of one's masculinity or femininity tied so fundamentally to the ability to father or mother a child. Sex, on the present accounting, is primarily a gift, not a talent to be displayed, or a right demanding exercise, or a power by which one proves his or her worth and so makes a mark on the world. Understanding sex as a gift, rather than as a need or an appetite or a tool, is a profoundly liberating experience which develops attitudes of appreciation, reverence and responsibility for the gift, as well as toward the giver and receiver of the gift. Such attitudes in turn foster a comfortableness and ease in regard to one's sexuality, a freedom rightly called the virtue of chastity which makes neither too much nor too little of human sexual experience.

Second, the sexual ethic proposed here has repeatedly stressed a normative ideal for sexual acts and relationships which is basically positive and open-ended, characteristics it receives from its vocational, social dimension. It is an ethic which points human beings toward the positive virtues and transforming power of human sexual acts and relationships, rather than emphasizing what is wrong about them. The question of the moral wrongness and sinfulness of human sexual behavior cannot be responsibly avoided, however, no matter how much one wishes to emphasize the positive goodness of human sexuality.[12] I have tried in Chapter VI to account for certain positive, humanizing qualities in human sexual experience, even where one must judge the actions to be morally wrong. I, for one, find it good news to discover that the grace of God is at work in human lives even in the midst of human folly and fragility. I find it even better news to discover that such human folly and fragility can be overcome without losing the same positive qualities.

Third, and last, I have stressed the importance of a way of life and of a life direction over the significance of isolated actions in trying to assess the moral quality of human sexual behavior. In practice that means that I have argued that not all sexual acts or relationships which contravene the normative ideal of sexuality are thereby serious sins. When combined with the responsibility assigned to personal conscience and the recognition of the fact of and need for continuing moral development as discussed in Chapters VI and VII, this understanding of sexual morality honors both the personal and ecclesial nature of Christian moral judgment. I find it good news to recognize that in our sexual journey we are neither alone nor swallowed up in some undifferentiated, corporate body.

One important consequence of the view of human sexuality articulated in these pages is that mercy, compassion and forgiveness will mark the Christian attitude and response to sexual sins far more than will anger, punitive demands, and rejection or even ostracism of the sinner.[13] Yet, at the same time, one's attitude toward sexual immorality and moral evil will not be one of tolerant indifference. Sexual sin is pitiable because it means the failure of a human person to realize important human possibilities and it marks the sinner as lost in his or her quest for human happiness and fulfillment. But sin is more than the failure to realize human possibilities, more than an error in judgment about what will bring happiness. Sin is at root always a form of active or passive idolatry,[14] a kind of disordered love which makes the loves of one's own mind and heart, or the loves of another's mind and heart, superior to the mindful heart of God. Sexual sin is no less idolatrous, for it gives to sexual pleasure and experience an importance that belongs only to the kingdom of God. The good news of the Christian sexual ethic proclaims that sexuality and sex are neither burdens nor the forbidden fruits of sin. Rather they find their meaning as gifts pointing us toward and moving us along the graced path to oneness with God and one another in Christ through the Spirit. That is why Christian sexual ethics deserves universal attention and effort and why it can be counted as good news for everyone.

NOTES

1. The classical biblical text in regard to God's desire that all be saved is 1 Timothy 2:1–6. See also Karl Rahner, "Universal Salvific Will," *Sacramentum Mundi* V, ed. Karl Rahner, *et al.* (New York: Herder and Herder, 1970), pp. 405–409.

2. Karl Rahner, "Concerning the Relationship Between Nature and Grace," *Theological Investigations* I (Baltimore: Helicon Press, 1961), pp. 310–317.

3. Schillebeeckx, *Marriage,* pp. xxviii–xxix.

4. For a style of sex education that seeks to communicate such a

view see James J. DiGiacomo, "All You Need Is Love," *America* 156, 6 (February 14, 1987), pp. 126–129.

5. *Lumen Gentium* 9–13, Flannery, *Vatican Council II*, pp. 359–365.

6. Hanigan, *As I Have Loved You*, pp. 27–28.

7. *Ibid.*, pp. 209–225, suggests that God's deepest passion is to become friends with us.

8. It is an interesting question whether or not certain social roles are a suitable basis for distinguishing sexual norms. I would suggest that in some cases they are. The question has relevance to the debate over clerical celibacy in the Roman Catholic Church, a requirement of priesthood in the Church today that is clearly not vocationally based.

9. It is a strong human propensity to measure our rights and obligations, our talents and achievements over against those of our fellow human beings. However appropriate it may be to do this in some cases, it is not proper to our life of grace. Paul urges the Romans: "Each of you must judge himself soberly by the standard of the faith God has given him," because "our gifts differ according to the grace given us" (Rom 12:3–6).

10. William Robert Miller, *A Harsh and Dreadful Love: Dorothy Day and the Catholic Worker Movement* (New York: Liveright, 1973).

11. While I am not fond of the language of continuous conversion because I think it obscures the foundational experience that is conversion, such language has become common to indicate the need for moral and spiritual growth, what the Catholic tradition more typically and accurately referred to as sanctification, a word which has its own problems of obscuring what it requires. In either usage, however, the concern is to recognize that life in Christ is life and so requires growth for continuing vitality.

12. The refusal to face the question of the wrongness of sexual acts is one of the weaknesses of the work by Kosnik, *et al., Human Sexuality,* p. 91, even while one may laud its effort to stress the positive values of human sexuality.

13. The model for Christian response to sexual sins can be found in the example of Jesus in the story of the woman taken in adultery, John 8:3–11. Archbishop John R. Quinn, "Toward an Understanding of the Letter ON THE PASTORAL CARE OF HOMOSEXUAL PERSONS," *America* 156, 5 (February 7, 1987), pp. 92–95, 116, has offered an interpretation of this letter which stresses both the positive growth possibilities and absence of hostility toward sexual acts that are less than perfect realizations of the normative ideal. His own positive interpretation of the letter indirectly indicates what is flawed about a letter that is focused on pastoral care.

14. Idolatry is the root and form of all sin, but is too often explained or imaged only as an active form of pride, arrogance, or ambition, stereotypical masculine sins. This kind of sin I refer to in the text as active idolatry. But idolatry can also have its passive side, letting others dominate, control, dictate to one as if they were God and submission to them was all important, stereotypical female sins. See Judith Plaskow, *Sex, Sin and Grace: Women's Experience and the Theologies of Reinhold Niebuhr and Paul Tillich* (Lanham: University Press of America, 1980).

THEOLOGICAL INQUIRIES SERIES:

Serious studies on contemporary questions of Scripture, Systematics and Moral Theology. Also in the series:

2961-9
5-02